PARENTING
FOR THE
'90s

PARENTING
FOR THE
'90s

PHILIP OSBORNE

Good Books®

Intercourse, Pennsylvania 17534

Figures 8.2 and 8.3, 10.3, 10.4, and 10.5 are adapted from
Parent Effectiveness Training by Thomas Gordon, © 1970; by
permission of David McKay Co., a division of Random
House, Inc.

"On Children" is reprinted from THE PROPHET, by Kahlil
Gibran, by permission of Alfred A. Knopf, Inc. © 1923 by
Kahlil Gibran and renewed 1951 by Administrators C.T.A. of
Kahlil Gibran Estate, and Mary G. Gibran.

Scripture references designated RSV are from the Revised
Standard Version of the Bible, copyrighted 1946, 1952, ©
1971, 1973.

Scripture references designated KJV are from the King James
Version of the Bible.

Scripture references designated NIV are from the HOLY
BIBLE: THE NEW INTERNATIONAL VERSION, © 1973,
1978, 1984 by the International Bible Society, used by
permission of Zondervan Bible Publishers.

Design by Cheryl Benner

Library of Congress Cataloging-in-Publication Data

Osborne, Philip, 1943–
    Parenting for the '90s/Philip Osborne.
        p.   cm.
    Bibliography: p.
    Includes index.
    ISBN 0-934672-73-3: $9.95
    1. Parenting. 2. Parent and child. I. Title.
HQ755.8.073 1989
649'.1—dc19   89-2009
                                                        CIP

PARENTING FOR THE '90s

Contents

List of Figures   6

Acknowledgements   7

Part I: Gaining Perspective on Parenting Advice   9

1. Balanced Parenting   13

2. Balance Among the Four Areas   23

3. Three Philosophies of Parenting   30

4. An Alternative Perspective on Parenting   46

Part II: The No Problem Area   58

5. Activities in the No Problem Area   65

6. Fighting the Television Battle   80

7. Keeping Sports in the No Problem Area   93

Part III: The Child's Problem Area   99

8. Listening   101

9. Encouraging Autonomy   125

Part IV: The Parent's Problem Area   143

10. Providing Information: Facts and Feelings   147

11. Taking Charge: Demands and
     Consequences   163

12. Using Punishment   189

13. Applying Behavior Modification   209

Part V: The Mutual Problem Area   233

14. Managing Conflict   235

15. Changing the Family System   253

16. In Summary   282

Questions for Thought and Discussion   288

References   308

Index   312

About the Author   317

List of Figures

1.1 Division of the Relationship Circle by the Child's Problem Line   14

1.2 Variability in the Location of the Child's Problem Line   15

1.3 Division of the Relationship Circle by the Parent's Problem Line   16

1.4 Variability in the Location of the Parent's Problem Line   18

1.5 The Four Areas of the Balanced Parenting Model   19

1.6 Parenting Strategies for Each Problem Area   22

2.1 The Goals of Discipline for Each Area   25

2.2 The Effects of Discipline Imbalance Among the Four Areas   27

3.1 Three Philosophies of Parenting   43

4.1 An Alternative to The Three Popular Philosophies: The Adult Believers Position   55

II.1 The Importance of the No Problem Area   60

II.2 Paradoxes of the No Problem Area   61

5.1 No Problem Area Activities   66

8.1 The Listening Skills   105

8.2 The Communication Process   112

8.3 Active Listening Feedback in the Communication Process   115

8.4 Good Listening Includes Delaying Suggestions Until the Timing is Right   120

8.5 The Parent's Solution to the Child's Problem May Not be the Same as the Child's Solution   121

9.1 Independence and Age of Child

9.2 Characteristics of Overly-Dependent Children   128

9.3 Levels of Expectations and Characteristics of Children   129

10.1 Restricted and Elaborated Styles of Language   150

10.2 The Parent as Sender and Child as Receiver of Message   154

10.3 The I-Message Communication Process   155

10.4 The You-Message   156

11.1   Parental Excuses for Misbehavior of Children   164
11.2   Parents Take Charge by Changing Themselves   165
11.3   Unassertive, Assertive and Aggressive Styles of Making and Turning Down Requests   170
11.4   Nonverbal Differences Among Unassertive, Assertive, and Aggressive Messages   174
11.5   Examples of Problems and Logical Consequences   180
11.6   Friendly Farmer Drives Combine   185
12.1   Uses of Punishment   205
13.1   Four Ways of Changing a Behavior through its Consequences   218
13.2   Potential Positive Reinforcers   220
13.3   Behavior Modification Procedures   225
14.1   Parenting Skills for the Mutual Problem Area   236
14.2   Managing Conflict Unassertively, Assertively and Aggressively   240
14.3   Conflict Management Case: The Homecoming Plans   250
14.4   The Goal of the Mutual Problem Area is to Manage Conflict in a Manner That Does Not Generate More Conflict Nor Suppress Conflict   251
15.1   Relationships as Linear Action   255
15.2   Relationships in Context of System   257
15.3   Fused, Distant and Differentiated but Close Relationships   261
15.4   Balancing Togetherness and Separateness Desires   263
15.5   The Dyad   270
15.6   The Dyad Under Stress   270
15.7   The Triangle   271
15.8   The Triangle Under Stress   272

Acknowledgments

Parenting for the '90s is the result of my teaching an undergraduate college level parent education course for many years, and during that time, never finding a book which seemed to me to adequately cover the subject. Many books on parenting are available, of course, but few offer the theoretical scope which yields perspective on the field of parent education and also systematic training in parenting skills. My hope is that those who counsel parents, offer programs in family life education, or who are parents themselves will find this book useful.

I am grateful to Jim Mininger, long-term friend and Academic Dean at Hesston College, and to the rest of the Administrative Cabinet for supporting my efforts in so many ways, including a leave-of-absence. I am appreciative also of the Nursing Department faculty who provided daily encouragement as well as a second office on campus so that I could get away from my regular office and the usual routine during the leave. And a big thank you to Kathy Goering, administrative assistant, who does so many things, all of them well.

I am indebted to many others on the faculty here at Hesston College or on the staff at Prairie View Community Mental Health Center: Jim Mininger and Marion Bontrager, for their reviews of chapter 4; Karen Weaver Koppenhaver, chapter 11; Marion Bontrager and Ron Guengerich, chapter 12; Dave Osborne and Doug

Penner, chapter 13; Randy Krehbiel, chapter 15; and Margaret Wiebe and Ruth Hartzler, librarians, for their help in locating sources.

Thanks also to former colleagues John and Naomi Lederach, now on the staff of Philhaven Hospital, for their encouragement to write.

I am indebted to the many students of Hesston College, their parents, and their children who supplied stories and suggestions for the book. Individuals who are complimented by the stories are identified. For stories which do not flatter the families involved, details and names have been altered to disguise identities.

Becky Springer, a student with outstanding skills in writing, provided invaluable help with every chapter of the manuscript. Thanks again, Becky!

I am appreciative also of the opportunity to work with Phyllis Pellman Good, editor of the book, along with her husband Merle who is the publisher. If the book is judged to be well-written, credit is due Phyllis for her painstaking attention to detail and knack for bringing audience and book together with the right choice of word.

My wife, Lorna, and our three children, Jeff, Julie, and Nathan were supportive of me throughout the time I was writing, in spite of the fact that the content exposes them to more public scrutiny than they would like to have. I appreciate their confidence and trust. Thanks, Julie, for your help with chapter 14.

Lorna has taught me much about parenting. Fortunately, she does it with a great sense of humor, and for that, too, I am thankful. I look forward to many more years of partnership as parents of adult children and as grandparents.

Philip Osborne
Hesston College
Hesston, Kansas
January, 1989

Part I
Gaining Perspective on Parenting Advice

Reading parenting advice is somewhat like reading the Foods section which comes in each Wednesday's edition of our daily paper. The reader gets good ideas about recipes and finds out about fads in foods. Using the recipes, however, has very little to do with providing the family with a well-balanced diet.

Nutrition has to do with a well-balanced diet. A cook has to know something about the basic four food groups in order to put the recipes together in a balanced way. Otherwise, the cook risks overdoing one part of the diet and overlooking others. Even the most attractive and savory dish loses its appeal if placed on the table too often, and other parts of the diet are slighted when too much emphasis is placed on one type of food.

The same is true of parenting advice. Parents need to know the basic four groups of parenting skills in order to be well-balanced in their parenting methods. There is no *single* method, technique or bit of advice which, by itself, serves parents adequately. Even the best technique becomes a problem if over-used. It loses its effectiveness, and other skills, which also need to be used at times, are not used enough.

So this book is not about *a* method; it's about methods. In fact, it is about *balancing* methods. It introduces parents to the four areas of the parent-child relationship and the skills that are needed in each. It also is about what happens when some skills are used too much and others are not used enough.

Knowing the four areas of parenting skills makes possible an evaluation of parenting programs (P.E.T., S.T.E.P., Behavior Modification and so on) and the advice of parenting experts (Dr. Spock and Dr. James Dobson, for example). If parents followed those varying points of view and advice, certain skills would be performed well, but in other areas competency would be weak, resulting in an imbalanced set of skills. This book will help enable parents to weigh the contributions and limitations of the experts.

The reader may be disappointed to find that this book does not contain many suggestions about how to handle specific problems, nor does it deal specifically with certain ages. What it does offer is a way of thinking about problems which is applicable across many situations and ages of children.

Problems with children, generally speaking, are of two types. One kind occurs because of normal developmental challenges; the problems are common, predictable and temporary. For example, in the late pre-school and early elementary years, many children become afraid when they are in their bedrooms alone at night. Specific suggestions are useful with this type of difficulty: a nightlight, open door, permission to sleep on the floor in another bedroom, reassurances of safety, prayers for safekeeping and so on. Parents generally are appreciative of suggestions like this and can implement them successfully.

Although developmental problems are not easy to manage at the time they occur, parents get through them with a little knowledge of child development, some common sense and a lot of patience. The problems eventually turn out to be self-correcting, because most children outgrow them.

The other type of problem is more complicated, however, because it is sustained by interactions within the family. These problems frequently start out as normal, developmental problems, but become more than that because of the reactions of the parents. Normal development is disrupted if parental anxiety is focused on the child.

From a family systems' point of view, this second type of problem exists because it fills some need within the family. By focusing on a child, the family is protected from dealing with more unsettling issues, often fears of the parents or conflicts in the marriage relationship.

With this kind of problem, there are no suggestions which will "fix" the child, because the problem exists in the pattern of family interactions, not simply within the child. Since the parents are part of the problem, they resist taking steps to change the situation, preferring to use the child's problem as a cover for the more significant issue.

I have learned that when parents ask for advice, they invariably think the problem they are dealing with is of the first type. If it is, they may be able to get the advice they want and the advice will work for them. But often the problem they are struggling with is seen by an observer to be of the second type. The advice parents get will not be what they want, or if it is, it will not work.

One of the goals of this book is to give parents some ideas about altering their approach to problems when their old approaches aren't working very well, and in fact, may be sustaining the problems. Ultimately, this is more useful than suggestions about how to handle specific situations.

Parenting for the '90s is divided into five parts. In the first part, the four groups of parenting skills are introduced, and the concept of maintaining balance among the groups is developed. Imbalance is illustrated with an analysis of the roles of the traditional father and the traditional mother. Three popular philosophies of parenting are reviewed next for their contributions to the balance.

A note to my readers about the tone of this book is appropriate at this point. One of my greatest disappointments in today's parenting literature is its own imbalance. This is due, to a great degree, because of the modern western insistence on separating the "secular" and the "religious." Rather, I have observed much overlap of the two worlds in my years of teaching and counselling. I also note that a majority of Americans hold church membership (a National Council of Churches survey in 1988 set it at 59%), yet in parenting literature we ignore this. On the other hand, books which do acknowledge a possible role for religious values in parenting often seem narrow and manipulative to me.

This book does not assume religious faith on the part of the reader, but I will not shrink from referring to the role of faith and values for some parents from time to time. My editors and I have diligently attempted to avoid any tone of manipulation on this subject. To act as though no one has found faith and values helpful in parenting would be false and imbalanced.

I note this here because I wish to have integrity in my writing. The final chapter of Part I, which readers may skip if they so wish,

presents a theological perspective on parenting which some readers
may find helpful.

The remaining four parts of the book cover the four areas of the
parent-child relationship and each will be introduced at that time.
Each part offers training in skills which parents need to be competent, and perspective on when to apply the skills so that they can
keep their balance amidst the pushes and pulls of daily life.

Questions for Thought and Discussion about this Chapter are on page 288.

1. Balanced Parenting

Parents have several different types of responsibilities in the care of their children. Competent parents are able to manage each kind of responsibility most of the time, and are balanced in their attention to each area. Many parents possess a mixture of parenting strengths and weaknesses, managing some of their responsibilities very well but struggling with others. Still other parents are weak in nearly all areas of parental responsibility.

I am placing the areas of parental responsibility within a conceptual framework called the Balanced Parenting Model. While this might sound too complicated or theoretical to be useful, it is not difficult to understand or apply. Living in harmony with someone is never simple, but for parents the means of living in harmony with their children are at least clarified when the parent-child relationship is viewed through the framework of the Balanced Parenting Model.

Parents who learn to use this model will understand better the different areas of parental responsibility and gain insight into what happens when the areas are out of balance. They will perceive the set of skills that parents need in each area and will discern when (if ever) it's appropriate to follow the assorted bits of advice about parenting which come from all directions.

The Problem Lines

In the Balanced Parenting Model, we will let a circle represent the parent-child relationship. A vertical line is drawn through the circle to divide it into two areas, one area for the times the child is feeling fine, and the other for the times the child is bothered about something (see Figure 1.1).

Figure 1.1
Division of the Relationship Circle by the Child's
Problem Line

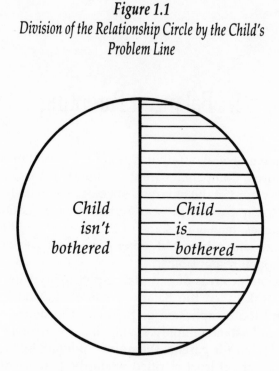

The area in which the child is bothered is called the Child's Problem Area. It covers a multitude of situations: problems with friends, brothers and sisters, school, possessions, responsibilities, and even problems within children themselves. Because of these problems children feel frustrated, deprived, disturbed, angry, puzzled, belittled, confused, inadequate, discouraged and so on:

Marilyn is out of money and can't buy the chocolate candy she wants.

David doesn't like it when Spot jumps on his lap.

Stan can't find his soccer shoes.

Ryan's friends didn't invite him to go to the rock concert.

Amy woke up hungry and is crying to be fed.

The area on the other side of the vertical line represents the times the child is feeling fine. In these moments the child responds appropriately and adequately to the demands of the situation and is satisfied:

Marilyn sits on the back steps eating the chocolate which she bought with her allowance.

David gets home from school and plays with Spot.

Stan practices kicking the soccer ball in the back yard.

Ryan goes to his room to play his favorite music on his stereo.

Amy is fed and playing contentedly with her toes.

Figure 1.2

Variability in the Location of the Child's Problem Line

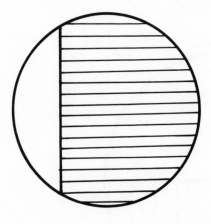
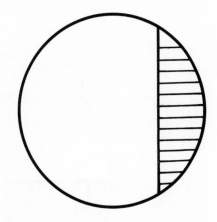

Bad day for child
Discouraged child
Poorly adjusted child
Many problems to cope with

Good day
Happy child
Well-adjusted child
Few problems to cope with

The vertical line is not located in the same place for all children, nor is its position always the same for one child (see Figure 1.2). Some children are easily discouraged. The problem line for them is farther to the left than it is for children who are less easily discouraged. Some children lack the social and intellectual skills needed to respond competently to challenges. They, too, have a larger area to the right of the problem line, compared with children who are more competent. Some children have more problems to contend with than others because of circumstances of health, finances or loss within the family. And for all children, some days seem to go better than other days. All of these conditions affect the location of the child's problem line.

Now visualize a horizontal line through the circle, dividing it once again into two parts (see Figure 1.3). The upper part is for the things which the child does which don't bother the parent. For example:

Figure 1.3
Division of the Relationship Circle by the Parent's
Problem Line

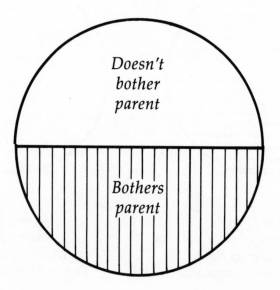

Marilyn offers her mother a bite of chocolate.

David fills Spot's water bowl.

Stan decides to play soccer in the recreation league.

Ryan does a homework assignment while listening to music.

Amy smiles at her dad.

The lower part represents all of the things which the child does which are upsetting to the parent. These things are called the parent's problems, and include the myriad ways parents are bothered by their children's behavior. When parents "own" the problem they feel disappointed, frightened, embarrassed, angry, impatient, disgusted, resentful and so on:

Marilyn smears chocolate all over her clothes.

David forgets to walk Spot.

Stan tracks mud into the house.

Ryan blasts the house with his stereo.

Amy's diaper is dirty and her father hates to change her.

In these situations, the parent is the one who is bothered, not the child. Ryan likes to rock the house with his music, and Marilyn was savoring her chocolate. Stan was oblivious to the mud. Not walking the dog was no problem for David, and Amy was just doing what babies do.

Note also that in this diagram the parent's problems have only to do with the child. The area below the parent's problem line does not contain the other things which might be bothering the parent—the flat tire on the car, the quarterly report which is due, Grandpa's surgery, the overdrawn checking account—but which are external to the parent-child relationship.

These other bothersome situations are not within the circle because the Balanced Parenting Model looks only at the parent-child relationship.[1] Since it does so from the parent's perspective, it serves as a pair of prescription lenses to put on to see more clearly the child in the relationship, and the manner in which the parent and child are relating. The parent's other concerns are also important, but are peripheral to this view.

The other concerns, however, will alter the location of the horizontal line (see Figure 1.4). When parents are worried, frazzled or ill

---

[1] The Balanced Parenting Model is useful in understanding other relationships as well as the parent-child relationship, when "the other person" is substituted for "child." For example, the model provides perspective on one's relationship with a spouse or colleague or client. But since this is a book about parenting, "the other person" in this book is always a child and the person using the model is assumed to be a parent.

Figure 1.4
Variability in the Location of the Parent's
Problem Line

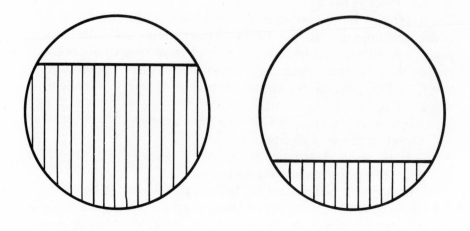

Bad day for parent   Good day
Unaccepting parent   Accepting parent
Difficult child   Easy child

they get irritated with things their children do, which on better days don't bother them. When parents have just returned home from a trip after missing their children, or when they are in a holiday mood, they tend to be more accepting of children's behavior than they are under usual circumstances. If the behavior takes place in public or in the presence of company, parents respond one way; if it occurs in private, they respond another way.

The horizontal line varies also when different children are involved. Some children are hard to live with, constantly setting their parents' teeth on edge. The horizontal line for these parents will be high because so much of what the children do bothers them. Other children are easy to take care of, charming those around them from birth. These parents will have a horizontal line which is low because they are bothered by very little of their children's behavior.

The characteristic intensity level, physical appearance, state of health, birth order, sex and age of the child involved all modify the location of the parent's problem line. In regard to birth order, for example, parents usually become more relaxed with younger children. I once asked my mother, who raised seven children, how she changed in her care of the younger ones as a result of her experiences with the older children. She thought for a moment and then replied, "I rocked each one more."

Parents are different, too, just like children, and their differences affect the horizontal line. Behavior that is a problem for one parent isn't a problem for another, even within the same family. Parents who are relaxed about the messes children make, or who are confident in their parenting expertise, have a larger area above the line than parents who are concerned about household tidiness, or who are worried about their proficiency.

Social class backgrounds, religious beliefs about children, current fads or adult peer pressure in parenting philosophies, expectations about appropriate child behavior, and experiences with one's own parents affect the position of the horizontal line.

Figure 1.5
The Four Areas of the Balanced Parenting Model

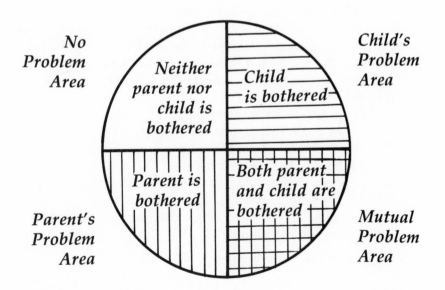

The Four Areas

Placing the vertical line and the horizontal line on the circle simultaneously yields four regions. These areas are the blueprint for the structure of this book (see Figure 1.5).

The first region, called the No Problem Area, is to the left of the child's problem line and above the parent's problem line. It represents situations bothersome to neither parent nor child. The child is content and the child's behavior is acceptable to the parent. Examples used earlier include:

> Marilyn sits on the back steps eating the chocolate which she bought with her allowance.
> Stan practices kicking the soccer ball in the back yard.

A second region contains the situations which bother the child but not the parent. This is the area above the parent's problem line, but to the right of the child's line, and is called the Child's Problem Area. Examples include:

> Ryan's friends didn't invite him to go to the rock concert.
> David doesn't like it when Spot jumps on his lap.

Another region embodies those situations which are upsetting to the parent but not to the child. This is below the parent's problem line, but to the left of the child's line and is called the Parent's Problem Area. Situations in the Parent's Problem Area include:

> Stan tracks mud into the house.
> Ryan blasts the house with his stereo.

The fourth area consists of circumstances upsetting to both parent and child. This is the region formed by the overlap of the areas below the parent's problem line and to the right of the child's problem line. It is called the Mutual Problem Area. The following situations fall into the Mutual Problem Area:

> Marilyn wants to bake brownies but she can't do it alone and her dad doesn't have time to help her.
> David wants to take Spot to Grandpa's, but his mother doesn't want Spot in the car with them.
> Stan wants to get a new pair of soccer shoes, but his parents think the kind he wants are too expensive.
> Ryan begins his 30 minutes of trumpet practice when his mother is on the phone.

Determining Problem Ownership

To use the Balanced Parenting Model in a particular situation, the first step is to decide who owns the problem. This is important because the appropriate parental responses are different for each area. The following questions are signs pointing to the owner of the problem:

Who is upset, bothered or hurt?

Who is experiencing a problem with whom?

Who would like to change the situation?

Whose rule is being broken or whose expectations are not being met?

Whose needs are not being met?

Who is being treated disrespectfully?

Is personal safety involved? (If so, the parent owns the problem; if the child is actually hurt, the problem is mutual.)

Parenting Goals of Each Area

The responsibilities of parents are different for each area. The primary goal of the No Problem Area is to develop the parent-child ties, so that the child feels a sense of belonging in a family where members care about each other and enjoy each other's company. They do this by taking advantage of No-Problem moments to play, work and celebrate together when neither parent nor child is upset. Stan's parents, for example, are carrying out responsibilities of the No Problem Area when they attend his soccer game.

The primary goal of the Child's Problem Area is to be supportive and encouraging when the child is experiencing problems. To do this parents need to be able to respond in ways which help the child to deal with the problem and the feelings brought about by the problem without taking over the problem as their own. In the example above, Ryan's friends didn't invite him to go to the rock concert. He needs help from his parents in dealing with his disappointment. But since the problem is Ryan's, his parents need to refrain from taking over the problem and solving it to *their* satisfaction.

The goal of the Parent's Problem Area is to get the child to change whatever it is that's bothering the parent. From the situations above, Stan's parents want him to stop tracking in mud, and Ryan's parents want him to stop playing his music so loudly.

The listening and encouraging skills used in the Child's Problem Area are inappropriate in the Parent's Problem Area because here the problem is the parent's and the solution rests with the parent — that is, it's up to the parent to see that the problem is corrected or doesn't happen again.

The goal of the Mutual Problem Area is to deal with conflict by searching for mutually satisfying solutions to problems, and to adapt to change when change is required. Either Marilyn or her dad or both need to adjust their plans, for example.

Figure 1.6
Parenting Strategies for Each Area

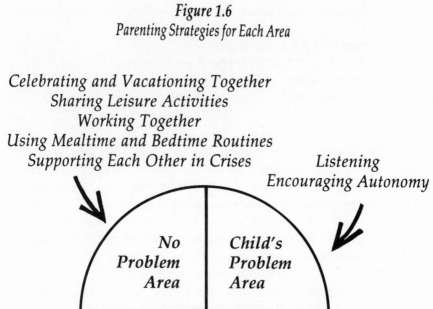

Celebrating and Vacationing Together
Sharing Leisure Activities
Working Together
Using Mealtime and Bedtime Routines
Supporting Each Other in Crises   *Listening*
                                Encouraging Autonomy

No Problem Area   *Child's Problem Area*

Parent's Problem Area   *Mutual Problem Area*

Providing Information: *Managing Conflict*
Facts and Feelings   *Changing the Family System*
Taking Charge: Demands and
Consequences
Using Punishment
Applying Behavior Modification

Questions for Thought and Discussion about this Chapter are on page 288.

2. Balance Among the Four Areas

When parents say they are "disciplining" their child, they usually mean that they are using punishment to correct the child. But to use the word discipline in this way is to give it a very narrow definition. Discipline does occur in punishment, but it also takes place in many other ways. It occurs through praise for achievement, encouragement following failure, the structure of the family's daily routine, and the influence parents have in pleasant conversation with their children. Scott Peck describes it this way:

> The parents who devote time to their children, even when it is not demanded by glaring misdeeds, will perceive in them subtle needs for discipline, to which they will respond with gentle urging or reprimand or structure or praise, administered with thoughtfulness and care. They will observe how their children eat cake, how they study, when they tell subtle falsehoods, when they run away from problems rather than face them. They will take the time to make these minor corrections and adjustments, listening to their children, responding to them, tightening a little here, loosening a little there, giving them little lectures, little stories, little hugs and kisses, little admonishments, little pats on the back. (Peck, 1978, p. 23)

Discipline includes what parents do in all four areas. It includes all of the things which the parent does because the child is valued and the parent-child relationship is important (the activities of the No Problem Area). It includes the many ways parents show support when the child is struggling (the parenting skills of the Child's Problem Area). It also includes the methods of correcting the child's misbehavior (the techniques of the Parent's Problem Area), which is what people usually mean when they talk about discipline. And finally, discipline includes the way the family manages conflict and adapts to change (the strategies of the Mutual Problem Area).

Discipline is a long-term process. It's the molding of character and values, self-control and relationship style which takes place throughout childhood and which helps produce the person that the child eventually becomes in adulthood. Discipline is the sum of everything the parent does to move the child in the direction of long-term goals.

The influence of parents includes the modeling which they provide for managing relationships in general. One long-term result of parental influence is that children use the relationships with their parents as patterns for dealing with other relationships in their lives. Relationships with their own children, their friends and work colleagues, and even their spiritual relationships are shaped by the parent-child relationship pattern.

For example, imagine a parent engaged in pleasant conversation with a child at the dinner table. The situation is in the No Problem Area, since the conversation takes place because the parent is interested in the daughter's activities and opinions, not because the parent desires to correct her. The parent's immediate goal might be to show interest in the biology test or play tryouts, and to support the child in her endeavors. But the long-term influence of the parent is that the daughter becomes a person who is able to express interest in the lives of her friends, just as her parent did with her.

This means that the methods which a parent selects for influencing the child in the immediate situation need to be consistent with the kind of self-discipline which the parent hopes is the eventual result.

For me, the long-term goal of the No Problem Area is to develop our children's abilities to establish and nurture relationships. If my attention to the No Problem Area is adequate, they will become affectionate, loyal and comfortable with others because they have been treated in an affectionate, trustworthy and accepting manner (see Figure 2.1).

My long-term goal of the Child's Problem Area is to develop our

Figure 2.1
The Goals of Discipline for Each Area

	The parent . . .	so that the child becomes . . .
No Problem Area	shows affection enjoys being with child plays reveals reverence and gratefulness to God	affectionate comfortable with others playful reverent and grateful
Child's Problem Area	listens supports encourages guides	expressive, honest supportive of others confident realistic
Parent's Problem Area	reasons shares own feelings demands socially acceptable behavior lets child experience consequences of misbehavior	reasonable respectful of feelings of others socially acceptable responsible
Mutual Problem Area	seeks conflict resolution assertively compromises, changes affirms importance of relationship values individuality of child	assertive willing to compromise, change trusting, rather than withdrawing emotionally differentiated, rather than emotionally fused

children's abilities to manage stress, and to be empathic and encouraging with others who are experiencing problems. For the Parent's Problem Area, my long-term goal is that our children conform appropriately to society, and also learn to change others tactfully and effectively. Finally, my long-term goal of the Mutual Problem Area is that our children learn to deal with conflict and adapt to change.

Importance of Balance Among the Four Areas

The skills that parents need in the four areas are independent of each other, at least to some extent. That is, a parent can be strong in some areas and weak in others, or strong in all areas, or weak in all areas. The areas are not totally unrelated, however, because strengths and weaknesses of one area affect what happens in the other areas.

For example, a parent who is good in the No Problem Area but whose methods in the Parent's Problem Area are poor has an advantage over the parent who is poor in both areas. The first parent gets by with poor techniques for changing the child's misbehavior because of the strength of the parent-child relationship. For the parent who has not developed a strong relationship with the child, on the other hand, the poor techniques are ineffective or make the relationship even worse.

Few parents are highly skilled in all areas. Most are better at some aspects of parenting than at others. Most parents are somewhat out of balance, and the array of parenting strengths and weaknesses each possesses determines the nature of the imbalance.

Imbalance occurs because parents tend to emphasize too much the areas of responsibility where their strengths and concerns lie and emphasize too little the areas which are more difficult or of less concern. Both the overemphasis and the underemphasis have negative effects, as shown in Figure 2.2. The goal of parents, in the Balanced Parenting Model, is to develop skills in all four areas and to maintain balance among them.

The traditional sex roles provide an illustration of the importance of balance among the areas. The mother traditionally has been better at the Child's Problem Area than the father has been. Mothers traditionally tend to be more aware of the child's day-to-day experiences and feelings and spend more efforts in nurturing the child, compared with the father.

On the other hand, fathers traditionally have been better at the Parent's Problem Area than mothers. They tend to be more successful in establishing the limits of the home and at clarifying the values and goals of the family.

But if a mother emphasizes too much the Child's Problem Area, smothering the child with attention, she impedes the development of the child's independence. And if she is weak simultaneously in the Parent's Problem Area, unable to adequately control her child's behavior, she becomes victimized by the child's whims and plays the role of martyr in her parenting style.

If the father emphasizes too much the Parent's Problem Area he becomes an autocrat, more interested in obedience and respect than

Figure 2.2
The Effects of Discipline Imbalance Among the Four Areas

	Results of Too Much Emphasis	Results of Too Little Emphasis
No Problem Area	Parent and child are emotionally fused. Parent is too pushy for togetherness. Parent is unable to relax with child; always "parenting." Family ties so strong, child unable to leave home.	Parent and child are apathetic to each other. Parent is too busy for togetherness. Parent is unaware of child; abdicates parenting responsibilities. Family ties so weak, child searches elsewhere for belonging.
Child's Problem Area	Parent interferes in child's problems. Parent smothers child with attention. Parent expects too little of child (or too much). Parent is so responsive to child's moods that child becomes manipulative.	Parent abandons child in time of need. Parent is cold, indifferent to child. Child's development is impeded (or hurried). Parent is callous, insensitive to child's moods.
Parent's Problem Area	Parent is autocratic. Parent is abusive to child. Parent orders, threatens, preaches. Parent resorts to coercive, punitive methods to control child.	Parent is martyr. Parent is abused by child. Parent makes requests apologetically. Parent is too afraid of child's reactions to take action.
Mutual Problem Area	Parent is quick to engage in power struggle. Parent assumes too much responsibility for determining beliefs, values, preferences of child. Parent is rigid, unwilling or unable to change. Parent doesn't want advice.	Parent is passive, avoids conflict. Parent is reluctant to express own values, beliefs, preferences. Parent is confused and insecure, feels like situation is out of control. Parent won't act on advice, doesn't accept responsibility for changing relationship pattern.

in an informed discussion of the issues which concern the family. And if he is simultaneously weak at the Child's Problem Area, he becomes a stranger to his children, unaware of their experiences and feelings.

What typically happens in this pattern is that the children feel more comfortable with their mother, so they go to her with their concerns. Since the father is not as informed about his children's concerns, his attempt to intervene in their lives sometimes turns out to be inappropriate. His wife criticizes him because she would have handled the situation differently in light of the additional information she had.

Since relationships among family members are dynamic (see Chapter 15 on family systems), the effect of the imbalance in their skills is that the imbalances become greater and greater. When the children have a concern about the father, they will speak to the mother about him, rather than directly to him. If she chooses to ally herself with them to protect them from their father, she becomes close to them, but does so by creating greater distance in the father-child relationships. Because of the closeness she feels with her children, she is reluctant to correct them. She leaves the "disciplining" up to him, setting up his interactions with them to occur when the children need to be corrected.

The result of this pattern is that the father withdraws from his children out of frustration and ineptness, the mother forms an unhealthy alliance with her children, and the parents become adversarial rather than complementary in their parenting styles. He focuses more and more on the Parent's Problem Area, she focuses more and more on the Child's Problem Area, and their parenting skills become more and more out of balance.

Either parent could alter this pattern by paying greater attention to the skills in which she or he is weakest in particular problem areas. For the traditional father, this would mean improving in the ability to listen and encourage (the Child's Problem Area); the ability to recognize the importance of moments of togetherness and to take advantage of them (the No Problem Area); and the ability to compromise and accept change (the Mutual Problem Area).

For the traditional mother, improving the balance would mean developing her ability to assertively establish the expectations of the home and to take action when expectations are not met (the Parent's Problem Area); and also improving her ability to deal with conflict in a manner which keeps family members close yet recognizes their individuality and which is not passive nor manipulative (the Mutual Problem Area).

The traditional sex roles are changing in the manner suggested in this analysis. For many parents today, whether male or female, single or married, the ideal is to possess the skills needed in each of the four areas and to keep the areas in balance.

The next chapter is about philosophies of parenting. Three common schools of thought are presented and evaluated from the perspective of the Balanced Parenting Model.

Questions for Thought and Discussion about this Chapter are on page 289.

3. Three Philosophies of Parenting

Psychologist X returned from a trip to find that the family's dachshund, named Sigmund Freud (Siggy), had become boss of the house in his absence. That evening when Mr. X told Siggy to go to his usual spot for the night, Siggy flattened his ears and growled, refusing to budge. Mr. X got a small belt to help him "reason" with Siggy. When the dog still would not obey the command, a fight between man and beast took place, with the man swinging the belt and the beast trying to bite the belt and the man. The struggle moved through the house, with Siggy growling but retreating until finally he was in the intended spot.

The following night Siggy complied immediately with the command, and has not taken such a defiant stand since. "Just as surely as a dog will occasionally challenge the authority of his leaders," Psychologist X concluded, "a little child is inclined to do the same thing, only more so."

On a rainy morning, Psychologist Y noticed that his daughter was leaving for school in the rain without her raincoat. He pointed this out to her and she claimed that she didn't need a raincoat. He explained that without a raincoat her clothes would get wet and she might catch cold, which concerned him. The daughter insisted that she didn't want to wear her raincoat.

In the discussion which ensued, Mr. Y found out that she didn't object to raincoats in general, but that she didn't want to wear her raincoat because it was plaid; other kids were wearing plain-colored raincoats.

Mr. Y still wasn't willing for her to be without a raincoat, so he asked her if she could think of a solution to the problem. The daughter suggested that she wear her mother's raincoat instead of her own. After gaining her mother's consent, she left for school that morning wearing a raincoat. The sleeves were rolled up because it was too large, but it was plain-colored.

The conflict with his daughter was resolved, Psychologist Y concluded, in a mutually satisfying manner, without using power and with both of them walking away from the incident feeling warmly toward the other.

Psychologist Z built a closed compartment about the size of a crib for his infant daughter. One side of the compartment, which could be raised and lowered like a window, was made of glass. The temperature and humidity inside the box could be controlled. Through experimentation Mr. Z discovered settings so comfortable that his daughter rarely cried.

The infant wore no clothing, except for a diaper, so that she would be more comfortable and less restricted in her movement. The mattress was a tightly stretched canvas, kept dry by warm air. A single bottom sheet operated like a roller towel; it was stored on a spool outside the compartment at one end and passed into a wire hamper at the other. A clean section of sheet could be pulled into place in seconds; the roll of sheet was ten yards long and lasted a week.

The walls of the box were insulated to keep out unwanted noise, and a curtain could be drawn over the window to reduce light and other visual distractions so that the infant could sleep undisturbed.

The baby was removed from the box for feeding and changing, and also each afternoon for a play period. The play period was extended as she grew older, and eventually the box was used only as sleeping quarters.

Psychologist Z recommends that other parents use a box like the one he designed using scientific principles to ease their job as parents and to improve the environment of babies.

Each of these true stories is told by three different prominent psychologists and each represents an influential philosophy of parenting. The first story is told by James Dobson in one of his films about parenting and also at the beginning of the book *The Strong-Willed Child* (1978, pp. 11–14). The second story is used by Thomas Gordon in Parent Effectiveness Training classes and also in the book by the same title (1970, pp. 196–197). The third story is from an article written in 1945 for *Ladies Home Journal* by B. F. Skinner (1945/1972).

Much of the advice which parents receive today is from one of the philosophies these stories represent. Given the importance of the three schools of thought, my goal in this chapter is to help parents gain perspective on parenting advice by recognizing its source. The chapter covers the development of each philosophy, the assumptions made by each one and the impact of each on the American family. In order to clarify the distinctions among the three, I present them in extreme forms.

Childhood as Evil and Parent as Disciplinarian

Background. The first philosophy of parenting, represented by Dobson, has roots which go back through the conservative Christians of this century to the Puritans, who emigrated from England to the New England colonies in the seventeenth century. They brought with them an austere moral code to combat the depraved human condition, and a stiff determination to carry out their beliefs. Children were expected to stand when adults entered the room and to remain silent until given permission to speak. They were to obey commands promptly and without protest, especially those of the father, the primary authority. Since children were valued for their economic utility, they were expected to work to help support the family.

When they made mistakes or showed lack of deference, children were beaten on the hands, back, buttocks or head. Beatings took place at home, in the school or at work, and often were severe.

The punitive treatment of children in former years, harsh by today's standards, wasn't due solely to the parenting philosophy summarized here. Child abuse and neglect also occurred because of ignorance and poverty. Life itself was harsh.

Nevertheless, this first parenting philosophy is still an important force in parenting advice today. The abusive techniques have been discarded, for the most part, but the assumptions about human nature which compel parents to correct their children remain unchanged.

Assumptions about human nature. More than the other two philosophies summarized in this chapter, the rationale of this position is theological, resting heavily on the doctrine of original sin formulated in the third century by Augustine. The doctrine is derived from Paul in the New Testament, who wrote that all persons share with Adam and Eve the fall from perfection.

John Wesley, the English clergyman who founded Methodism in the eighteenth century, held this view of the nature of children. In a "Sermon on the Education of Children" (about 1783), he exhorted parents to:

> ... teach your children, as soon as possibly you can, that they are fallen spirits; that they are fallen short of that glorious image of God, wherein they were first created; that they are not now, as they were once, incorruptible pictures of the God of glory; bearing the express likeness of the wise, the good, the holy Father of spirits; but more ignorant, more foolish, and more wicked, than they can possibly conceive. Shew them that, in pride, passion, and revenge, they are now like the devil. (Wesley, 1783/1973, pp. 61–62)

Dobson's parenting philosophy begins with the belief that children are evil by nature. In *Dr. Dobson Answers Your Questions* (1982), he responds to the query, "Many people believe that children are basically 'good.' . . . Do you agree?"

> If they mean that all children are worthy and deserving of our love and respect, I certainly do agree. But if they believe that children are by nature unselfish, giving, and sinless before God, I must disagree. I wish that assessment of human nature were accurate, but it contradicts scriptural understandings. Jeremiah wrote: "The heart is deceitful above all things, and desperately wicked: who can know it?" (Jer. 17:9). (p. 44)

Assumptions about the causes of problems in the home. In this point of view, misbehavior of children is caused by their sinful nature. They naturally want to go their own way. Willful disobedience is evidence of this, so the child's will is a focus of attention in this tradition, as explained by Dobson:

> The entire human race is afflicted with this tendency toward willful defiance. God told Adam and Eve that they could eat anything in the Garden of Eden except the forbidden fruit.

Yet they challenged the authority of the Almighty by deliber-
ately disobeying His commandment. Perhaps this tendency
toward self-will is the essence of "original sin" which has
infiltrated the human family. It certainly explains why I place
such stress on the proper response to willful defiance during
childhood, for that rebellion can plant the seeds of personal
disaster. (Dobson, 1982, p. 122)

Goals of parent education. Since willfulness is the problem, the
goal of parenting is to overcome defiance, and gain submissiveness
and trust. Wesley's sermon illustrates this, too:

To humour children is, as far as in us lies, to make their
disease incurable. A wise parent, on the other hand, should
begin to break their will, the first moment it appears. In the
whole art of Christian education there is nothing more important than this. The will of a parent is to a little child in the
place of the will of God. Therefore, studiously teach them to
submit to this while they are children, that they may be ready
to submit to his will, when they are men. (Wesley,
1783/1973, pp. 59–60)

Dobson speaks of shaping the will, rather than breaking the will,
but otherwise his message is similar to Wesley's: "I am recommend-
ing a simple principle: when you are defiantly challenged, win
decisively. When the child asks, 'Who's in charge?' tell him" (Dobson, 1970, p. 50). Dobson's tough stance on this issue is revealed in
the titles of some of his books: *Dare to Discipline* (1970), *The Strong-
Willed Child* (1978), and *Parenting Isn't for Cowards* (1988).

According to Dobson's view, the reason it's so important to win in
the contest of wills is that the parent-child relationship is based on
the respect which winning engenders. "Nothing brings a parent and
child closer together than for the mother or father to win decisively
after being defiantly challenged" (Dobson, 1970, p. 35). After letting
the child know who is in charge, "take him in your arms and
surround him with affection. Treat him with respect and dignity,
and expect the same from him. Then begin to enjoy the sweet
benefits of competent parenthood" (1970, p. 50).

Dobson draws a parallel between this sequence of events in the
parent-child relationship and the divine-human relationship:

Remember that He [God] revealed His majesty and wrath
and justice through the Old Testament before we were permitted to observe Jesus' incomparable love in the New Testament. It would appear that respect must precede loving

relationships in all areas of life. (Dobson, 1982, p. 118)

View of punishment. In the struggle to subdue the child's will, physical punishment sometimes is levied. Scriptures about the use of the "rod" are used to justify the punishment of those who fail to meet parental demands. One such scripture is from the Old Testament book of Proverbs:

> Withhold not correction from the child: for if thou beatest him with the rod, he shall not die. Thou shalt beat him with the rod, and shalt deliver his soul from hell. (23:13–14)

(For a fuller discussion of the "rod," see Chapter 12 on punishment.)

Dobson does not recommend that parents use techniques which are harsh and oppressive in their resolve to correct their children. But he does recommend physical punishment:

> The parent should have some means of making the child want to cooperate, other than simply obeying because he was told to do so. For those who can think of no such device, I will suggest one: there is a muscle, lying snugly against the base of the neck. Anatomy books list it as the trapezius muscle, and when firmly squeezed, it sends little messengers to the brain saying, "This hurts; avoid recurrence at all costs." (Dobson, 1970, p. 38)

He recommends spanking under certain circumstances:

> In my opinion, spankings should be reserved for the moment a child (age ten or less) expresses a defiant "I will not!" or "You shut up!" When a youngster tries this kind of stiff-necked rebellion, you had better take it out of him, and pain is a marvelous purifier. (Dobson, 1970, p. 27)

Dobson suggests that parents use a switch or belt to end defiance, and not the hand, because "the hand should be seen by the child as an object of love rather than an instrument of punishment" (Dobson, 1982, p. 159).

Impact on parent education. Dobson and the philosophy he espouses have had enormous influence on the American family, especially in the 1980s. His first book, *Dare to Discipline*, which appeared in 1970, has gone through three editions and over 40 printings, sold over 2.5 million copies and been translated into 12 other languages. Several other books which followed were best-sellers. Dobson's films have been viewed by an estimated 80 million persons and his daily radio program ("Focus on the Family") is carried by over 1200 stations, with a listening audience estimated to be one to two million persons. The headquarters of "Focus on the

Family," which receives 160,000 letters each month, now employs over 500 people (S. Becraft, personal communication, February 23, 1988 and March 22, 1988).

Childhood as Good and Parent as Communicator

Background. The second parenting philosophy is traced to Jean-Jacques Rousseau, whose 1762 book, *Emile*, emphasized the natural goodness of children. The premise of the book is that a young tutor takes a child, Emile, into the country to get away from the corrupting influences of his family and society. There the child learns from nature and is protected from formal training for the first twelve years of life.

In regard to the physical care of children, Rousseau argued that children should be breast-fed by their mothers, which is the natural manner of nourishing them. At the time, many infants were separated from their parents because of the belief that mothers lost vital fluids in breast-feeding. Infants were viewed as parasites, feeding at the mother's expense, which motivated parents to place their infants with wet-nurses if they could afford to do so.

Rousseau also argued against the practice of "swaddling," binding the infant with strips of cloth:

The limbs of a growing child should be free to move easily in his clothing; nothing should cramp their growth or movement; there should be nothing tight, nothing fitting closely to the body, no belts of any kind. (Rousseau, 1762/1965, p. 86)

Rousseau's suggestions for how to educate children were radical for their day. Instead of training through instruction, he wrote, adults should allow children to learn at their own pace following their natural curiosity:

Train him gradually to prolonged attention to a given object; but this attention should never be the result of constraint, but of interest or desire; you must be very careful that it is not too much for his strength, and that it is not carried to the point of tedium. (Rousseau, 1762/1965, p. 90)

In regard to moral education, Rousseau advocated an absence of training: "Give your scholar no verbal lessons; he should be taught by experience alone; never punish him, for he does not know what it is to do wrong" (Rousseau, 1762/1965, p. 80).

Rousseau's book outraged philosophers because it elevated feeling above reason, and it outraged the church because it barely recognized religion. Nevertheless, its thesis was revolutionary: children are different from adults, and deserve to be valued and understood for what they *are* rather than what they will become. A century later this point of view resulted in the child-study movement, in which children began to be studied with scientific methodology. Its influence was felt also in the creation of programs to protect children: orphanages, shelters for street children and various other asylums for children; laws which set the minimum age and maximum number of hours per day for child labor; and compulsory education laws.

In the twentieth century, this philosophy found expression in the Progressive Education movement of the early part of the century, and again in the humanistic psychology movement about 1950. In the 1940s clinical psychology was highly diagnostic and Freudian. Carl Rogers, in his book *My Philosophy of Interpersonal Relationships and How It Grew* (1980), experimented with a warmer, more empathic manner of therapy in which the therapist reflected back to the client, in a nonjudgmental way, the feelings the client was expressing. The techniques of "client-centered therapy" which he developed revolutionized individual counseling and spawned a parent education program (1980).

In the 1950s Thomas Gordon was working as a clinical psychologist, using the techniques of his colleague, Rogers. It occurred to him that the children he was seeing were not necessarily psychologically disturbed, nor were their parents. They were experiencing problems in their relationships because they were misinformed about what goes on in human relationships.

Gordon decided that parents could relate to their children in a healthier, more therapeutic manner if they were taught to use the communication skills employed in counseling. He began such a program in 1962 and Parent Effectiveness Training was born (Gordon, 1980).

Assumptions about human nature. Rousseau claimed that all of nature, including human nature, is good:

> God makes all things good; man meddles with them and they become evil. He forces one soil to yield the products of another, one tree to bear another's fruit. He confuses and confounds time, place, and natural condition. He mutilates his dog, his horse, and his slave. He destroys and defaces all things; he loves all that is deformed and monstrous; he will have nothing as nature made it, not even man himself, who must learn his paces like a saddlehorse, and be shaped to his

master's taste like the trees in his garden. (Rousseau 1762/1965)

Under Carl Rogers, this natural goodness came to mean a trust in self. One's feelings generated in the course of life are to be valued and not denied:

> I have moved a long way from some of the beliefs with which I started: that man was essentially evil . . . that the expert could advise, manipulate, and mold the individual to produce the desired result . . . . I have come to prize each emerging facet of my experience, of myself . . . . the feelings of anger and tenderness and shame and hurt and love and anxiety and giving and fear—all the positive and negative reactions that crop up . . . . I don't expect to act on all of them, but when I accept them all, I can be more real. (Rogers, 1980, p. 43)

Obviously, Rogers believes that being "real" is a good thing to be. He trusts human nature to unfold in a positive way, if provided an accepting environment.

Assumptions about the causes of problems in the home. In this point of view, problems are caused by "nontherapeutic" messages in the home. These messages tend to:

> make people feel judged or guilty; they restrict expression of honest feelings, threaten the person, foster feelings of unworthiness or low self-esteem, block growth and constructive change by making the person defend more strongly the way he is. (Gordon, 1970, p. 35)

When children hear these messages, they become resistant to efforts to change them. Parents then become more coercive to bring about change, which creates resentment, and the problems worsen.

Goals of parent education. In programs based on this philosophy, parents are taught skills of communication—to listen accurately and empathically, to provide feedback in nonthreatening ways and to resolve conflict to the point of mutual satisfaction. These skills enable parent and child "to relate to each other with mutual respect, love, and peace" (Gordon, 1970, p. 306).

View of punishment. Gordon argues against the use of punishment for philosophical reasons. He rejects the notion that parents need to rely on their superior power to influence children:

> My own conclusion is that as more people begin to understand power and authority more completely and accept its use as unethical, more parents will apply those understand-

ings to adult-child relationships . . . and then will be forced
to search for creative new nonpower methods that all adults
can use with children and youth. (Gordon, 1970, p. 191)

Not all persons of this philosophical bent take the radical position
that Gordon does. Some, like Fitzhugh Dodson (1970), accept brief,
nonabusive physical punishment as a means of communicating a
message which doesn't get through in other ways.

Impact on parent education. Gordon's impact on the American
family has been immense, particularly in the 1970s. Like Dobson's
first book, his first book — *Parent Effectiveness Training* — was published in 1970. The book has sold over two million copies and has
been translated into more than a dozen languages. Over 20,000
individuals have been trained to lead P.E.T. workshops, and more
than a million persons have enrolled in P.E.T. courses (D. M. Lucca,
personal communication, March 2, 1988).

With his daughter, Judy (the subject of the raincoat story), Gordon
wrote a sequel, *P.E.T. in Action* (Gordon, 1976). He also adapted his
parenting program to fit teachers (*Teacher Effectiveness Training,*
Gordon, 1974) and leaders (*Leader Effectiveness Training,* Gordon,
1978).

Few of today's young parents and college students have read
P.E.T., and in fact most have not heard of it. Yet those who are
reading about parenting almost inevitably are being influenced by
Gordon's ideas, because the techniques of P.E.T. (identification of
problem ownership, active listening, "I messages" and mutual problem solving) have become standard in parenting advice.

Childhood as Neutral and Parent as Environmental Engineer

Background. The third philosophy of parenting looks on the
child, not as a soul to be saved or as a partner in communication, but
as an organism responding to its environment. John Locke (1632–
1704) is credited with setting the foundation for this philosophy. He
argued against the notion that children are born with innate ideas.
Instead, they are born like a *tabula rasa* (blank slate) which is filled in
by experience.

Differences among children, Locke maintained, are due to differences in upbringing:

I have seen children at a table, who, whatever was there,
never asked for any thing, but contentedly took what was
given them: and at another place I have seen others cry for
every thing they saw, must be served out of every dish, and

that first too. What made this vast difference but this, that one was accustomed to have what they called or cried for, the other to go without it? (Locke, 1690/1973, p. 25)

This emphasis on the environment was carried in the twentieth century by the behaviorist branch of American psychology. John Watson, known as the father of behaviorism, is famous for this claim of 1914:

Give me a dozen healthy infants, well-formed, and my own specified world to bring them up in and I'll guarantee to take any one at random and train him to become any type of specialist I might select—doctor, lawyer, artist, merchant-chief, and yes, even beggar-man and thief, regardless of his talents, penchants, tendencies, abilities, vocations, and race of his ancestors. (Watson, 1914/1958, p. 104)

B. F. Skinner devoted a lifetime to studying the effects of environmental conditions on behavior, and led behaviorism to such prominence that it was the major force within American psychology from the 1940s to the 1960s. In 1943 he published *The Behavior of Organisms*, which was based on years of experimentation with pigeons and rats. It became the definitive work in the study of learning by conditioning, and it also demonstrated the power of positive reinforcement in the control of behavior.

To solve specific problems in the home or school, Skinner advocated an experimental analysis of behavior to find out what works. The procedures for altering behavior, based on Skinner's principles of reinforcement, came to be called *behavior modification*. Behavior modification has been applied to a wide variety of situations, and is the basis for numerous parent education programs.

Assumptions about human nature. In this third philosophy, the natural condition of childhood is seen not as evil or good, but as neutral. Children are capable of doing bad or good things; what they do is what they have learned to do.

The radical form of behaviorism espoused by Skinner isn't concerned with the issue of human nature. Humans, like other animals, are products of their environments:

More and more of the behavior of organisms, including man, is being plausibly related to events in their genetic and environmental histories. If other sciences are any guide, human behavior may ultimately be accounted for entirely in such terms. (Skinner, 1964/1972, p. 51)

Skinner refers to such concepts as the human will, wishes, emotions and attitudes as "mentalist" ideas, which, if properly understood would be unnecessary. For example, of free will, he states:

> A sense of freedom is another of those inner attributes which lose their force as we more clearly understand man's relation to his environment. Freedom—or, rather, behavior which "feels free"—is also the product of a history of conditioning. (Skinner, 1964/1972, p. 53)

Assumptions about the causes of problems in the home. Today's behaviorists would still agree with Locke's statement regarding parental responsibility for the manners and abilities of their children:

> We have reason to conclude, that great care is to be had of the forming of children's minds, and giving them that seasoning early, which shall influence their lives always after. For when they do well or ill, the praise or blame will be laid there: and when any thing is done awkwardly . . . it is suitable to their breeding. (Locke, 1690/1973, p. 19)

In this point of view, parents train children to behave. If their behavior is judged to be inappropriate, it is because the home environment (or society in general) failed to provide the conditions necessary for children to learn the appropriate behavior. Therefore, there are no bad or good children, but there are bad and good environments.

Goals of parent education. Since parents are the most significant part of the child's environment, behavioral models of parent education focus on increasing parental skills in shaping desirable behavior in their children. Parents are taught to view learning as the problem, and also as the solution. Behavior that is inappropriate can be unlearned; behavior that is appropriate can be learned to take its place. The techniques which parents are taught deal with observing the specific behavior in question, and altering the consequences of the child's behavior to bring about the desired behavior.

View of punishment. This philosophy tends to oppose punishment for empirical reasons. The data of experimental research reveal that punishment isn't as effective as parents commonly think it is. Under certain conditions punishment is effective, but undesired side effects sometimes accompany it. Furthermore, positive reinforcement is so powerful that it usually will achieve the desired end without punishment. (See Chapter 12, "Using Punishment," and Chapter 13, "Applying Behavior Modification.")

Impact on parent education. Behavior modification was used widely in the 1960s in parent education programs. In the 1970s it began to fade from public consciousness, because behavior modification was never adopted by ordinary American families to the extent that Dobson's and Gordon's concepts have been. Most people today have heard of "behavior mod," and reject it for philosophical reasons, although they don't understand it. Their image of behavior modification tends to be the image portrayed by the mass media, which is inaccurate—punitive and inescapable control by a totalitarian government.

In professional settings behavior modification remains the strategy most frequently employed for such problems as autism, hyperactivity, self-injurious behavior, bedwetting, phobias, language deficits, aggressiveness, withdrawal and tantrums.

In recent years several programs for teaching parents to be more assertive have been developed. These programs are based in part on a behavioral model of parenting, with roots in the learning theory of Skinner.

Evaluating the Three Philosophies of Parenting

From the perspective of The Balanced Parenting Model, the three philosophies of parenting all overemphasize certain aspects of parenting and underemphasize others. By itself each philosophy would lead parents astray, that is, towards an imbalance of parenting skills.

The strengths of the first philosophy, represented by James Dobson, are in its emphases on the No Problem Area and the Parent's Problem Area. Dobson's motivating talks prod parents to place parenting responsibilities high on their list of lifestyle priorities, persuading parents that there is no more important task than that of molding a child's character (the No Problem Area).

Parents who are weak with the skills needed in the Parent's Problem Area need the courage and firmness which Dobson recommends. I have seen parents, for example, who are so afraid of their children's displeasure that they are unable to take any kind of corrective action. I know parents who want so badly to make their children happy that the children are allowed to make everybody around them miserable.

But the emphasis which is Dobson's strength becomes its weakness when it is overemphasized. Shaping the will through demands for obedience and punishment for disobedience is but one small slice of the discipline pie. To make obedience the major emphasis leads parents to power struggles which aren't always necessary; they

Figure 3.1 Three Philosophies of Parenting

Illustrative Story	Siggy's Challenge	The Raincoat Problem	Baby in a Box
Nature of Childhood	Evil	Good	Neutral (tabula rasa)
Role of Parent	Disciplinarian	Communicator	Environmental Engineer
Contributors	Augustine John Calvin John Wesley James Dobson	Jean-Jacques Rousseau Carl Rogers Thomas Gordon	John Locke John B. Watson B. F. Skinner
Assumptions about the Causes of Problems	Problems are caused by will-fulness which is inherent in human nature.	Problems are caused by poor human relationship skills.	Problems are because bad habits have been learned and good habits have not been learned.
Goal of Parent Education	Parents are taught to shape the child's will by overcoming defiance and gaining submissiveness and trust.	Parents are taught to listen and speak effectively and to resolve conflicts through mutual respect.	Parents are taught to extinguish undesirable be-havior and to shape desirable behavior.
View of Punishment	Accepted within limits. Justified with biblical references about the "rod."	Generally opposed for philosophi-cal reasons. Punishment is dis-tasteful.	Generally opposed for empirical reasons. Punishment is ineffective, has undesirable side effects or is unnecessary.
Key Terms	Authority Obedience Respect Willfulness Discipline	Realness Acceptance Mutual respect Active listening I-messages Conflict resolution	Learning Environment Scientific analysis Training Shaping Reinforcement Extinction

become so focused on the child's willfulness that they aren't able to perceive other means of gaining compliance. And too many parents cross the fine line from punishment to child abuse in responding to misbehavior, compelled by their belief that the evil nature of children requires that kind of response.

The second philosophy, represented by Thomas Gordon, is strong in the Child's Problem Area. In my opinion there still is no better book than *Parent Effectiveness Training* (P.E.T.) for helping parents gain the skills they need to be supportive when their children are struggling. Unless parents have had some training in how to listen, they tend to rely on such old methods as lecturing, scolding and blaming, which drive their children away.

The P.E.T. program has a great deal to teach parents about how to love their children, although it doesn't place the parent-child relationship in any religious context, in contrast to the first philosophy.

Concerning P.E.T. James Dobson writes:

> . . . it is my view that the great flaws in Tom Gordon's philosophy far outweigh the benefits. They are . . . (1) his failure to understand the proper role of authority in the home; (2) his humanistic viewpoint which teaches that children are born innately "good," and then learn to do wrong; (3) his tendency to weaken parental resolve to instill spiritual principles systematically during a child's "teachable" years. All things considered, therefore, I would not recommend that Christian parents attend the P.E.T. program unless they are braced for the contradictions and deficiencies I have outlined. (Dobson, 1978, p. 177)

The influence of such statements is unfortunate if the skills of P.E.T. are lost to parents of the Dobson tradition. They need the skills P.E.T. offers for maintaining balance among the four areas of parenting responsibility.

Of course, P.E.T. is not the solution to all problems. It is weak in the Parent's Problem Area. Gordon teaches the use of the "I message," which is an important technique, but not enough by itself. Parents need more than a single technique for dealing with problems in the Parent's Problem Area. The "I message" requires mutual respect to be effective, and some children do not respect their parents to the extent required.

The strength of the third philosophy of parenting lies in the Parent's Problem Area. Behavior modification has become an essential tool for those in the helping professions who work with children lagging in intellectual and social development. Parents of mentally and socially handicapped children are grateful for the gains made possible by the systematic use of reinforcement.

Parents who are weak in the Parent's Problem Area can benefit from the training to be more assertive which the behavioral branch of psychology provides. It also informs parents of the various effects of punishment, enabling them to use punishment selectively or avoid it altogether.

But the applications of the behavior modification philosophy of parenting, as important as they have been, form only one small part of discipline, even in the Parent's Problem Area. For example, parents of children whose behavior is normal can get by without using behavior modification, since there are many other methods for dealing with the Parent's Problem Area which are less contrived and less complicated (see Chapters 10 and 11).

This philosophy contributes very little to the parental skills of the Child's Problem Area, because it pays scant attention to the child's feelings as a cause of behavior. And because it tends to reduce human behavior to mechanistic responses, the behavioral model overlooks the way family members affect each other in a dynamic, interlocking system of relationships. Thus, it contributes very little to the No Problem and Mutual Problem Areas.

The philosophy of parenting that shapes this book is eclectic. To be eclectic means to select concepts from several positions without ardently supporting any one position. I reject all three philosophies of this chapter as single understandings and methods, yet am willing to borrow from each of them the skills which help me pursue my parenting goals. **Parenting for the '90s,** therefore, teaches methods originating from a variety of sources, and explains where the methods are appropriately applied in order to maintain balance in discipline methods.

As I acknowledged in Chapter 1, the parenting experience is affected by the religious values of parents. In Chapter 4 I explore this further.

Because the position developed in Chapter 4 has theological underpinnings, some readers may want to skip Chapter 4 and continue with Part II, the No Problem Area. While the Balanced Parenting Model does not hinge on the material covered in Chapter 4, I do provide basic background there for my own reasons for selecting from other sources and then applying those skills.

Questions for Thought and Discussion about this Chapter are on page 289.

4. An Alternative Perspective on Parenting

When Jeff was a baby, I was feeding him with a bottle one day while visiting with a neighbor. The neighbor's philosophy of parenting was the conservative Christian philosophy reviewed in the previous chapter, so when Jeff forced the nipple out of his mouth and refused to take it again, he said, "Look at that! His sinful nature is showing up already." Although I didn't argue with my friend, I perceived the event from a different perspective.

Background. Persons taking the position of my neighbor tend to place the human race into two classes of people—the lost and the saved. Children are thought to be born into the former because of their sinful human nature. The implication of this position for parents is clear—children should be moved from the category of the lost to the category of the saved as soon as possible.

One means of meeting the spiritual obligations of parents, from the point of view of those who emphasize the evil nature of children, is to see that children are baptized. According to this view, baptism saves children (or signifies their salvation), and marks the end of their vulnerability to eternal damnation. By the time of the Middle Ages, therefore, infant baptism was required by law in the state churches of Europe.

Since the Reformation in the sixteenth century, the Christian church has been divided on the issue of infant baptism. Some of those who rejected infant baptism replaced it with child evangelism and retained the sense of urgency about converting children from their naturally evil condition. (For example, read again the quotation of John Wesley in Chapter 3, page 33: ". . . teach your children, as soon as possibly you can, that they are fallen spirits.")

Another group of reformers rejected infant baptism on the basis that Jesus' call to repentance and a life of discipleship was a message for adults, not children. Those taking this adult-believers position argued that children cannot make the kinds of decisions required for membership in the kingdom of God, nor can anybody else make the decisions for children. Jesus' invitation to children in the New Testament book of Mark was to come and be blessed, not repent and be baptized:

"Let the little children come to me, and do not hinder them, for the kingdom of God belongs to such as these. I tell you the truth, anyone who will not receive the kingdom of God like a little child will never enter it." And he took the children in his arms, put his hands on them and blessed them. (10:14b–16; NIV)

Those who hold the adult-believers position today maintain that the New Testament calls for the Christian nurture and teaching of children, but not for their conversion or baptism. Children are neither lost nor saved, but "safe" under the atonement of Christ until the "age of accountability," at which time they will be responsible for making the decisions of faith for themselves. Although the age at which their status changes is not specified, it is assumed to accompany the physical, intellectual and social changes which mark the passage from childhood to adulthood.

Assumptions about human nature. In the story which begins this chapter, my friend was convinced that Jeff's willful, sinful nature revealed itself when he pushed the nipple out of his mouth and wouldn't take it anymore. But the assumption from an adult-believers position is different. Jeff may have been distracted, full or even stubborn. But there is no reason to interpret what happened as a struggle between good and evil. Jeff was developmentally immature and was responding to his world within the limits of his capabilities. And even though he was just an infant, he was a separate individual, with his own will and a set of characteristics which made him different from all other persons, including us his parents.

As Jeff grew older his will sometimes led him to misbehave and he needed to be corrected. But that same will sometimes led him to run across the room, jump on my lap and give me a hug. And what makes those moments special is that they are voluntary, not automatic. Even God prefers such acts to be voluntary, according to the Genesis account of the Creation, because he made Adam and Eve with the capacity to make decisions. Children are people like Adam and Eve and all of us — they are not robots or puppets.

The adult-believers position acknowledges that we all sin, just as Adam and Eve did. But the capacity to choose to relate to God and to one another lovingly is necessarily accompanied by the capacity to choose to reject and disappoint. It's impossible to have only one choice — that's not a choice. Human nature was created with potential for both good and evil, and this is the way God wanted it. According to the Genesis account, "God saw all that he had made, and it was very good" (1:31a; NIV).

Goals of parent education. If an adult-believers perspective on parenting does not focus on the necessity to correct children from their naturally evil state, what does it focus on? It focuses on the parents themselves. This sounds odd, but it is consistent with the emphasis on the decisions of adults. Adults have children and so the hope of parents is that their children will grow up someday to be adult believers like themselves. *Like themselves.* There's the catch. What kind of adult believers will the children be if they grow up to be like their parents?

Horace Bushnell, a nineteenth century theologian, wrote about the connection between the faith of the parent and the faith of the child:

> If we narrowly examine the relation of parent and child, we shall not fail to discover something like a law or organic connection, as regards character, subsisting between them. Such a connection as makes it easy to believe, and natural to expect, that the faith of the one will be propagated in the other. (Bushnell, 1867/1973, p. 146)

This notion was understood by the Amish farmer who, when asked what he raised, replied "I raise Amishmen."

The connection between parent and child is not due solely to either heredity or to the parent's ability to parent; it also depends on the parent's own spiritual renewal:

> When a germ is formed on the stem of any plant, the formative instinct of the plant may be said in one view to produce it; but the same solar heat which quickens the plant,

must also quicken the germ, and sustain the internal action of growth, by a common presence in both. So, if there be an organic power of character in the parent . . . (it) demands the realizing presence of the Spirit of God, both in the parent and the child, to give it effect. (Bushnell, 1867/1973, p. 150)

This is why the adult-believers tradition places primary emphasis on "regenerated marriages, homes, and congregations that make possible the nurture of children in the values of the Christian way" (Jeschke, 1983, p. 143). For example, in this tradition the "child dedication" service which is held when the child is an infant or toddler is not a dedication of the child at all. It is a dedication of the parents and congregation; they dedicate themselves to the task of bringing up a child in the faith.

John Drescher (1979), author of books on family relationships, makes this distinction in the book *If I Were Starting My Family Again.* He writes that he used to pray solicitous prayers for his children — that they would become more obedient, pleasant, loving and so on:

. . . it struck me that this kind of praying must stop . . . I was praying for the wrong person.

I stopped praying like that for my family. I realized that if my children were to know Christ's love, then I, as their father, needed to experience more of Christ's love and make that love visible. If they were ever to learn true love in relationship to others, then I needed divine aid to demonstrate true love in all my relationships with the family and others. So my prayers turned to "Lord, make me fit to live with, loving, and kind, as you are to me." (Drescher, 1979, p. 34)

Specific misbehaviors of children are of concern and need to be corrected. This book addresses methods for correcting and influencing children in each of the four areas of parenting skills. But parental concern for children goes beyond teaching them what behaviors are socially proper and what are improper. The larger concern is the gradual induction of the child into a lifestyle — a lifestyle of Christian discipleship. Discipline is ultimately a matter of discipling. (The two words have the same Latin roots.)

Therefore, my job as parent as seen from the perspective of the adult-believers position was to cherish Jeff as a child of God entrusted to my care, nurturing him in the faith by living my own life of Christian discipleship with him by my side. I did not have to worry about altering his sinful nature, as my neighbor would have done.

On Children

And a woman who held a babe against her bosom said, Speak to
   us of Children.
And he said:
Your children are not your children.
They are the sons and daughters of Life's longing for itself.
They came through you, but not from you,
And though they are with you, yet they belong not to you.
You may give them your love, but not your thoughts.
For they have their own thoughts.
You may house their bodies but not their souls,
For their souls dwell in the house of tomorrow, which you cannot
   visit, not even in your dreams.
You may strive to be like them, but seek not to make them like you.
For life goes not backward nor tarries with yesterday.
You are the bows from which your children as living arrows are
   sent forth.
The archer sees the mark upon the path of the infinite, and He
   bends you with his might that His arrow may go swift and far.
Let your bending in the archer's hand be for gladness;
For even as He loves the arrow that flies, so He loves also the bow
   that is stable.

Kahlil Gibran

Assumptions about the causes of problems in the home. In regard to problems in the home, this perspective acknowledges first of all that parents have no guarantee that there will not be problems. Even God had problems with Adam and Eve. Parents do not have control over the disposition the child is born with nor all of the choices the child makes. Respect for the individuality of the child is accompanied always by apprehension and sometimes by disappointment.

From this point of view, parents need not take all the blame (nor all the credit) for how their children turn out. Children are ultimately responsible for their choices. This relieves parents of some of the responsibility they likely feel for their children, but it doesn't let them off the hook entirely. The kinds of persons parents are does affect the kinds of persons children become, and parents *are* responsible for *their* own choices.

When John Drescher was writing about the moment he realized that he was praying for the wrong person, he went on to say what a difference the change in focus made:

> It suddenly seemed that my wife and children changed. A new atmosphere of love pervades the house and even the car when we go driving. The children seem kinder. And it all started when I stopped praying for them and began to pray for God to give me a new attitude. . . . My wife and children are as much in my prayers as ever. But now my prayers are primarily prayers of thanksgiving for each member of my family. And I believe that God desires this kind of praying because it also honors him who gave each one to me. (Drescher, 1979, p. 35)

An incident reported in the news reminded me of how much children learn through daily life with their parents. A five-year old boy awoke one morning to find his mother sick in bed. Since she was unable to chauffeur him and his two-year-old sister as she usually did, he decided to do it himself. He took the car keys from his mother's purse, opened the garage door, put his two-year-old sister in the back seat, moved the front seat all the way forward so that he could just touch the pedals, started the car, backed it out of the garage, and then maneuvered it safely through rush-hour traffic. A patrol officer saw the car moving through traffic seemingly without a driver. The young boy noticed the flashing light and siren of the patrol car and pulled the family car to the curb. Realizing that the situation needed an adult presence, he told the officer, "My mommy can't come here because I have the only car. I can drive. I'll go get her" ("Open Road," 1987).

What a tremendous amount he had learned in five years! He was able to use driving skills which were picked up without lessons or practice, knew the family's daily routine, had constructed a mental map of the city, understood traffic patterns, and was fluent in English. In addition he had developed a sense of empathy and care for his mother, responsibility for his sister, respect for law enforcement officers and confidence in himself.

Some years ago, studies at Northwestern University by psychologist James Bryan shed some light on how the modeling effect occurs. He compared the effects of what adults *say* with what they *do*. In one experiment, children heard an adult talk about why one should give to the March of Dimes (for example, "Children should help other children."). Other children heard him talk about why one should not give (for example, "Children don't have to help other children."). Half of the children in both groups then saw the model actually donate to the March of Dimes and half saw him walk out without donating. The children were then observed to see what impact the experimental conditions had on their donations.

The researchers found that the children were influenced by what the adult *did*. When he gave, they were more likely to give also. What the adult *said* made no difference in whether or not the children donated, but it did affect what children said to other children about giving. It was as if two different domains were being modeled: children did what the model did and said what the model said, but what the model said didn't necessarily affect what the children did (Bryan, 1969).

Not satisfied that this was the whole story, Bryan followed that study with one in which the adult's statements were changed from the "oughts" of the earlier study to comments about how he felt about giving, as in "It feels good to give." This time his *word* as well as his *deed* influenced the donations of the children (Bryan, 1971).

These studies suggest that parents are more likely to pass on their faith when they live it, and especially when they enjoy living it. If children do not adopt the values of the parents, it may be because the values are not genuinely valued.

View of punishment. Traditionally, adult-believers groups have used physical punishment, even many of those who follow a lifestyle of nonresistance and deplore the use of violence to resolve conflict. Those who use it maintain that physical punishment in the home and violence between adults or nations do not belong in the same category, as long as the punishment of the child is not abusive.

There are others, however, who include physical punishment with the forms of violence they oppose. They believe that the traits they value (humility, conformity, respect, reverence, unselfishness, generosity and nonviolence) can be instilled without punitive measures. (Some argue this more strongly, maintaining that these values cannot be instilled through punitive means.) The values are caught by children in the course of growing up because the values are so deeply ingrained in the parents themselves, as suggested by the following young adult:

> I think most of what I learned at home is the result of learning by imitation. For instance, my parents never used threats of violence to scare us and I never heard them talk that way to anybody else. I don't think they ever said, "If you do that, I'll whip your hide!" or some similar expression which I heard in other homes. I think that their quiet discipline rubbed off on me, for I too am gentle.

Horace Bushnell took the same position, arguing eloquently for spiritual discipline as an alternative to physical punishment:

> I would not undervalue a strong and decided government in families. No family can be rightly trained without it. But there is a kind of virtue, my brethren, which is not in the rod—the virtue, I mean of a truly good and sanctified life. . . . There are . . . many who talk much of the rod as the orthodox symbol of parental duty, but who might really as well be heathens as Christians; who only storm about their house with heathenish ferocity, who lecture, and threaten, and castigate, and bruise, and call this family government. They even dare to speak of this as the nurture of the Lord. . . . By no such summary process can you dispatch your duties to your children. You are not to be a savage to them, but a father [parent] and a Christian. Your real aim and study must be to infuse into them a new life, and, to this end, the Life of God must perpetually reign in you. (Bushnell 1867/1973, p. 151)

What can be stated with certainty is that there has been considerable disagreement among adult-believers groups about punishment. For a fuller treatment of the issues involved, see Chapter 12, "Using Punishment."

Impact on parent education. In contrast to the three popular

Figure 4.1
An Alternative to the Three Popular Philosophies: The
Adult-Believers Position

Illustrative Story	Refusal to Take the Bottle
Nature of Childhood	Developmentally immature. Potential for both good and evil. Theologically "safe" in spite of human sinful condition, until "age of accountability."
Role of Parent	Nurturer
Contributors	Anabaptist branch of Reformation Horace Bushnell John Drescher
Assumptions about Causes of Problems	Immaturity of child Choices, individuality of child "Values" of parents not genuinely valued
Goal of Parent Education	Nurture faith in child through daily life together. Cherish child as gift of God. Correct child's misbehavior using methods consistent with beliefs about relationships.
View of Punishment	Divided—some accept role of punishment in the nurture of children; some maintain punishment is inconsistent with the value of nonviolent means of solving problems.
Key Terms	Nurture Education Age of accountability Modeling effect Children "in the midst," "by your side"

philosophies which have had significant impact on contemporary families, the perspective of this chapter has had very little effect. It is partly because those who come the closest to this position in practice do not talk about it much; they emphasize deed rather than word, ethics rather than creed.

For contemporary adult-believers groups, the perspective of this chapter may help to clarify the connection between their theology and their childrearing practices. And to those of a different religious background who are dissatisfied with the conservative Christian emphases on evil and punishment, the behaviorist branch of psychology which ignores religious thought, and humanistic psychology which cares about people but is not connected to faith, the position of this chapter offers an alternative way of thinking about parenting.

My hope is that, regardless of religious background, persons will be challenged by this perspective to consider what it means to live with children by their side.

Questions for Thought and Discussion about this Chapter are on page 292.

<u>Children Learn What They Live</u>

If a child lives with criticism,
    He learns to condemn.
If a child lives with hostility,
    He learns to fight.
If a child lives with ridicule,
    He learns to be shy.
If a child lives with jealousy,
    He learns to feel guilty.
If a child lives with tolerance,
    He learns to be patient.
If a child lives with encouragement,
    He learns confidence.
If a child lives with praise,
    He learns to appreciate.
If a child lives with security,
    He learns to have faith.
If a child lives with approval,
    He learns to like himself.
If a child lives with acceptance and friendship,
    He learns to find love in the world.

—*Dorothy Law Nolte*

A Prayer of Parents

Help us to the stature of good parenthood, O God. We pray that we may let our children live their own lives and not the ones we wish we had lived. Therefore, guard us against burdening them with doing what we failed to do, and when tempted to seek balm for old wounds, strengthen us against our self-justification.

Help us to see today's missteps in perspective against the long road they must go, and grant us the grace of patience with their slow pace, lest in our impatience we force them into rebellion, retreat, or anxiety.

Give us the precious wisdom of knowing when to smile at the small mischiefs of their age and when to give them the haven of firmness against the impulses which in their heart they fear and cannot master.

In time of needed punishment give us a warm heart and a gentle voice so that they may feel the rule of order as their friend and clasp it to their souls to be their conscience.

Help us to hear the anguish in their hearts through the din of angry words or across the gulf of brooding silence, and having heard, give us the grace to bridge the gap between us with understanding warmth before speaking our own quick retorts, and stay our tongues also from the words which would chill their confiding in us.

Still our voices and smooth from our brows all that mars infectious serenity and joy in living; rather let our faces so shine that these adult years will seem to them a promised land toward which to strive.

We pray that we may raise our voices more in joy at what they are, than in vexation at what they have done; each day may they grow in sureness of themselves.

Help us to hold them with such warmth as will give them friendliness toward others; then give us the fortitude to free them to go strongly on their way.

Then as we see them striding forward eagerly, self-sure, friendly, and in good conscience, our grateful hearts will swell with joy.

Amen.

*—adapted from a prayer by
Marion B. Durfee*

Part II
The No Problem Area

In the No Problem Area the child is not in a struggle with the parent nor worried about other matters, and the parent is not bothered by the child's behavior.

Of the four areas in a parent's relationship with a child, the No Problem Area is the most important. Those moments when parent and child are together and neither one is upset offer opportunity for creating a sense of family in which members enjoy each other's company and care about each other.

If this sense of family is created, problems will be manageable when they arise, even if the parent's techniques are not the best. On the other hand, if this sense of caring for each other is not created, no technique or method will work well in dealing with a problem.

Abidin (1982; also Stinnett & DeFrain, 1985) describes the parent-child relationship as a savings account. The things which build the relationship are deposits into the account. Those things which damage the relationship are withdrawals. If the withdrawals are greater than the deposits, the relationship is bankrupt. When a parent-child relationship is nearly bankrupt, the parent will have to rely more and more on coercive techniques to manage the child's behavior, and less and less on goodwill and respect. This in turn leads to an even poorer relationship. Finally, in a bankrupt relationship, no technique will be effective; the account needs to be replenished first.

In *Secrets of Strong Families* Stinnett and DeFrain describe the strengths of the strong families which they studied as a

pool of resources that they draw on when times are difficult —rather like we save money for a "rainy day." In contrast, unhealthy families are worn out and depleted on a daily basis by the stress of poor relationships. When a crisis comes along, the unhealthy family must add it to the burden they already struggle with. No wonder the extra load is sometimes too much. (Stinnett & DeFrain, 1985, p. 137)

From the perspective of the Balanced Parenting Model, the goal of parenting in the No Problem Area is to increase its size. As the vertical line moves to the right and the horizontal line moves down, the No Problem Area enlarges and the other three areas necessarily become smaller (see Figure II.1).

Figure II.1
The Importance of the No Problem Area

When the No Problem Area is small (top), living together generates continuous mutual problems because minor matters escalate into conflict. Both parents and children attempt to solve problems through manipulation and coercion. Attempts are met with resentment, resistance and rebellion. The No Problem Area continues to shrink in size. Eventually an emotional cutoff takes place and the parent-child relationship dies from neglect.

When the No Problem Area is large (bottom), problems which arise are more easily managed. Both parents and children rely on mutual respect and support to solve problems. The relationship is valued more because of what they have been through together and the No Problem Area grows even larger.

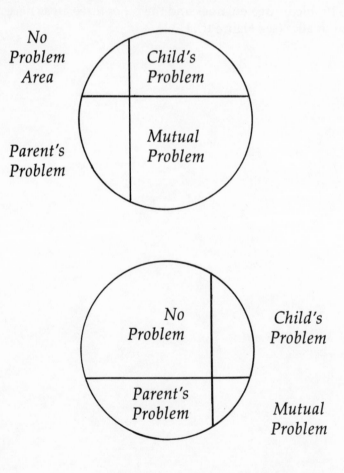

Paradoxes of the No Problem Area

There are a number of features about the No Problem Area which are paradoxical and which make it unique among the four areas.

1. Of the four areas, the No Problem Area is the most important, yet it is the most overlooked. This is because parents tend to think of "discipline" as correction or even punishment, without regarding the interpersonal context in which the correction takes place. Thus they fail to see discipline as the control that is molded in many ways by living with children; they fail to see that children are willing to be influenced in a relationship which they value. What often happens is that the more parents focus on the correction-punishment aspect of parenting, the less successful they are in reaching their goal of discipline.

2. Success in the No Problem Area doesn't have to do with parenting "methods." It's more likely to occur when parents get out of the parent role and relax, treating their children in a friendly and respectful manner, just as they would treat a good friend whose company they enjoy.

3. Activities in the No Problem Area aren't necessarily planned in advance, although parents can make them more likely to happen. No Problem Area moments tend to occur when parents are relaxed and attentive enough to respond to the child's initiatives. The moments can't be forced; they often contain elements of surprise and spontaneity.

4. No Problem Area times don't necessarily cost money, although they often happen in a change of setting and routine which sometimes does cost money (for example, a family vacation trip). They can be as cheap — and as priceless — as an exchange of affection or a walk in the park.

5. No Problem Area moments don't necessarily take much time, although some time together is required. In the 1970s, as more mothers went to work outside the home, the issue of time spent with children became an important one. If mothers weren't as available as before to spend time with their children, perhaps they could make good use of the time they did have. "Quality time" became the goal. Here, however, time itself is not the main issue, since families can spend two weeks vacationing together and be miserable.

A teenaged daughter of divorced parents related an incident which occurred at the end of her summer visit with her dad as he was moving from one state to another:

When we came to the place in the trip where he headed south and I needed to go north, he simply stuck me on a bus. He just didn't want to spend another day traveling with me, even though I had done nothing wrong.

The amount of time together is not the critical issue in this incident, since she had just spent part of the summer with her dad. The more important issue is that she was not feeling loved and so she interpreted his decision about saving time as an indication of his lack of commitment to her. Therein lies the paradox. No Problem moments require very little time, but they do require emotional attachment, and persons who are emotionally attached will spend time together and will capture more of the brief moments.

Scott Peck explains the connection between time and love this way:

When we love something it is of value to us, and when something is of value to us we spend time with it, time enjoying it and time taking care of it. Observe a teenager in love with his car and note the time he will spend admiring it, polishing it, repairing it, tuning it. Or an older person with a beloved rose garden, and the time spent pruning and mulching and fertilizing and studying it. So it is when we love children; we spend time admiring them and caring for them. We give them our time. (Peck, 1978, p. 22)

6. The goal of No Problem Area activities is not to teach children lessons, but through the activities they will learn a great deal. No Problem Area moments are "teachable moments." Since parents and children are not experiencing conflict with each other, there is less reason to be critical, on the one hand, or defensive on the other; children are more open to being influenced. And one of the things they will learn through No Problem Area activities is how to develop and maintain relationships, an important by-product of the experience.

7. The parenting role requires that parents initiate No Problem Area activities for the sake of their children, but parents profit at least as much as children do through the activities. The companionship of children is a fringe benefit to parenthood. Furthermore, when the parent-child relationship account is adequately supplied, problems which arise at other times are more easily resolved, so that parents who initiate No Problem Area activities are making it easier on themselves in that the rest of their responsibilities as parents will be more manageable.

8. No Problem Area activities sometimes are the result of tragedies. While failures, illnesses, accidents and other stressful events are not desired, they sometimes improve the parent-child relationship and are remembered with appreciation. This is because stress which is external to the relationship drives family members together for mutual support.

9. No Problem Area times are important in the moment they occur, but are equally important later in the remembering. For children, an event happening once can be remembered as a "tradition." Family jokes and stories, family photographs, family traditions and private memories all become part of the family heirlooms. The retelling of earlier No Problem Area times is an important No Problem Area activity itself.

10. It is never too early and it is never too late in a child's life for No Problem Area activities. Parents, especially fathers, often wish that they had spent more time with their children when they were younger or had been more attentive to them. College students often wish their parents had been better at this. I am continually surprised by how many young adults are unable to remember being hugged, kissed or told they are loved by their parents. But it's never too late for either child or parent, at any age, to initiate No Problem Area activities. When these moments are rare, the impact they make as deposits into the relationship account is even greater than when the account is plentifully supplied.

Questions for Thought and Discussion about this Chapter are on page 292.

Figure II.2
Paradoxes of the No Problem Area

1. Of the four problem ownership areas, the No Problem Area is the most important, yet it is the most overlooked.
2. Success in the No Problem Area doesn't have to do with parenting "methods."
3. Activities in the No Problem Area aren't necessarily planned in advance, although parents can make them more likely to happen.
4. No Problem Area times don't necessarily cost money, although they often happen in a change of setting and routine.
5. No Problem Area moments don't necessarily take much time, although some time together is required.
6. The goal of No Problem Area activities is not to teach children lessons, but through the activities they will learn a great deal.
7. The parenting role requires that parents initiate No Problem Area activities for the sake of their children, but parents profit at least as much as children do through the No Problem Area.
8. No Problem Area activities sometimes are the result of tragedies.
9. No Problem Area times are important in the moment they occur, but are equally important later in the remembering.
10. It's never too early and it's never too late in a child's life for No Problem Area activities.

5. Activities in the No Problem Area

In order to find out more about the raw materials for building parent-child relationships, I asked many people—children, college students and parents—to disclose their memories of happy times with either one or both of their parents. Many of their stories clustered under these categories: family trips, holidays and other celebrations, shared leisure activities and spontaneous fun, working together, meals and bedtimes, and (surprisingly, since I had asked for "happy" memories) mutual support in times of crisis.[1]

Family Trips, Holidays and Other Celebrations

No Problem Area activities are those times when the child has the parent's presence and attention without stress. Perhaps this is why many of the happy memories evoked by my question had to do with family vacation trips. On vacations, away from the normal daily routine, parents are less pressured, more leisurely. Family members spend more time together than usual, in a car, cabin, or on a beach or hiking trail; make decisions together about where to eat, spend the night, what to do during the day; and adjust together to life without

[1] I have collected written and spoken stories over a period of many years in parenting workshops, college classes and interviews with children. The collection has been for my own use as a source of anecdotes in teaching. I regret that the methodology for determining the clusters of memories lacked the rigor required to provide data analyses to those who might want them.

Figure 5.1
No Problem Area Activities

1. *Family trips, holidays and other celebrations*

2. *Shared leisure activities and spontaneous fun*

3. *Working together*

4. *Meals and bedtimes*

5. *Mutual support in times of crisis*

the usual conveniences and responsibilities. Doris, a college student, wrote:

> Foremost in my mind are our yearly vacations to the mountains of Pennsylvania. We went to my uncle's cabin, which had gas lanterns, an outhouse and no running water. Two bedrooms accommodated Mom, Dad and the seven kids. One night late, a bear came scratching on our door. We talked about that memory for years.

For many years our family has spent a week in the summer in Colorado. We spend a weekend with our good friends and do some shopping in Denver, and then head for a cabin at Rocky Mountain Camp on the backside of Pike's Peak where we stay several days.

In the morning we hike, always including a trip to the top of Sentinel Point, a climb both exhausting and exhilarating. At the top we eat the lunches we had packed and take naps between the rocks where the wind can't reach us but the sun does, and then make the descent. After hot showers at the main camp we return to the cabin to read, watch chipmunks, hummingbirds and deer, fix supper, play games and go to bed early.

There is nothing unusual about this vacation routine, but for our family these experiences have been important. They are deposits into our No Problem Area savings account. Members of other families recount similar happy memories. Joi wrote of her family:

> Each year in May we went to Michigan for a week of mushroom-hunting. This was not just my immediate family, but grandparents, aunts and uncles and cousins, too. All of us kids got out of school. We went to the woods each day and

there was always a contest: who got the most, the largest, etc. In the evenings we swam, had campfires and went riding in the dunes. We did this every year until I went to college and it's a special memory for me.

Family vacations are not without problems, of course. But even the things which go wrong become good stories for telling later when family members can laugh about what happened. One student wrote:

I'll never forget Dad's photographic skills on our trips. First he'd look through the camera on the tripod, then order us to turn this way or that, look into the sun, put our hand here, etc. Then he'd set the timer and rush back. No matter what, he always looked stiff and posed. It makes me laugh now. Those were good times.

In addition to family trips, holidays and birthdays were mentioned frequently as happy memories. Deb wrote:

The first special memory that pops into my mind is Christmas. We always have a candle-lit dinner in which we fondue beef and chicken. Before the meal, we all hold hands and everyone usually prays. My dad always closes that prayer time. After everyone helps clean up the kitchen after the meal, we gather in our family room to hear the Christmas story which is read by Mom. After this, Dad hands out the presents to everyone and we go from youngest to oldest, opening just one present at a time. The rest of the evening is spent "playing" with our gifts.

At Bobbie's house, birthdays

. . . were always a big deal. Mom would decorate a cake for us and prepare our favorite meal. I remember getting to go shopping with her a couple of days before my birthday and picking out my favorite cake mix and flavor of ice cream. I always liked to choose new flavors that we had never tasted before and got more and more disappointed as I got older that we had already tried them all. Birthdays were special because, for one day, I got the attention I craved.

These stories of family vacations and holidays illustrate activities in the No Problem Area which were repeated year after year by these families. Many happy memories, however, were of events which took place only once. In fact, some events are important because they aren't ordinary occurrences, and they are remembered happily if parents help to give the moments their due value.

Especially important are events marking developmental *rites of passage*. Lori remembered the day her driver's permit arrived in the mail:

> I was in the field mowing alfalfa when my dad and some of the family drove up in our truck. I wondered what was wrong. Dad got out of the truck and waved for me to come. I jumped off the tractor and ran to the truck. He stood there grinning, so I asked what this was all about. He handed me the permit and keys, then told me to get in and drive, because this was cause for celebration.

Ramona remembered appreciatively her parents' presence at a rite of passage in her religious development:

> I remember looking at my parents right after I'd been baptized. We all embraced for a few seconds, but the love we shared with one another was felt long after the embrace was over.

Also remembered with fondness is parental support at times of achievement — often music recitals, school plays and athletic competition. Larry, for example, remembered a track meet in his fourth grade year:

> My favorite event was the 880. That year I found myself a meet away from advancing to the Junior Olympics. The gun shot and I had a good pace — and finished second, good enough to go on. What stands out in my mind is that when I crossed the finish line, exhausted, my father reached out and gave me the biggest hug and kiss imaginable. That was special, even though I told him, "Dad, take it easy, all the people are watching!"

Parental presence at these events is a clear signal of support.

The mutuality of such support is illustrated by a story of Kim, who wrote in college:

> One memory that I will hang on to forever is the day my mama graduated from college with a degree in nursing. I remember many times during my high school years that we would sit at our big dining room table and study together. Finally the day arrived and I think I cried more at her graduation than at my own. We were so proud of her. And she looked good in her cap and gown!

One of the things which happens in the No Problem Area is that parents teach children how to love, how to develop and maintain relationships, as Kim so clearly has learned.

Shared Leisure Activities and Spontaneous Fun

Activities in the No Problem Area need not cost as much nor take as much time as family vacations. Sometimes they involve spending time together in favorite activities, going for walks, picnics in parks or simply playing together. This was the content of many of the happy memories I solicited. Brenda, for example, remembers that she did things which she enjoyed with both of her parents:

A special memory I have with my mom is when we would make music together. She would play the piano and I would sing. Sometimes I would play the flute and she would sing. I felt proud to have a mother who would sit down and spend time with me in that special way. I remember taking motorcycle rides with my dad. It was just him and me riding all over the Indiana countryside.

Some of Lorna's best times with our children have been going shopping and going out to eat. With her, riding 30 minutes to the mall involves more than simply getting there; shopping is more than taking care of the items on the list, and sitting at a table in a restaurant is more than eating. Each offers opportunity to be together in No Problem Area moments, and she has helped us to value these times.

Happy memories sometimes are formed when parents step out of their adult roles long enough to have fun in a moment of childlikeness. I once asked our children what they remembered about a trip our family took in 1974 from Kansas to Tennessee and back. Since the purpose of the trip was to attend my Ph.D. graduation ceremony, I assumed that their memories would be about this eminent event. But not so. The memory which emerged first and which was recounted with the greatest pleasure was of a picnic lunch at a roadside park. I was eating a bologna sandwich, and inadvertently got a dab of mustard on my cheek. The kids pointed this out, with some amusement. So I opened the sandwich up, smeared mustard on my other cheek and, spurred on by their cheers, on my forehead as well. Before long, we all had mustard on our faces.

They have a similar kind of memory about one of our summer trips to Colorado. The hike to Sentinel Point takes us up a valley which at one point is precipitous and full of huge boulders, with water running around and over the rocks. We always stop at this spot, captivated by its beauty, to rest, get a drink or splash in the water. On one occasion, the kids were playing in the water with their shoes and socks off. They begged us to join them, but I wasn't about to get my clothes wet in ice-cold water at an altitude of 10,000 feet, on our way to the top of Sentinel with its cold winds. But Lorna finally gave in to their persistence. I looked over at her, realized what she was doing and thought, "Why not?" The kids still laugh today about the time we stripped to our underwear in order to play with them in the stream without getting our clothes wet.

The content of other happy memories has to do with being allowed to do something — steer the tractor, push the accelerator of the car, bake cookies, host a party. Their parents' consent in these instances left the children feeling good about being trusted.

One of my favorite memories of this type is of an event that took place just before Julie took Driver's Education. Two of her friends and she were talking one evening about the upcoming course, and it was clear that they were eager to get through it to get their licenses. But it was also clear that they had some anxiety about the "stick shift" part of the course, since none of them had had any experience with vehicles with standard transmission. So I suggested that they practice. I drove them to the football stadium in a car with stick shift, gave them a lesson in the use of the clutch, and then let them learn by doing. They took turns grinding gears and jerking the car through the parking lot for an hour.

Since peers are increasingly important to children as they age, No Problem Area activities are more likely to involve their friends as children get older. Lorna and I found this to be an unexpected fringe benefit to parenting. We didn't realize how much we would enjoy getting to know our children's friends, and through them, their parents.

Children value this too, as is evident in the happy memories people recalled about parent-child-friend interactions. For example, Christine, who grew up in Kenya, wrote:

> When I reached high school age, I was sent to boarding school. My mother, who realized how important my boarding school friends had become for me, would invite me to bring friends home. One time I brought half of the field hockey team. Mom made us steak, potatoes, green beans and corn for supper. Then we ate *all* the ice cream for dessert.
>
> Since we had been playing at a hockey tournament all day, we were hot and sunburned; she brought vinegar and Noxzema to cool our skin and ran hot baths. I will always remember all the work she went to and how special that was.

Parents can learn things about their children and their friends by offering to host, sponsor or chauffeur them to their activities. When our children were early adolescents, they liked to spend an afternoon at a mall with their friends, walking the mall, shopping and going to a movie. But they needed a way to get there since they couldn't drive yet. So I volunteered to take them, drop them off and pick them up at a certain time. In the car they would turn the radio to their favorite station, turn the volume up, of course, and then talk and giggle and talk some more. I would disappear into my chauffeur role but would keep one ear open for an occasional bit of information.

A few years ago we finished a family room in our basement. It has become one of the best investments we ever made. It gives our children a place to be with their friends, without being too close to the rest of the activity of the household. We have enjoyed the visits with the friends as they come and go, and don't mind making popcorn, juice or fresh cookies. It won't be long before our children leave home and we will miss their friends as well as them.

We also have come to value associations with the parents of our children's friends. Visiting at games, getting together after games, traveling together to tournaments or meeting for coffee during church activities all provide opportunity for sharing experiences with people with whom we have a great deal in common. (Besides enjoying the conversations and fun, Lorna and I have discovered that maintaining contact with our children's friends' parents is like taking out an honesty insurance policy. Our children are less likely to mislead us about their activities when we know the other parents well enough to compare notes about what we've been told.)

Working Together

Another cluster of happy memories of childhood experiences has to do with working with mom or dad—helping water the trees, wash the dishes, make hay, bring in the cattle, dig potatoes and wait on customers in the family store. Rhonda, for example, wrote:

> A special memory from this past summer was working with my mom. She wallpapers for a few interior decorators; we decided that this would be a good job for me to have for this summer, so that's what I ended up doing. I wasn't terribly excited about it at first, because it didn't sound like much fun. We really did have a good time, though, and it gave us a chance to be together, which was especially important since I was leaving for college.

Similar experiences were recalled by Steve, who helped his parents and grandparents in the summers in their greenhouse business:

We each had our own tasks. Dad would mix the ground with various nutrients while Mom waited on customers. I helped with various things and each year was given added responsibilities. I got a lot of fulfillment out of this.

It was more than the work involved in these instances, however, which caused them to turn out to be pleasant memories. I have heard many other stories about working with parents which are bad memories, still told with resentment years later.

Psychiatrist Allen Wheelis, in *How People Change*, tells about a summer in his childhood many years ago when his dad was terminally ill with tuberculosis. In an attempt to teach Allen to work hard and be responsible in their last summer together, his father demanded that Allen cut the grass in an area of several acres with a straight-edge razor. The task took the entire summer, broken occasionally by protests from young Allen and reprimands from his father. The legacy left by Allen's father that summer did include a sense of responsibility and need to achieve, but it also included a loss of playfulness and the indelible message that he was a "low-down, no-account scoundrel" (Wheelis, 1973, p. 73). Fifty years later, Wheelis is still nagged by the memory of himself standing before his father on the glassed-in porch, being judged to be unworthy.

Although I know that the father in this story was unusually severe, the story haunts me, serving as a reminder to do what I can to keep experiences of working with my children in the No Problem Area. For Allen and his father, work drained their relationship account, and I don't want this to happen to us.

In order for work to replenish a parent-child relationship, parents need to respect the limits of the child's abilities. This is obvious, but still difficult to put into practice. When children are little, "helping" mom or dad may not be much real help at all; in fact the job may be easier without such help because of the messes and mistakes which are made. But the experiences of "working" side by side — making cookies, washing dishes, shopping for groceries, pulling weeds, changing the oil in the car or whatever it is that parents are doing — can be enjoyable ones, provided that parents allow children to contribute to the process at their level of ability and to learn by doing. Before shopping for groceries, for example, children can help make the list and, in the store, help locate the items.

One summer Nate and I spent a month building a deck on the

back of the house. In the beginning he helped by carrying boards and hammering, while I measured, cut and leveled. Before the deck was finished he was measuring and sawing while I hammered and carried boards. We both were proud of our work even though it would not have passed inspection by a skilled carpenter.

Too much pressure from time constraints or quality control makes it difficult to enjoy working together. We can get so focused on the task itself that we are not able to relate in a relaxed manner, and the experience no longer fits the No Problem Area.

A few months ago I took Nathan with me to the car wash; I wanted him to learn to wash the car there and I thought he might appreciate the experience. I gave him a brief lesson in using the sprayer, turned it over to him and put in two quarters, telling him he would have to work fast. But when the time was up, there was still soap all over the car. I was upset. "I told you to work fast! You should be able to rinse it before the time runs out." Yelling at him because of fifty cents was thoughtless and I regretted it almost immediately. Actually he had done a good job for the first time, probably as good as I did the first few times — when time ran out on me too. Later I apologized for my impatience.

Lorna is better than I at being available while working. While she is folding laundry, getting ready to go somewhere, working in the kitchen or whatever she is doing, one of the children often is nearby. She doesn't press for conversation, but keeps working, with one eye and one ear open to them. As she responds to their initiatives, they talk.

Our children are teenagers, but the same attentiveness is important with younger children, even those too young to talk. This is the lesson of notable research by Burton White and his colleagues at Harvard University. White began his research over 20 years ago, asking the question, What do parents of young children do which causes some children to turn out to be more competent than others?

The researchers found that it is not the number of educational toys, the amount of time parents spend on the floor in parent-child play, or lessons in numbers or the alphabet that makes the difference. Parents of competent children encourage them to play independently, but are responsive to the many times during the day their children approach them for comfort, assistance or to share the excitement over some discovery or achievement. These parents often are busy with their other responsibilities, but maintain enough awareness of their children playing nearby that they can respond

with eye contact, smiles and comments when the children occasionally initiate brief moments of interaction (Meyerhoff & White, 1986).

White's research teaches us that No Problem Area moments can
be as brief as the time it takes to smile at a child on the other side of
the kitchen counter, part-way up the ladder or behind the tomato
vines.

Mealtime and Bedtime Routines

Because of television, and also because both parents in so many
families work outside the home, mealtime is much different from the
way it used to be: Families today tend to spend less time together in
the kitchen, because they use food which is prepared quickly, eat out
often, sit down together for a meal irregularly, if at all, and watch TV
while they eat. The dining table has been replaced by the "family
room" (which in most cases means "TV room"), as the most important setting of family activity.

One college student wrote of the absence of family mealtimes in
his childhood:

> Dad worked in a sales position which required him to be
> gone for weeks at a time. Mom worked full-time as a teacher
> in the local school. She would dress me while I was still
> sleeping to drive me to my grandparents for the day. They
> were very strict as guardians, which I resented. So every day,
> when the chance came, I left for the trailer court nearby to
> play with the children there. I would skip dinner so I didn't
> have to go back. That was my life for years.

Another wrote about the intrusion of television into her family's
mealtime:

> When we eat is the same time the news is on and Dad has to
> see the news. I despise having to have the TV on when we
> eat, but when I tell them, they don't seem to understand.

On the other hand, one of Brenda's favorite memories has to do
with eating with her parents:

> I always enjoyed going out with just Mom and Dad. In
> restaurants we seemed to get along perfectly and had great
> conversations. Getting to know each other in that way was
> very special to me.

In her book *Traits of a Healthy Family*, Dolores Curran (1983) notes
the importance of mealtimes. The strong families she studied tend to
eat together regularly, valuing this enough that it gets high priority
in their schedules. They use the mealtime as a time of sharing and

caring. Family members are sufficiently aware of the events going on in each other's lives that they can ask specific questions. Instead of asking, "How was your day?" for example, they are able to ask, "Was your biology test as hard as you thought it would be?"

Curran found that the table conversation of the strong families includes all family members. No one is left out. There often are interruptions as the conversation gets lively, but no one person is the one who usually is silenced. While gentle teasing and humor are common, criticisms and putdowns are out of place, and parents do not use mealtimes for scolding.

We have tried to preserve mealtime as an important family activity, as the families Curran studied have done. We do not watch TV, listen to the radio or read the newspaper while we eat together. We usually begin the meal with a prayer, through which we express thankfulness, and the mundane events of the day are cast in the perspective of a world much larger than our own.

I'd like to be able to say that we eat together once or twice a day and that our mealtimes are full of stimulating conversation and words of appreciation, but after the children became involved in high school activities we simply weren't that successful. There is no doubt that all of us value mealtime, however, and we have been able to maintain the tradition of Sunday dinner together. One of the things we do at that time is preview our schedules for the new week and make plans for additional meals together.

Bedtime routines, like mealtimes, are remembered as happy times by some young adults. Memories of bedtime include being tucked in at night, stories and prayers, sitting on Dad's lap while he read, laying head on Mom's lap, singing and being comforted after a hard day.

The process of settling down for the night has emotional, social and spiritual dimensions, as well as physical aspects, all of which are important. If the day is ending in a No Problem way, that is, without issues to be dealt with, the bedtime serves as a time for reviewing the events of the day and previewing approaching events and the feelings the child has about those events. It is a time for physical expression of love for one another. And it is a time for reading stories and, the always popular activity, telling stories from the parents' own childhood. That enables children to think of their parents as persons who once were children like themselves and who sometimes got into trouble, were embarrassed or did funny things.

Psychotherapist Clayton Barbeau tells of the time in his childhood when he burned the family house down by playing with matches, and the impact this had on his children when he told them about it. He became more of a real person, more approachable. Nothing they did was as bad as the thing he had done!

In homes where faith is practiced, if the parent-child relationship remains stressed because of things that happened during the day, parents who seek to follow the biblical injunction to "never let the sun go down on your anger," can discuss what happened and seek reconciliation in the bedtime ritual.

Whether the day ends with problems or without them, bedtime can be a time for parents and children to make connection with the divine Presence in their lives. Bedtime prayers, even in the simple contemplative manner of children, are important in asking forgiveness about past occurrences, seeking courage for pending events, charting a course of action consistent with the family's values, or expressing gratitude for the loving family to which they belong.

The nature of the bedtime ritual changes as children get older, but the importance of having a ritual never lessens. Lynda remembered how much she enjoyed the physical closeness in being carried, even after she was too big to be carried under normal circumstances:

I remember as a child, while coming home from somewhere, I would fall asleep in the car. Dad would carry me in over his shoulder and would put me to bed. I often pretended that I was asleep so that I wouldn't have to walk in.

When our children were in the late teen years and stayed out later, Lorna and I expected them to come to our room and awaken us if we were asleep. Sometimes this extended to a visit about the events of the day, especially if we had not seen them earlier in the day because of busy schedules. And we still hug and kiss them regularly, although not as often as we did when they were younger.

Children need routine expressions of affection and care at all ages, even during their high school and college years. At the very least, they deserve the courteous "good night" which is extended to guests in the home.

Mutual Support in Times of Crisis

There are times when family members help one another struggle through a stressful situation. These occasions fit the No Problem Area because the stress is from an external source and is not due to conflict in the relationship itself.

Lori recalled the unifying effect on the family from taking care of a sick cow:

> I remember when Judy, our best cow, went down with coliform mastitis. She lay down and would not walk. We worked her legs, talked to her, fed her apples, gave her large doses of medicine, and prayed desperately over her. When she finally struggled to her feet and stood by herself, as a family, we hugged each other and the cow. We felt victorious.

When the children themselves are the ones who are ill or injured, they remember the care of their parents with appreciation. Another young adult wrote of her third grade year:

> I woke up in the middle of the night from having a seizure. I was scared since this had never happened before. My parents heard me struggling and came running into my room. After a few seconds, the seizure quit. We didn't know what to think. After it happened a few more times, I was hospitalized for tests. During the time I was in the hospital or in the following months when I would wake up early in the morning with a seizure, my parents were always there for me. My sickness brought the three of us closer together and I remember this as a time of happiness, even though what happened was not so happy.

Other memories are of back rubs, special diets and special places for bed rest. With a smile, Greg remembered his dad's get-well gift after an accident which happened near the Fourth of July:

> My dad and I were riding a motorcycle, and we blew a tire and laid it over. He was unharmed, but I had a deep gash near my knee. It wasn't Dad's fault, but I knew he felt guilty about it because when I was laid up in my room, he showed up with a bag of fireworks, even though he doesn't like fireworks and thinks they are a waste of time and money.

As parents provide the extra attention which is needed in times of illness, these unfortunate events become deposits into the parent-child relationship account.

When children observe their parents deal with stressful situations they learn that life is not stress-free, even for adults. Parents too feel guilty, discouraged, defeated, angry and frightened, and need the support of those who care about them. Rhonda learned this from her mother:

> Mom often stayed up late sewing and I would go in and talk with her. We talked about everything and it wasn't always

me talking and Mom listening. In fact, many times I would listen to how she was doing. I think this drew us closer together because I understood better why she was acting the way she was. I think we as children always expect our parents to be kind, confident and understanding, but we need to realize that parents are people too, and that they have their bad days and feel depressed at times.

Mutual support requires family members to need each other. This does not mean that children should be expected to "parent" their parents; sometimes parents hold unrealistic expectations about this and then become abusive when their children aren't capable of meeting their emotional needs. For the most part, children are on the receiving end. But as they are cared for, children learn how to be caring persons, and, in time, the support becomes mutual.

Another result of stressful events is that children learn how to manage stress by observing their parents in crisis. Lori wrote about such an event:

Last summer in the harvest fields I experienced the dreaded breakdowns. Since most people would blow up under the pressure, I asked Dad if he was mad, and he replied, "Being mad is not going to solve anything." He remained calm and thought of a way to fix the problem. That experience meant so much to me; I admire his qualities of patience and calmness and hope I can carry them out in my life.

If parents rely on divine guidance in the midst of life's stresses, that becomes apparent to children. Lynda remembered a routine of her family when they lived in New York City:

My dad would take the subway to work every morning. Mom and I would walk him to the door to say goodbye. Before he left, we would put our arms around each other and pray. We would pray for Dad's safety and other things. We did this every day and it really has stuck in my memory. It also taught me to pray.

The value of a lived faith, like that of Lynda's family, is under-scored by research of Nick Stinnett and his colleagues (Stinnett & DeFrain, 1985), who found "spiritual wellness" to be one of six major qualities of the hundreds of "strong" families which were studied: ". . .over and over again the strong families talked about an unseen power that *can* change lives, *can* give strength to endure the darkest times, *can* provide hope and purpose" (p. 100).

Relationships in families can be stabilized by religious faith. Family members share a moral code and sense of priorities; concern for others, forgiveness and contentment grow out of a religious orientation which is not self-centered; and their religious affiliations and rituals form part of the family's identity. The processes of clarifying a moral code and priorities, assisting those in need, seeking reconciliation, expressing gratitude and worshipping together all can make significant contributions to the relationship accounts of the No Problem Area.

Through vacationing, playing, working, eating and worshipping together, family members cache No Problem Area experiences in the storehouse of happy memories. The memories create an inheritance, one which is bequeathed in the lifetime of the parents and enjoyed by both generations. There are no tax breaks for doing this, but neither are there income requirements. It is too good a deal to pass up.

Questions for Thought and Discussion about this Chapter are on page 292.

6. Fighting the Television Battle

Television has come to have tremendous impact on family life. Most parents are concerned about its effect, especially the extent to which the content of television programs influences their children's values. I am concerned about the values that are portrayed, but I am equally concerned about the *quantity* of television viewing. The television sits in our home like an animal with a voracious appetite for time, consuming huge portions of daily and weekly routines.

Nearly every American household (98 percent) has a television set (Parke & Slaby, 1983). It is turned on an average of 7 hours a day, and individual members of the household watch an average of 4 hours a day (Murray & Kippax, 1979; Steinberg, 1985). That is over 1000 hours a year. The only activities at which we spend more time are sleeping and full-time employment (Singer, 1983).

When family members watch TV together, the experience can contribute to the relationship account of the No Problem Area. It has this potential if the family exercises restraint in the amount of time spent watching TV and discrimination in the programs viewed.

With indiscriminate or excessive amounts of viewing, however, the activity contributes very little to the relationship account. Family members watch TV side by side, but the experience wouldn't be much different if they were doing it alone or with a group of strangers since they interact very little.

This is the point of a poem submitted anonymously by a reader to an Ann Landers' column:

TeeVee

In the house
Of Mr. and Mrs. Spouse
He and she
Would watch Teevee,
And never a word
Between them was spoken
Until the day
The set was broken.
Then, "How do you do?"
Said He to She.
"I don't believe we've met.
Spouse is my name.
What's yours?" he asked.
"Why, mine's the same!"
Said She to He.
"Do you suppose we could be. . . ?"
But the set came suddenly right about
And they never did find out.

Marie Winn, in *The Plug-In Drug* (1977), suggests that the reason little interaction occurs when people watch television may be because passivity is induced by the activity of watching itself, regardless of the content of the show, rather than being made difficult because of the focus of attention on the program. Persons viewing television excessively become "narcotized," she claims. They become physically relaxed, passive, in a kind of trance. It is difficult for others to get their attention or to get them to leave the TV in this state. When they do leave, there are withdrawal symptoms including grouchiness and restlessness.

There is no doubt that interaction while viewing is difficult, whether due to induced passivity or restriction of attention. But that difficulty alone is not the whole of the problem. The activity of television viewing also prevents other kinds of activities from happening. Part of the four-hour daily television regimen could be used for the things families used to do before television came along, some of which contributed to the No Problem Area. Many years ago a national study found that television owners sleep less, read less and talk less. They also spend less time in religious activities, leisure travel, socializing with friends and reading newspapers (Robinson, 1972, 1981). This is called the "preemptive" effect of television (Myers, 1987).

A thirteen-year-old girl in Wichita, Kansas, recently completed a year without TV to win a $500 bet with her mother. The experience altered her life dramatically. She reported an initial period of boredom, but then learned cross-stitch, embroidery and candlewicking. She took more time doing her homework and her grades went up. She became more involved in church and school activities and sports and table games. She also noticed that she spent more time in conversation with her mother and her friends (Tanner, 1988).

Researchers in Canada, taking advantage of a natural occurrence, reported similar effects of television viewing. Children in a town which was unable to receive television because of its location were compared with children in two other towns, one which received one station and one which received four. The researchers found that children in the first town were more likely to participate in community activities and scored higher on tests of reading fluency and creativity. Four years later, after television had arrived, children in the first town were no different in their test scores than children of the other two villages (Williams & Handford, 1986; Corteen & Williams, 1986; Harrison & Williams, 1986).

Finally, the problem of excessive television viewing includes the resentments which hamper relationships among family members when viewing interferes with household responsibilities. Children drag out of bed in the morning or are too tired to do what they need to do because they stayed up late the night before watching TV— and they likely will repeat the pattern that evening. Parents become frustrated with this pattern, nag to get their children out of it, then feel defeated by the cycle of inertia which can seem nearly impossible to end. I get angry if our children tell me they don't have time to help with a task in the kitchen or yard, when I know that they already have spent considerable time that day in front of the TV. And I resent the illnesses, school absences and medical bills which so often follow by a few days the late-night movie-watching of groups of friends.

Besides the concern about the *amount* of television viewing, what it preempts and what it does to relationships among family viewers, the other major concern has to do with the effects of the *content* of TV. Values inconsistent with the parents' are played out hour after hour in the family's own home. The impact seems overwhelming, and it may well be.

Parental influence will be inadequate to counterbalance television's influence if the goal of parents is to stem the tide of social change in order to preserve an earlier or traditional way of life. This can't be done. What we can hope to do, however, is help our children become tied to an ethical system so that they can rise and fall with the tide without being swept away. We do this not with simple exhortations about good and evil or with strict rules to control behavior, but with discussions about the basic ethical question— What happens to people? With television the important questions are, what happens to people in television programs, and, what happens to people who watch television heavily?

Violence. We know that 80% of the programs on TV contain violence, which comes at the rate of five violent acts per hour during prime time. This rate has remained fairly constant from the late 1960s through the middle 1980s (Gerbner, Gross, Morgan, & Signorielli, 1986). By age 16, the average child is estimated to have witnessed over 13,000 killings on television (Liebert & Schwartzberg, 1977)!

The regularity with which violence occurs is indeed numbing. In one experiment, researchers confirmed that viewing violence breeds indifference to violence. Children who watched violent shows were more apathetic than children who had not viewed the violent shows, when exposed to the film of an actual brawl or when actually observing two children fighting (Drabman & Thomas, 1976).

I remember once watching a program which included a political execution in another part of the world. It was done by beheading with a saber, with the condemned person in a large black bag, bent over, head on a rock. I was horrified because I wasn't used to this kind of violence. I am used to people being blasted with large caliber revolvers, blown up in explosions or knifed, or dying in cars which tumble end over end, go over cliffs or over the ends of wharfs into harbors. Since we become immune to the horrifying effects of violence, directors come up with ever more graphic portrayals to keep viewer responsiveness high. What a moral tragedy it is when we no longer are capable of being disturbed by the terrible things people do to each other.

Dozens of studies have found that watching violence amplifies the viewers' aggressive behavior, with both immediate and long-term effects. In an experiment with institutionalized, delinquent boys, physical attacks increased sharply in cottages where boys viewed violent films, compared with the week preceding the violent film series (Park, Berkowitz, Leyens, West, & Sebastian, 1977).

A study by Eron and Huesmann (1984), carried on over 20 years, found that the amount of viewing of televised violence by boys at the age of eight was somewhat predictive of their aggressive behavior when they reached age 19 and even of criminal records when they turned 30. Another study covering several years found a significant increase in homicides during the week following heavyweight fights; the increase was attributed to the influence of the mass media (Phillips, 1983).

Children in a town which was unable to receive television showed a significant increase in physical and verbal aggression after television arrived; children in two other towns which received television earlier showed no such change during the same period (Joy, Kimball, & Zabrack, 1986).

Not only does viewing violence increase aggressive behavior, it affects the way people view the world. Gerbner and his associates (1986) surveyed both adolescents and adults and found that heavy viewers of television (four hours a day or more) are more likely than light viewers (two hours or less) to exaggerate the frequency of violence in the world around them and to fear being personally assaulted. These perceptions may be to some extent self-fulfilling, since there is evidence that children who believe that life is more violent are more aggressive themselves (Huesmann, Lagerspetz, & Eron, 1984).

As an example of a distortion which comes to be believed, television portrays law enforcement officers as frequently firing their guns at those they are trying to apprehend and dodging bullets themselves. But in reality, officers rarely fire at someone. A recently retired Kansas Highway Patrolman reported that he drew his gun about five times, never had to fire at someone, nor did anybody ever fire at him in his 30-year career.

I remember how frightening TV can be. Some years ago Lorna and I lived for two years in another country without TV. Soon after our return to the States, we watched a suspenseful drama together one evening. It scared us so badly that we had trouble sleeping for the next several nights, worrying about someone coming in through a door or window. But we eventually adjusted to such a view of the world once again, watching TV and sleeping in spite of the frightening possibilities.

The research evidence on the effects of watching violence, barely summarized here, is overwhelming: it affects the behavior, beliefs and feelings of the heavy viewer. If we choose to be heavy viewers of television, we do so, it seems to me, at the risk of losing our capacity to object to violence.

Berkowitz and Alioto (1973) found that aggressive behavior is more likely to follow the viewing of filmed violence if the film justifies the violence it shows. But I don't find this reassuring, since much of the violence is portrayed to be justified. That's the problem. On television, violence is the method of choice for solving human problems.

More reassuring to me is a study which found that children who watch violence on TV in the presence of adults who condemn the violence are less likely to behave aggressively in later situations (Horton & Santogrossi, 1978). Concerned parents can find hope here—and a prescription for conscientious objection to televised violence.

Sex and marriage. Another area of concern about which we must talk with our children is the way sex and marriage are treated on television. The frequency of sexual innuendos increased tenfold during the last half of the 1970s (Sprafkin & Silverman, 1981). Most allusions to sexual intercourse occur between unmarried couples or involve a prostitute (Fernandez-Collado & Greenberg, 1978; Lowry, Love, & Kirby, 1981).

Characters in leading roles, unless the show is about the household itself, are usually unmarried. Few characters are portrayed to be contentedly married if the show is about their work in business, law enforcement, medicine or whatever it is that they do. Even though they are highly attractive, successful and willing to get involved, they are always available to fall quickly into a new relationship without jeopardizing a prior one. And they fall just as quickly into bed, without a long-term commitment to one another, since the leading characters need to be available again the following week to repeat the pattern.

Where are the people who are successful in both work and marriage? Where do we see couples whose sexual involvement grows out of their mutual need for intimacy, care and trust over time? There are a few shows with characters who are admirable exceptions, but not many.

I know of little research about the effects of heavy viewing of television's treatment of singleness, marriage, sex and work, but surely, the effects are substantial. Unless we object to the distortions and model an alternative in our own lives, our children's lives may be disappointingly similar to what they have absorbed from television.

Parenthood. With a few exceptions, most television characters who are parents are unmarried, divorced or widowed, as if a more traditional situation can't be entertaining. During the 1988 season, programs included a gruff granddad who took in his widowed daughter-in-law and her children; two unrelated grandparents with their adult children and grandchildren; a single woman suddenly thrust into the position of being guardian to her younger sister; the young daughter of a recently deceased woman who is cared for by two men, either one of whom could be her biological father; a couple with four children, three of them adopted and all of different cultural backgrounds; an alien father who returns to Earth to help his teenage half-human, half-alien son; and a family that adopts a creature from outer space.

During 1988 four movies involving babies were released almost simultaneously. Perhaps the Baby Boomers (Americans born between 1946 and 1960) of the movie industry are becoming more concerned with parenthood as they approach the end of their best childbearing years. If these films mark a trend, I welcome it. But the characters in these films acquired the duties of parenthood because babies were inherited, left on a doorstep, kidnapped and the unplanned result of teenage sex.

We need to point out to our children the way parenthood is distorted on TV by the absence of couples who choose to bear and raise children together, because it is such an enormously gratifying part of life.

Sex-role stereotypes. The most common movie plot involves a male who is handsome, powerfully built and quick to engage in combat. He operates independently and his supervisor can't quite keep him under control as he goes outside normal procedural bounds to solve problems quickly and forcefully. He would get into trouble, except that he succeeds in the job he sets out to do and emerges a hero.

The plot also involves a female who is attractive physically.

Usually she is in her late twenties or thirties, younger than the leading male who is in his forties or fifties. She is resourceful and uses good judgment, except for her tendency to fall under the influence of a male who scoffs at social custom.

The two are attracted to each other from the first moment they meet, but initially she is unavailable. Sometimes she is on the side of evil and sometimes she is on the side of social propriety, but in either case, she is just out of his reach. Before the movie is over, however, the male hero wins her over to his side, which is the side of impropriety with underlying goodness. In doing so he frees her from the domination of another male, often the villain, sometimes her father.

When the hero takes her into his arms for the first time she resists him, but he forcibly kisses her. She pushes him away at first, but within moments is holding him tightly, her passion unlocked by his dogged pursuit.

Sound familiar? We've all seen this theme, or variations of it, hundreds of times. And it is built out of stereotypes which we need to point out to our children. The leading female is younger than the leading male because she is at her peak of physical beauty in her late twenties and thirties, and our culture values beauty. He is in his forties or fifties because at this time he is at his height of power, influence and wealth, which our culture also esteems. In the real world, such an age difference is likely to suggest an affair or remarriage; in reality, the more common pairing is of two persons of nearly the same age. The wife will live, on the average, ten years as a widow because of the differences between men and women in life expectancy. But even the popular Cosby show cast an actress in the role of Mrs. Huxtable who is many years younger than her television husband, thus denying the nearly common age of most spouses.

The stereotypical leading role for males includes elements of a boy who never quite grew up, who is unwilling to work cooperatively as an equal with others, and who won't keep the rules. He solves problems, but can't be counted on to meet other obligations.

The stereotypical leading role for females is, in part, a little girl who hasn't quite grown up either. She doesn't take charge of her own life as an adult, but waits to be rescued by a knight, however tarnished his armor might be. And the notion that women really want to be overpowered and conquered sexually fits more appropriately scenes of rape than scenes of romance.

Commercials, like story plots, are built on stereotypes, including

the traditional sex role stereotypes. Common sense would suggest
that watching this repeatedly affects behavior, and experimental
evidence bears this out. Female subjects who viewed non-traditional
commercials subsequently were less conforming than those who
watched traditional ones. The non-traditional commercial viewers
were also more self-confident in delivering a speech (Jennings, Geis,
& Brown, 1980).

A common theme in commercials is that good-looking, successful
men and women have fun together because of the products they
buy. Want to join them? Buy the products. Unless we object repeatedly to such materialism and model an alternative lifestyle ourselves, our children are likely to be heavily influenced by the
350,000 commercials they will see during their growing up years
(Myers, 1987).

So the problems associated with TV viewing are substantial. How
can parents fight the TV battle?

Occasionally, one hears of families that attempt to solve the
television problem by not having television. Such was the case of the
family of a college student who related this incident from her
conservative childhood:

> We never had a TV in our home. However, I remember my
> older brothers buying an old, large, black and white TV.
> They put it in the barn. It remained there for several weeks,
> until my mother found out. My dad would not have cared,
> but Mom could not tolerate it. She pulled the TV from the
> barn and pushed it to the front of the house, a distance of
> about 150 feet, to an old well. She got a stick and literally
> demolished it before pushing it into the well!

What a vivid demonstration of the mother's feelings about "the
world," as some traditional religious groups refer to secular influences. But in the end, her methods didn't work very well. Her sons
sneaked the television into the barn, and the daughter who witnessed the incident reported that she went through a period of
excessive television viewing after she left home.

There are families who don't have TV and are quite content, but
most parents don't attempt to solve the problem this way. Personally, I wouldn't want to be without television, and I'm skeptical that I
could keep our children from television, any more than the college
student's mother was able to keep her children from it. Television
pervades life today.

An alternative to eliminating it from our lives is to become intelligent consumers of TV and not television addicts. This is a formidable challenge which many parents are not willing to accept. For those who are, the following strategies are useful.

1. The most forthright plan of action is to place limits on viewing. The limits can be of several types: (a) Parents can restrict the amount of viewing time per day. For example, they can establish a rule of no more than one or two or three hours of total viewing time. (b) Parents can place constraints on the time of day for viewing. For example, they can prohibit viewing before school or after 9:00 p.m. (c) Certain kinds of programs can be prohibited: R-rated movies, soaps, cartoons or shows full of sex and violence or whatever parents find most objectionable. (d) And finally, parents can make viewing contingent on the completion of other activities: homework must be done first, household chores finished, or dressing and making the bed must happen before watching in the morning.

In order for the restrictions to limit viewing effectively, parents must be resolute in holding children to them. As all parents know, this is difficult; most of us wear out and give up at times. Expect the battle to be a never-ending one; be prepared to turn the set off, unplug it or put it out of commission for a time if necessary.

Boundaries are essential for young children who don't have the internal resources to make all of the viewing decisions themselves. As children get older, however, they want to make more of these decisions for themselves, and these kinds of limitations are less successful. It's hard for us as parents to give up the restraints when we see our children exercise poor judgment without the restrictions, but we must do this eventually. So we parents need additional strategies for not only fighting the TV battle but also to move towards the long-term goal of helping our children become persons who are intelligent consumers of television.

2. Locate the TV strategically in the house. The extent to which the television pervades the daily routine depends in part on how easy it is to turn it on and watch it. In many households the television is on all day long, a constant part of the home environment. Some families have multiple sets so that viewing is possible in practically every room of the house. The family tends to spend less time with the TV if it is located out of the main flow of traffic, and where it cannot be seen from the dining table.

3. Buy a video cassette recorder (VCR). This appliance makes possible control over television programming which wasn't possible before. Now families can watch what they want to watch, when

they want to watch it. If we "fast forward" through the opening segment and commercials, a 30-minute program is reduced to about 20 minutes, another advantage of the VCR.

With a VCR our family watches no more than we did before, we are more discriminating about what we watch, and we feel less vulnerable to the intrusion of the TV schedule into our schedule.

4. Teach your children, by admonition and example, the distinction between "watching TV" and watching a particular program. "Watching TV," for many people, means watching it out of habit for a couple of hours before going to bed, regardless of what's on; flipping through the channels to catch a little of this and a little of that, without much interest in any of it; or having it on constantly, either to be watched or as a part of the background to whatever else is going on in the house.

If we and our children are to be discriminating viewers, and not TV "junkies," we have to clarify our preferences and not treat all programs alike. I am aware, when I am honest with myself, that some programs I like, some programs I strongly dislike, and to the vast majority, I am indifferent. In order to let my viewing behavior be guided by these preferences, I plan in advance what I will watch. When the weekly TV program guide arrives in the Sunday paper, I go through the schedule and circle any programs I want to watch if I have time. If there is a program I don't want to miss, I set the VCR to tape it.

A similar process is needed in making decisions about movies. Parents have considerable help in this regard, since movie reviews are carried by most newspapers and magazines and also on television. I also subscribe to a couple of small magazines which are devoted to previewing television specials and movies, and include background information about the issues involved and discussion questions.

When I read about a movie that I think I'd like to see, I jot its title on a little slip of paper which I carry in my billfold. Then if Lorna and I feel like watching a movie, I select one which is on my list at the video rental shop, without wasting time looking through their entire supply or selecting one just because it happens to be there to catch my eye.

5. Remind your children that every time they sit down to watch TV they are not only deciding to watch TV, they are also deciding to not do something else. For example, when they decide to stay up late Friday night to watch a movie, they simultaneously are deciding to

shorten their Saturday because they will sleep in and not have as many hours to do other things. If they decide to stay up late to watch TV, they simultaneously are deciding to be tired the following day, unable to put forth their best efforts at whatever else they do. Choices are involved, and priorities are determined in the way the choices are made.

6. Talk about what you like and dislike about television with your children. Although I don't expect our children's preferences to be the same as mine, that doesn't mean that I am silent about what I like and dislike. I want them to know why I react as I do.

Years ago parents could keep their children protected from the evils of "Hollywood," yet they talked very little themselves about the issues of concern, especially sex and marriage. Today it is impossible to keep children as sheltered and naive as they used to be kept. In order for parents to maintain a hope of counterbalancing society's sway with their own influence, they have to talk more than parents of previous generations did about the issues of importance to them. We must talk about the violence which is portrayed, the treatment of sex and marriage and the ways people are stereotyped. Parental objections to what is portrayed in programs are influential (Horton & Santogrossi, 1978). We need to analyze commercials with our children; research indicates this helps children to be more realistic about the credibility of advertising (Cohen, 1980).

7. Watch television and movies with your children. There are benefits to TV — it's not all bad. TV can introduce us to people we've never met, places we've never been and things we've never seen. Television is capable of teaching healthy attitudes about ourselves and other nationalities and races; it keeps us informed about what is happening around the globe. It can teach new skills, including reading, spelling, standard English, vocabulary, gardening, exercising and many other things. A five-year-old boy, for example, was able to rescue his six-year-old playmate from choking because he had seen the Heimlich maneuver demonstrated on TV ("You Can Bet," 1986). Television also is cheap and convenient entertainment.

Our children's choices of movies and television programs often aren't the same as ours, with their choices more likely to be what is currently popular. The ones we like, they generally (but not always) like too, whereas the reverse of this is not true; so if I am paying, I reserve the right to strongly influence the decision about what we watch together. Since they see more movies than Lorna and I do, they will probably get to their first choice anyway.

The movies I prefer tend to be about relationships portrayed at least somewhat realistically, and which move me, leaving me at the end with a warm feeling and the desire to put more into my own relationships. Examples from the 1980s are "Ordinary People," "On Golden Pond," "Stone Boy," "Trip to Bountiful" and "Four Seasons." Our teenagers know what I prefer and occasionally recommend a movie to me, one which I would have passed off as teenage mindlessness, but which they assure me is a good film about relationships. So I will see it too, partly because I might like it as well as they, which happens sometimes, and partly to see what it was that they liked, to understand them better.

Good discussions about the show and about "quality" often follow our watching a movie together. Although I want our children to be influenced by our values, I don't assume that their values will be the same. They are a younger generation, growing up in a different historical setting. I must respect their point of view as teenagers, if I expect them to respect mine.

Rather than take the differences too seriously, I think it's better to assume that common sense doesn't have to be pounded into their heads, and to laugh at some of our less significant differences: who likes to talk during a show and who doesn't; who likes to read the credits at the end and who doesn't; who likes to be scared and who likes to be moved to tears; who likes certain stars and who likes others; and who likes buttered popcorn and who likes plain.

Knowing that in the long run our children's values will turn out to be similar to ours, provided that we maintain well-balanced relationships with them, helps us to take ourselves less seriously in the present moment.

Well-balanced means that we make regular deposits into our relationship accounts by taking advantage of No Problem Area moments. If we do that, our children will enjoy other kinds of activities with us, they will be influenced by the values we live, and they won't watch television excessively to fill a void in their lives.

But we must put the time monster in our homes on a restricted diet, so that fewer No Problem Area moments are eaten up.

Questions for Thought and Discussion about this Chapter are on page 293.

7. Keeping Sports in the No Problem Area

The happy memories which I gathered from people sometimes involved sports activities with their parents. Randy, a college student, wrote in a letter to his dad:

> I remember our first sport was high jump. Thanks for building me an adjustable high jump with the old mattresses for soft landings. Together we won the high jump contest from first through third grade. I also remember training for and running the Pike's Peak Marathon. Although at age six I didn't win the race, we both had a lot of fun and we also had something to be proud of. I remember the many years we played basketball together. Although I never used your famous hook shot, you taught me to enjoy the game and that helped tremendously.

Through sports, Randy and his dad made deposits into their relationship account.

Like Randy and his dad, I enjoy basketball, and the gym has been the setting for hundreds of hours of play with our three children, taking them with me when they could barely walk to sit on the side while I played; playing with them when they were older; coaching their teams in late childhood; playing with them and their friends, and inviting them to play with me and my friends; and attending their games in high school and college.

I find it almost impossible to put into words the pleasure I get in being in the gym with them. I suspect that other aficionados of sports will understand.

For many families, however, experiences in sports have been withdrawals from their relationship accounts. It's not uncommon for children to participate in a sport because their parents want them to, even though they don't have the inclination to do so. A kindergarten teacher once told me of a father, who at the beginning of the school year, asked that she train his son to be left-handed — so that the son would become a left-handed pitcher!

Parents volunteer to help in the assignment of players to recreation league teams in order to get their children on the best teams. They call the coach and school board members to complain that their children aren't getting enough playing time. And most of us have witnessed parents creating ugly scenes at ballgames, castigating umpires, opposing players, coaches and, sometimes, even their own children when the outcome of a play isn't to their liking.

When parents make such inappropriate demands of their children and place such undue emphasis on winning and achieving public acclaim, sports are no longer playful but are burdensome and unlikely to contribute to the No Problem Area.

Philosophers of play (e.g., Huizinga, 1949/1955) define it as an activity engaged in voluntarily because of its inherent enjoyment. Normal social roles are suspended; order is derived from the rules of the game itself which are established by common agreement. This definition is abstract, but I understand its meaning because of personal experiences.

For years I have participated in noon-hour basketball with a group of men from the central Kansas community where we live. We play each Monday, Wednesday and Friday, year-round, and miss only on occasions of unavoidable conflict. As I reflect on why we do this so regularly, I come to the conclusion that we don't do it for cosmetic reasons, although it does help to keep off some pounds. We don't do it for reasons of health, although I'm sure it is the reason for my efficiently slow heartbeat and quick recovery to resting heart rate. We don't do it for friendship, because we don't affiliate off the court; in many cases, we know very little about each other even though some of us have played together for nearly 20 years. And we don't play for the sake of winning and gaining public esteem, since there are no observers, statistics are not kept, nor is there a record of wins and losses since teams are organized anew each day.

I conclude that we participate in noon-hour basketball because we enjoy playing basketball together. The enjoyment is inherent in the activity itself—in making the right pass, playing tough defense, hitting a string of five in a row, watching with admiration the one whose quickness, surehandedness or court sense makes him unusually adept at practicing the craft of basketball. After an hour of play we return to our respective offices, drained but looking forward to our next recess from the normal routine of the day.

Children today don't play like this as much as children used to play. Less common are the games town kids played in backyards, driveways and empty lots, or that farm kids played in barnyards, haymows and pastures. Today air conditioning keeps children indoors and television occupies their time.

At the same time that informal play has diminished, organized activities have increased. Unfortunately, a sense of playfulness is missing too often from sports activities arranged for children by parents and other adults, especially in the pre-teen years.

There are exceptions. Each spring for many years Gerry Sieber, Hesston (Kansas) College's soccer coach, has organized soccer games for Hesston's elementary school children. Children are assigned to teams in a manner designed to equalize the teams, and members of the college soccer team serve as coaches and referees. Matches are scheduled for late Wednesday afternoons and Saturday mornings. Parents take their lawn chairs and blankets to the playing fields to watch their children and to visit with one another. In order to minimize the competitiveness of the activity, the results of the matches are not reported in the local paper, won-lost records are not kept and no awards are given.

The children's enjoyment of this activity is obvious from the level of their participation; 16 teams are formed out of an elementary school enrollment of about 250 children.

In high school, the role of sports becomes more complicated since organized sports are more than play at this age. Adolescents need recognition of their emerging status in the community, and competitive games have always served this purpose. Track and field events and baseball are not modern inventions; we inherited earlier versions of them from the ancient Greeks, in the former case, and Native Americans, in the latter. Through such games, proud parents, in ancient and modern societies alike, watch their children display the evidence of growing up. The community celebrates the prowess of its young people, and grown-ups make room for another cadre of young adults who will join them in the bleachers in years ahead for the social events which home games render.

One problem with sports arises when parents overlook the many other ways by which youth express their individuality and develop competencies. Recognition through sports can become so important to parents that children who have neither the desire nor the ability to excel in sports feel pressure to do so anyway. The stage of the parent-child relationship is thus set for failure and disappointment, resentment and manipulation. Struggles regarding sports inevitably become withdrawals from the relationship account.

In communities and families where sports are given excessive regard, those children who are not involved in organized sports may feel neglected. And in fact, they may be. But that fact alone does not make me altogether critical or supportive of athletics. Some people are so reactive to the issue that their criticisms are like letting air out of the one inflated tire rather than pumping up the three flat ones to achieve balance.

I, too, am appalled by the physical and emotional abuse children receive sometimes from coaches. I deplore what happens to parents when they get too emotionally involved in their children's activities. And I think it's tragic when young people feel worthless if they aren't outstanding in athletics.

On the other hand, I am glad for the structure which after-school activities and organized summer recreation provide in the lives of teenagers; I can't imagine what teen life would be like without this. And I appreciate the discipline demanded of individuals by coaches. Achievement requires this kind of dedication. I wish more teachers would show the enthusiasm, intensity and personal attention in the classrooms and laboratories which coaches show on the courts and playing fields.

One solution to the problem of overemphasis on sports is to stress sports less, but an equally important solution is to recognize other arenas of achievement. Who tells the high school juniors, who spend so long in front of mirrors before going out, that their appearances are pleasing? Who commends the achievement of the teenagers who can diagnose and fix the mechanical problems of their cars? Who appreciates the breath control and lip and tongue techniques of the young flutist and trumpeter who spend many hours refining their skills? Who even notices the discipline of the young paper carrier who has the morning paper on the community's porches before others are up? Who responds thoughtfully to the probing questions of the young philosopher?

The answer is, of course, that parents can do this, but few do it enough. I know that I don't. It's easier when I remind myself that throughout childhood, and especially in adolescence, our children are discovering what their distinctive qualities are and are developing in a wide array of important ways. They test themselves constantly by playing to an imaginary audience. That's why teenagers are so self-conscious; each is performing and waiting for the response, hoping for applause.

For those in sports and music, the audience sometimes is real. Each spring when the music department of the local high school produces its musical variety show, I am impressed with the impact it has in the lives of the young performers. By objective standards the performances are not spectacular; few if any from our small town will go on to be professional entertainers. But the music teacher stretches them to their limits musically, and helps them to overcome their inhibitions on stage. Then when they perform before an appreciative community audience, we see that a miracle has taken place. Teenagers, who a few months before were self-conscious and awkward in public, are doing lively dance routines, solos and other numbers with smiles on their faces, enthusiasm in their voices and exaggeration in their movements, enjoying every minute of it.

Those not in sports or music need applause too, from an appreciative audience of at least one or two persons — their parents. If they have that, they will be secure enough in their sense of self that sports will not become unduly important, whatever their level of interest or ability or participation.

Each of our three children is unique, as are all children, of course. Julie's interest in athletics has never been sustained for long. I used to take her to the gym with us to help her develop her basketball skills, but we reached the limit of her interest fairly quickly and I did not push her beyond that. Julie is Julie — bright, creative, artistic, socially involved and an interesting person, but not interested in athletics except as social events.

Jeff has always been very intense. As an infant he demanded to be fed immediately upon waking. When he approached the age of walking, he pulled himself up, climbed over the furniture and toddled across the floor, falling often. In spite of bruises, he would pull himself up and do it again and again. At age five he learned to ride a bike in the same manner — with determination along with cuts and bruises.

In contrast, Nathan as an infant remained content for an hour in his high chair in the morning without being fed. Approaching the age of walking, he waited until one day he began to walk, without falls. At age five he refused to get on the bike that Jeff had used at that age. He refused again when I suggested he try it shortly after his sixth birthday. In first grade his friends rode bikes and Nate ran along behind them. Finally, following his seventh birthday, I got the bike out again. He agreed to try it with my help, but insisted that he wasn't going to get hurt. And he didn't. He just started riding without taking a spill.

We were not surprised, then, that their differences in personal style affected their approach to sports. Jeff wanted to try everything, practiced hard, set high standards for himself and reached them. He hung out at the gym, attended all of the community games and the older high school and college players were his heroes. Nathan clearly disliked baseball and didn't care much for running. He liked basketball, however, and went to the gym often enough to develop exceptional skills in that sport. But he doesn't often attend a game other than his own. Even though Julie never achieved a high level of skill in any sport, she maintained strong participation as a reserve player, cheerleader, manager and fan.

Lorna and I are thankful that our three children are different from each other and different from us. They all need our seal of approval as they differentiate themselves from us and from each other more and more as they grow older.

Lorna, who does not enjoy sports to the extent that I do, long ago helped me to realize that if basketball is to affect my relationship with our children positively, it will be through our enjoyment of the game, not through pressure on them to play or criticism of their play. So I attend all of their games that I can, even road games, with pleasure, not complaint; compliment them rather than criticize; never interfere between them and their coaches; and keep playing with them for fun as often as I can.

Questions for Thought and Discussion about this Chapter are on page 293.

Part III
The Child's Problem Area

Lorna works as an operating room nurse, a high stress occupation. Many times she comes home bothered about something that happened during the day — problems with people or policies or just the pace of activity. What do I do? I'm tempted sometimes to call up surgeons and tell them how nurses should be treated, or to call the administrator and express an opinion about how a hospital should be run. But the problems are not mine to "fix"; she is the one who has to respond to the situation. What she wants is for me to listen to her complaints. She also likes me to rub her feet at the end of a long day. Nothing more.

The same is true of children. When they experience problems, they need to be listened to empathically and supportively.

To say that a situation is in the Child's Problem Area doesn't mean that the parent does nothing about it. It means that parental responses are directed to helping the child deal with the problem. Sometimes the assistance takes the form of intervention in the situation on the child's behalf, but very often it takes other forms: listening empathically, or offering encouragement and guidance.

Sharing personal experiences is not easy, especially for young children whose conceptual and language abilities are not well developed, and for those of any age whose feelings have been discounted. That's why listening skills are so important. Unless parents have had some training in listening, they tend to respond to children who are having problems in ways that shut children up, instead of open them up, and in ways that are discouraging rather than encouraging. Parents also tend to take over too many of the child's problems or rush in too quickly with solutions.

Chapter 8 describes the listening skills that are so important to the Child's Problem Area and Chapter 9 contains suggestions for helping the child to become a mature, resourceful person.

Questions for Thought and Discussion about this Chapter are on page 293.

8. Listening

"Hi, Frank. It's nice to see you," I greeted a former classmate who was on campus visiting his daughter who was in her first year of college. "How's everything going?"

"Just fine. Jeannie seems to be getting along well. She just told me she is really enjoying college."

"I'm glad to hear that," I replied.

"So was I! She got off to a rocky start."

"Oh?" I was pleased that his daughter was getting along well now, but curious about her rough beginning.

"One Sunday evening about a month into the fall semester she called us. As soon as I answered the phone she started crying and couldn't even talk for a little while. She was discouraged about several things and a little homesick, too, I think. She had just received the lowest score she had ever had in her life on an Anatomy and Physiology test. She was starting to wonder if she should drop out of the nursing program. She and her roommate were barely speaking to each other at that time, and Jeannie was staying away from their room as much as possible because of the tension. She didn't like the campus job which was a part of her financial aid package and she had just found out that she wouldn't be able to spend Thanksgiving weekend at home because of a choir program. And if all that wasn't enough, she told us that her high school boyfriend and she were breaking up.

"The more she talked, the more upset her mother and I became. Linda was on another phone crying almost as much as Jeannie, and I was trying to figure out what to do about the situation. Finally, I said, 'Jeannie, I'm really sorry about all this. But I don't know what to do about it.'

"Jeannie stopped crying immediately and said, with surprise in her voice, 'Do? You don't have to do anything. I just want to tell you how awful I'm feeling this week.'

"Well," Frank concluded, "hearing her say that she didn't want me to do anything but listen was a relief. And it also taught me to respect her struggles. She's grown up a lot this year."

There are several reasons why it is so important that parents listen to their children. First of all, children need to develop confidence in their own abilities to solve problems. Parents show respect for the struggles of children when they listen empathically and supportively, as Frank and Linda did with Jeannie that night. When their struggles are respected, children become more capable of dealing with problems they encounter in life. Parents can never remove all difficulties for their child, nor should they attempt to. Since trouble inevitably will come, it is important that parents help children to manage problems and to learn from them.

A second reason for listening to children is that many times their dilemma is alleviated by airing it to someone else. Sigmund Freud noticed long ago that his patients often overcame emotional problems by talking about them. He called this the "talking cure," and the process of gaining emotional relief through therapeutic conversation he called "catharsis." The parenting skill called "active listening" is one of the main ingredients of psychotherapy, so when parents listen to their children, they do the same thing that the helping professionals are paid to do.

Mindy's mother aided her in dealing with painful events in the seventh grade by listening:

> I tried out for cheerleading along with four other girls. Later that day the principal called the students together to announce the results. I was the one who didn't make it. I was shocked and embarrassed. Afterwards while walking down the hall I could hear people laugh at me. About this same time my friend wrote a note in which she called me some names. I had no idea why she was mad at me. I felt betrayed and alone. There was no one I could talk to except my mom.

Negative feelings like resentment, disappointment or confusion tend to become less powerful when they are acknowledged, sometimes disappearing almost like magic. Listening helps free children of such troublesome feelings by "talking them out," or "getting them off their chests."

The third reason why listening is so critical is that it prevents misbehavior. The more skillfully parents help children with their problems, the less likely children are to make problems for others. Negative feelings like resentment, disappointment or confusion don't necessarily go away when they are suppressed. Many times they are acted out in inappropriate ways. Troublesome behavior often stems from:

- feeling rejected, belittled or ignored
- feeling disappointed, defeated or overwhelmed
- feeling frightened
- feeling bored

For example, imagine yourself driving down the highway at night. A car approaches and wanders across the center line. You swerve onto the shoulder at the last moment to avoid a crash. Instantly, you become weak and shaky, shocked by how easily you could have been injured or killed. In a few more moments you are angry at the other driver. Was the driver drunk? Sleeping? Careless? Too old to be driving safely? People like that shouldn't be on the road, you tell yourself. You are so angry that you would like to do something about it, even something out of your usual character.

The point is that you reacted to the situation initially with fright, protectiveness and shock. Your anger was a secondary reaction. What you need in that situation is a law enforcement officer or a friend who takes seriously your feelings about the terrible thing the driver did, threatening your life. Perhaps something should be done about the problem of the other driver, but it's unlikely that you'll solve it yourself by acting out of revenge or spite, the secondary reactions. However, if there is no one who will listen to you empathically and supportively, you might do just that.

It is the same with children. Even though they are different from adults in cognitive and language abilities, they are like adults in feelings. When a child expresses dislike or anger or resentment about school, almost certainly something happened earlier which resulted in the resentment. Perhaps it was due to struggles to achieve, as it was with Lori:

Reading class made no sense to me. I made it to third grade, but was placed in a low reading group. I lost all confidence in myself. I began hating school and anything connected with it, to the point of gagging myself in the morning so that I would be "sick" and wouldn't have to go. In sixth grade I was placed in the lowest section and my best friend was in the top section. She stopped talking to me. Finally I was placed in a special education reading class where I learned how to read. Through those years my parents listened to my complaints, but they never understood completely the pain that I felt.

It is important that children be permitted to express their struggles with hurt, disappointment and fear. They also need guidance in dealing with the stressful situations. Fortunately for Lori and those around her, she never vented her feelings of defeat in destructive ways. Through the encouragement of her parents and her own resilience, she never gave up and eventually became an outstanding student.

The fourth reason for listening to children is that the process of listening develops a loving relationship. When the things they say are valued, children feel valued. And when they feel valued, they feel loved. Scott Peck describes the effect of listening to children as a cycle of love:

. . . the more extraordinary you realize your child to be, the more you will be willing to listen. And the more you will learn. . . . And the more appropriate your teaching, based on your knowledge of them, the more eager your children will be to learn from you. And the more they learn, the more extraordinary they will become. If the reader senses the cyclical character of this process, he or she is quite correct. . . . Value creates value. Love begets love. (Peck, 1978, p. 126)

Gayle remembers her mother with affection as she talks about problems she has had in high school trying to choose between two guys:

Through this whole mess Mom has really been a support. She cried with me and spent many hours just listening while I worked through the situation. She could have told me what to do, but she hasn't. She shows respect for me by letting me know that guy problems can be hard. I might have one boyfriend too many, but I have one terrific mother!

Her mother's listening leaves Gayle feeling loved.

This chapter covers nine skills, in groups of three, used by good listeners. The first three are invitations to the child to talk: Being Available, Observing Nonverbal Messages, and Opening the Door. The next three are skills for conversation, which help the parent to listen accurately without putting the child on the defensive: Conversing About "It," Paraphrasing Content (Playing Back Content), and Listening Actively (Playing Back Emotion). The last three skills have to do with the parental response to the child's problem itself: Delaying Suggestions, Responding to Legitimate Dependency, and Granting Wishes in Fantasy.

Figure 8.1
The Listening Skills

Inviting the Child to Talk
1. *Being Available*
2. *Observing Nonverbal Messages*
3. *Opening the Door*

Conversing Without Creating Defensiveness
4. *Conversing about "It"*
5. *Paraphrasing Content (Playing Back Content)*
6. *Listening Actively (Playing Back Emotion)*

Responding to the Problem
7. *Delaying Suggestions*
8. *Responding to Legitimate Dependency*
9. *Granting Wishes in Fantasy*

Being Available

Effective listening begins with the parent's attention. The parent who is rarely with the child, or who is lost in thought when present physically, is not likely to learn much about the child's problems. That is the way it has been in Mark's home, as he remembers it:

> It may be hard to believe, but my parents are always helping someone else and not me. Both of them are ministers and they are constantly on call or in meetings. "I have a meeting tonight, Mark. See you later." That's the way it's always been. I don't think they have ever asked me if something was wrong.

In a discussion about conversations with parents, one teenager said that when she talked to her parents, what she said went in one ear and out the other. The reactions of the other teenagers who were present suggested that this experience is as common as the cliche itself. Some said that their parents were so busy they had little time to talk. Others sensed that their parents' unavailability may be due to the parents' discomfort with conversation.

Children are more likely to talk if their parents convey an attitude of availability by greeting the child in a friendly manner, making eye contact, readily putting down the paper or turning down the volume of the radio or TV, or if busy working, keeping one eye and ear open to the child's initiatives for conversation.

Parents who are tired will have to make extra effort to truly be "present" when the child is talking. The level of concentration required to listen well is difficult to achieve when the body and mind are weary. But being available, even briefly, is important. Cheryl remembers how much she desired this and how slowly time passed when it was put off:

> When my dad would get home from work my mom would always tell me to leave them alone, since they hadn't been with each other all day. I was hurt by this; after all, I hadn't seen Dad all day either. It seemed like forever before I heard my parents go into the kitchen which meant that I could join them.

Since the days and weeks are tightly scheduled for many parents, they may find it necessary to reserve time for conversation by going out to shop or eat with their children, planning specific mealtimes to eat together at home or using the bedtime routine for sharing with each other.

Observing Nonverbal Messages

Social scientists claim that individuals communicate nonverbally at least as much information as they express verbally. Parents who "listen" to the nonverbal messages as well as the verbal, therefore, are able to respond to their children more appropriately. For example, if Bobbie's parents had paid more attention to the embarrassed look on her face, they would not have laughed at her in front of company when she backed into the tub of water in the yard. If Vanna's divorced father had watched her face with care, he would have seen how crestfallen she was when he declined the invitation to her high school graduation reception.

Parents who are good listeners are alert to the nonverbal signs that something is bothering the child:

- silence around others, retreats behind closed doors
- slamming of doors or other objects
- general irritability
- dejected posture, sighs
- teariness
- restlessness, fidgetiness
- absent-mindedness, detachment
- averted gaze, somber expressions
- changes in sleeping or eating habits
- headaches, stomachaches

Matter-of-fact statements made by parents about what they are observing tell children that their parents care about what happens to them. Such openers also invite children to talk about their problem if they would like to do so:

"I'm sorry. That was embarrassing."

"I can see the disappointment in your face."

"You seem to be down in the dumps."

"Looks like you've had a rough day."

"I noticed tears in your eyes."

"I guess you wanted to be alone after school."

"You've been having trouble sitting still."

"Concentrating seems to be hard for you right now."

Sometimes a parent notices that the child is bothered about something, but does not offer to talk about it. The notion that children need to "cry it out" on their own when they are bothered should be dismissed. Norie remembers how bothered she was as a child by the death of her cat. One morning she found her cat mortally injured and told her dad. He ended its suffering but nothing was ever said about the tragedy because, as Norie tells it, "They thought it would upset me to talk about it. It took me a long time to get over it by myself."

Attention to nonverbal signals is especially important with young children who don't have the capacity to talk about what is bothering them. When our children were infants, Lorna said she could identify at least five different kinds of cries: a hungry cry, a not-feeling-well cry, an in-pain cry, a bored-come-get-me cry, and a betrayed-mad cry. Each sounded different to her ears and each called for a different response.

If the parent misinterprets the sign, the child will indicate this in some way, verbally or nonverbally. If the parent interprets the sign accurately, the child still might not be willing to talk about it or even admit it. But whether or not the child lets the parent in on the problem, the child will appreciate being noticed and invited to talk.

Opening the Door

When children indicate that they are bothered by something, parents can open the door to more conversation with brief expressions that communicate interest, acceptance and warmth:

"I see."

"Oh."

"No kidding."

"Mm-hmmm."

"Tell me about it."

"I'd like to hear about it."

"Let's talk about it."

"You did, huh?"

"I'm listening."

"Sounds like you've got some feelings about this."

"Tell me what's on your mind."

Notice that these responses tend to be brief statements, rather than questions. They all say, "I'm available to listen if you want to talk about it," opening the door to conversation and inviting the child to enter. Parents generally rush in too quickly with probing questions and advice.

Larry came home from sixth grade with a note saying he was suspended for five days for fighting:

I also had a black eye because I had lost. When Mom saw me she said, "What happened to you?" I handed her the note and then she started yelling at me. I started crying and went to my room. She called me back and said, "I want to hear what happened." Then she listened to me and finally gave me a hug. That's all I wanted in the first place.

Without openers, conversation doesn't take place.

Conversing about "It"

Psychologist and author Roger McIntire (1985) suggests that parents think of conversations as being about Me, You and It. Parent-child conversations are kept going more easily, he maintains, if they talk about "It" (whatever it is that caused the child's concern) rather than focus on the parent (the "Me") or the child (the "You").

For the parent to talk expansively about Me (self) is not appropriate, since the problem is the child's and not the parent's. The child will become bored or skeptical about the parent's desire to listen if the parent gets carried away with storytelling or "I can top that" responses to the child.

On the other hand, children like to talk about themselves only to a point. As the conversation approaches the child's shortcomings and failures, it becomes too threatening, and the child will end the conversation rather than risk the parent's criticism.

The alternative is to talk about the "It," which seems safe and comfortable. This is one of the secrets of people who are good conversationalists — they keep the conversation from becoming too personal and threatening by viewing the problem as an "It" — a third thing, neither you nor me.

They do this by responding to the other person's problem as though it were a mistake or unfortunate set of circumstances, rather than an intentional and personal failure. They do this also by conversing matter-of-factly about what happened without using the conversation to teach the other person a lesson by scolding, moralizing, judging or blaming.

Monte's parents, unfortunately, weren't very good at this, and a car accident was more than they could handle with poor listening skills:

> I went to a private high school about 30 miles from home which made it necessary for me to drive my sister and me to school each day. One morning a front tire blew out on our car. I couldn't control it and the car rolled three times before resting top-down on a fence. My sister was badly injured. I didn't have even a bruise and I honestly believe I could have handled it better if I had been the one hurt. My dad was furious with me, constantly asking me "Why?" Life was hell for me for months. I was treated just the opposite of how my parents would have told me to treat others. The family fell apart because of this mess and I haven't had a good relationship with Dad since. I decided to go to college as far away from home as possible.

How much better it would have been if Monte's dad had been able to talk about the accident as an "It" without laying blame, and with more sensitivity to how Monte, too, was affected by the mishap.

One might comment about "It," so as to diffuse the focus on the child:

"It's too bad that happened."

"Things like that can really be disturbing."

"What a rotten day!"

"That's rough."

Paraphrasing Content (Playing Back Content)

Parents paraphrase the factual portion of the child's message by putting it into their own words and sending it back to the child:

"So you really told her off."

"They didn't want you to play with them, huh?"

"The report is due Wednesday."

This listening skill is simple, but for listeners who are so busy mentally constructing a response that they miss what the other person is saying, it is not easy to apply.

Paraphrasing the content serves several purposes. It prompts the child to keep talking, because the parent is interested in learning more and is withholding judgment and advice. And it keeps the parent from jumping to conclusions as Melodie's mother did:

As a child in Yorkshire, England, I decided to do something about poverty. I persuaded a friend to help me raise some money. We cleaned about 10 gardens one day and earned about three pounds each. I took the money home and put it under my pillow to send off the next day. But my mom happened to find it the next morning when she made the bed and assumed that I had taken it from her purse. I explained to her where it came from, but she wouldn't believe me. When my father came home I got the money back and we sent it off. But I was terribly disappointed by my mother's reaction.

Effective listening includes keeping on the conversation track without getting sidetracked by incorrect assumptions and unnecessary scoldings.

Listening Actively (Playing Back Emotion)

The listening skill of responding reflectively to the child's emotion is the most important parenting skill of this entire book. It is essential for dealing with the Child's Problem Area but contributes to the tactfulness and sensitivity with which parents relate to children in the other three areas as well.

In counseling psychology this skill is called "reflective listening" because the counselor serves as a mirror to reflect back to the client the emotion which is being experienced. In the Parent Effectiveness Training program it is called "active listening" (Gordon, 1970, p. 49). The process of identifying the emotion with which the child is struggling and feeding it back to the child is an active one, and not passive as the mirror analogy suggests. Faber and Mazlish (1980) refer to the skill with the descriptive phrase, "give the feeling a name."

Suppose that a ten-year-old son dallies in getting ready for church one Sunday morning. His parent tries to hurry him, but he continues to dawdle and the parent gets increasingly impatient. Finally the son says, "I don't want to go to church!"

Common responses of parents to a statement like this might be:

"Well, you're going whether you want to or not!" (ordering)

"You shouldn't talk like that." (moralizing)

"I've about had it with you!" (threatening)

"When I was your age, I had to go two or three times a week. You only have to go once." (lecturing)

"You're acting like a little baby." (shaming)

"Think you're too good for church?" (ridiculing)

"You know you don't mean it. You like church." (disagreeing)

"Well, you can go even if you don't want to. I'm sure that once you're there you'll feel better about it." (advising, solving the problem)

Each of these responses cuts short the communication process because the parent finds out nothing about what is behind the child's declaration. Each statement says, in effect, "I know what is good for you. What you think or feel about this is not important." The result of responses like these is that the child becomes increasingly defensive about his feelings; to him his feelings are important and not to be denied.

Active listening is an alternative to the typical responses of parents illustrated above. It is such an important means of dealing with the child's feelings that without it communication breaks down and ultimately the relationship itself is broken.

Regarding the situation in which the ten-year-old doesn't want to go to church, it is important that the child's problem about going to church be explored, even though the parent might feel so strongly about going to church that it is not a matter for negotiation. If the parent refuses to listen to the child's feelings about this issue, and if this discounting of the child's feelings is characteristic of the parent-child relationship, eventually the child may feel that he has to break relationship with his parents in order to declare his own individuality.

In terms of the communication process, active listening consists of feedback from listener to speaker, which shows that the listener is paying attention. When a child experiences some particular event and wants to share a response to that event with another person, the child has to encode the experience in some way in order to communicate it (see Figure 8.2). The code is a combination of words, facial expressions, tone of voice and so on. The message which is communicated is only an approximation of the experience, of course, since the event was experienced subjectively, that is, internally and personally. This is the nature of human experience — each of us lives in a private world. We give each other glimpses into our subjective worlds, but we cannot leave our own and enter that of another.

Figure 8.2
The Communication Process

Child   Parent

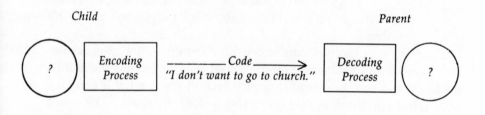

Child experiences something   Parent receives the message
and sends a coded message   and decodes it in order to
about the experience.   understand the experience.

Adapted from Parent Effectiveness Training *(p. 52) by Thomas Gordon, 1970. New York: Peter H. Wyden. Copyright 1970 by David McKay Co., a Division of Random House, Inc. Adapted by permission.*

Therefore, the task of the parent in active listening is to decode the message which the child is sending in order to understand better the experience of the child. The parent does this by making a guess about the emotion being experienced and then feeding it back in a tentative statement. A guess about the event which elicited the feeling can also be a part of the feedback response. These two parts of an active listening response are constructed in the parent's mind using the following formula:

"You feel _____ because/when/about _____."

When parents first begin to use this formula to practice active listening, they tend to have some difficulty in identifying the feeling. Sometimes this is because it's a response they are unaccustomed to making and find it awkward. Other times the difficulty is because they are more comfortable with opinions than feelings and are reluctant to give active listening a try.

There are several aids for identifying the feeling which the child is experiencing in the feedback response. First, if the word "that" is inserted into the formula ("You feel that church is boring"), the parent is identifying an opinion or thought, not a feeling. Second, if the word "like" is inserted into the formula ("You feel like not going to church today"), chances are that the parent is off-target again. This may be the identification of an opinion, rather than a feeling, or it may describe what the child wants to do, but it doesn't name the feeling involved. Third, if "You think" can be substituted for "You feel" ("You feel church is boring" and "You think church is boring") and the statement still makes sense, a thought is being identified, and not a feeling.

On the other hand, if "You are" can be substituted for "You feel" ("You feel bored" and "You are bored") and the statement makes sense, the response *does* identify a feeling. The list included with the discussion questions for Chapter 8 at the back of the book is useful in identifying emotions so that the overworked word "frustrated" is used less often.[1]

The parent doesn't necessarily say the words of the formula aloud, because the feedback statement might sound awkward if the formula were followed literally. For example:

"You feel angry when someone picks on you."

---

[1] Active listening is as appropriate for responding to positive emotions as it is for responding to negative emotions (for example, "You look pleased with things" or "I'll bet you can hardly wait!"). But since this chapter is about the Child's Problem Area the focus is on the negative emotions.

"You're feeling hurt because you hit your finger with the hammer."

"You're feeling hungry because it's about time to eat."

Rather than following the formula in a literal way, parents can listen actively by "naming the feeling" in a more natural way. For example:

"Boy, you sound mad!"

"That must have hurt."

"You're really hungry, huh?"

"That wet diaper is uncomfortable, isn't it."

"You seem to be pretty discouraged about that art project."

Each of these responses feeds back to the child the decoded feeling message, completing the communication circuit.

In the example about going to church, the child wants to communicate to the parent something of what going to church means to him on this particular morning. So he chooses the words, "I don't want to go to church," as a way of encoding the message. The parent attempts to decode the message by listening to the words and observing the nonverbal clues which accompanied the words.

There are many reasons why a ten-year-old boy might send a message like this. Perhaps he isn't feeling well. Maybe he is more tired than usual. Maybe he gets bored at church. Maybe he was scolded recently by his Sunday school teacher or was threatened by one of his classmates. It's possible that he isn't comfortable with the shoes he has to wear to church. Maybe he is so worried about returning to school on Monday that he'd like to curl up in bed and not go out of the house on Sunday. Perhaps he is upset by the Sunday morning tension among the rest of the family members.

A number of possibilities exist, so the parent guesses one which seems to be likely and tries it out, feeding the message back to the child in a tentative statement (see Figure 8.3).

If the active listening response is on target, both speaker and listener receive confirmation that communication has taken place. If the response is not on target, the speaker is given opportunity to correct the communication error by sending the message again. Only the speaker knows when the message has been received accurately, since it is the speaker's message that is being transmitted in the communication process. Since there can be many possible interpretations of the message, the listener decodes by feeding back an interpretation which seems likely to be accurate, and then awaits correction. That is why active listening responses are tentatively

Figure 8.3
Active Listening Feedback in the Communication Process

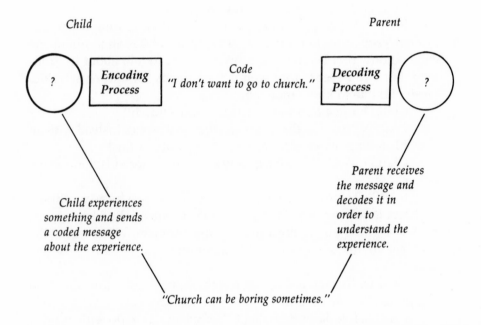

Child   Parent

Encoding Process

Code
"I don't want to go to church."

Decoding Process

Child experiences something and sends a coded message about the experience.

Parent receives the message and decodes it in order to understand the experience.

"Church can be boring sometimes."

Parent *"reflects"* back content/and or emotion in tentative statement.
If accurate, communication has taken place.
If inaccurate, child sends message again or corrects feedback.

Possible meanings of coded message:

- *gets bored at church*
- *too tired to get up and get ready*
- *best friend has chicken pox and won't be there*
- *doesn't like his shoes*
- *isn't feeling well*
- *doesn't like teacher*
- *worried about school problem*
- *was scolded last Sunday*
- *bothered by tension in family on Sunday morning*

stated.

The parent who reported this incident said it went something like this:

CHILD: I don't want to go to church!

PARENT: You don't, huh? [a door opener]

CHILD: I sure don't. Do I have to go?

PARENT: [tempted to respond with a door-closing order, but instead keeps the door open by making an observation about the child's nonverbal behavior and inviting him to talk about it] Probably. But I've never before seen you get ready for church so reluctantly. I'd like to know more about this.

CHILD: I just don't want to go. I hate church!

PARENT: [resists the urge to lecture and replies instead with an active listening response] You feel strongly about this!

CHILD: Well, I'm not the only one. The other kids don't like it either.

PARENT: [now realizes that the problem must be an in-church problem involving other kids, and not an out-of-church problem; makes a guess about the cause of the problem, referring to the problem in the impersonal "It" manner] Church can be boring sometimes.

CHILD: Church is OK, but not Sunday school. How about if I just go to church? [referring to the worship service]

PARENT: [knows now that the problem has to do with Sunday school, but still doesn't know what the problem is about, so guesses again] Sunday school is boring sometimes.

CHILD: Yeah. But in our class you sure can't mess around.

PARENT: [confused about whether or not boredom is the problem, so paraphrases the content of the child's last statement] Kids can't mess around in *your* class.

CHILD: Not with just two kids. Last Sunday there were only two of us there.

PARENT: [paraphrases content] Oh. So your class was really small last Sunday.

CHILD: Just Michelle and me. And Mrs. Moyer. Everybody else was on vacation.

PARENT: [realizes that the problem has to do with class size and not boredom and makes another tentative guess about the feeling] I suppose you miss the others when they aren't there.

CHILD: I guess so. I wish I could be gone when they aren't there. The bad part is that Mrs. Moyer asks all those questions.

PARENT: [finally able to name the feeling] It must have been pretty uncomfortable with just you and Michelle and Mrs. Moyer. I see what you mean about not messing around.

CHILD: Do I have to go?

PARENT: [firmly but warmly] Yes. When you're older you can decide for yourself, but for now you have to go. But I understand why you don't want to go. We've got the same problem with our class in the summer. [pauses and then continues with a smile] Maybe we should put our two classes together.

CHILD: No way! [pauses and then says] At least when summer is over, we'll get rid of Mrs. Moyer.

PARENT: [active listening response, followed by a delayed suggestion] You're looking forward to that, huh? Think you can put up with her questions for a few more Sundays?

CHILD: [now smiling, too] I guess I can — since I don't have any choice anyway.

The active listening response is a statement — although tentative — rather than a question because statements contribute to the process of communication at a different level than questions do. A small child or a computer can ask questions, but only a person who has been listening carefully to another can say, in effect, "I hear you. You are feeling _____. I know what you are going through." And for the speaker, being heard is not the same as being questioned.

Although parents tend to ask too many questions, questions are not to be avoided altogether. They can be useful, especially open-ended questions which aren't answered with one or two words (yes – no, etc.). A yes – no type of question opens the door to conversation, but only by a crack.

Asking *what* happened is better than asking *why* it happened or *why* the child is feeling a certain way. Many times "why" questions can't be answered — the child may not be able to articulate what the problem is or can't give a reasonable explanation for it. (Nor can adults, very often.) The boy who didn't want to go to church probably wouldn't have been able to explain why at the beginning of the conversation. The conversation helped him as well as his parent understand what he was feeling and why.

Even if the reason is known, the child may be reluctant to tell because of fear that a smart, brave or proper child shouldn't feel this way and therefore the reason isn't good enough. So tentative statements are preferred because they put the child on the spot less than probing questions do.

Parents sometimes are cautious about naming children's feelings, for fear of making the feelings worse. They tend to want to talk children out of their bad feelings, instead of acknowledging them. If a child hits his thumb with a hammer and comes crying into the house, parents typically respond with such responses as, "Be a big boy (or girl)," "Don't cry," "It'll be better soon," or "Shush — it can't hurt that bad." Each of these denies the child's pain. The result of this kind of response is that the child is likely to cry harder than ever; after all, the parent still hasn't been convinced that it hurts.

A more comforting response is to acknowledge the hurt: "Oh, that must have hurt!" "That's too bad." "I'm sorry that happened. Let's have a look." Ironically, the pain seems to be more tolerable and leave more quickly when parents accept the expressions of feeling without trying to hurry the child out of the discomfort.

This is as true of emotional discomfort as it is of physical discomfort. When children hear words for what they are experiencing, they are comforted. Someone understands what they are going through.

Sometimes parents are reluctant to use active listening responses because they think that to do so they must "agree" with the child. So as they listen, they are busy figuring out who is right and who is wrong in the child's problem situation. And if they decide that the child is wrong and shouldn't feel that way, the parents are unable to respond in the active listening manner. Patti remembers conversations with her dad this way:

> I always feel defeated when my dad and I argue. I feel like I am being told that my feelings are wrong because they aren't the same as his. Several times I have said how I felt about something and Daddy would say, "That's wrong." So I quit talking and then he gets mad because I won't talk. I tell him why and he again tells me that's not the right attitude to take and that he's not always telling me I'm wrong. Right there he's doing it again.

Feelings are neither right nor wrong. They are involuntary, internal responses to situations and often are transitory. Suppose that I dislike the color of the walls in one of rooms where I teach and so I say one day as I enter the room, "I sure don't like the way this room is decorated. If I had to be in here all day, I think I'd become ill." Am I right or wrong? Neither. If the issue is whether or not the colors of the room are in vogue or aesthetically pleasing to interior designers or people in general, then my statement is subject to correction. But if the statement expresses my feeling about the colors, it is indisputable. It is my subjective response to the situation and not subject to evaluation by others. Others may respond differently to the room, of course, but that doesn't mean that my feeling is wrong—or that theirs are wrong. My feeling simply exists—as children's feelings do.

The goal of active listening, therefore, is not to determine rightness or wrongness, or even to come to an agreement, but to understand the child better. And as a parent comes to understand a child more fully, the parent will discover that the two of them respond differently very often. This is inevitable since feelings which are generated in two individuals are never identical. By accepting a child's feelings as legitimate expressions of the child's own individuality, parents give permission to the child to become differentiated from them, which emotional maturity requires (see Chapter 15 on family systems). Children need recognition of their feelings, not agreement or disagreement.

Of course, what children do about their feelings—their actions —*can* be judged to be right or wrong, good or bad, appropriate or inappropriate. Respecting children's feelings doesn't mean that their behavior is always acceptable. Often it isn't. Parents can accept a child's feelings, while still insisting on certain behaviors.

Delaying Suggestions

Perhaps the most difficult block to effective listening is the desire to give advice. Parents generally want to help their children overcome problems as quickly as possible, so they lose no time in trying to talk children out of their negative feelings or passing on their suggestions about how such situations should be handled.

Like parents, college students generally assume that the basic ingredient of helpfulness is passing on wisdom to a friend in time of need. When they practice withholding or delaying advice while listening to a friend's problems, they are surprised at the effect, as this student was:

> I was sitting outdoors with the guy I have been dating and he was unusually quiet. I said, "You seem a little sad tonight." [nonverbal observation] He then told me about his best friend's recent marriage, and how he resented his wife taking that friend away. With a few encouragers [door openers] from me he revealed that he was actually scared of being alone and even more so of going back to college after being out for a few years. The conversation ended with him crying

in my arms. It was incredible! I had offered no solutions or advice; I had merely listened.

The problem with advice is not that parents shouldn't give it—children need the advice of their parents. The problem has to do with the manner in which advice is offered, especially the timeliness of it (see Figure 8.4). Children are more open to receive advice if it is delayed. If offered too quickly, before the child's feelings about the problem have been adequately explored, the advice is less likely to be appreciated or implemented.

Figure 8.4
Good Listening Includes Delaying Suggestions Until
the Timing is Right

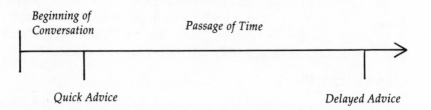

Remember that the problems under consideration here are problems in the Child's Problem area. For problems in the Parent's Problem Area, strongly worded advice, even demands, are appropriate. But when the child owns the problem, the parent's task is to help the child deal with the problem without taking over the problem and solving it to the parent's satisfaction. The parent does this by listening with empathy and encouragement and leaving the solution, as much as possible, with the child. If the parent responds to the situation with quick advice, admonishments, little sermons and so on, the parent is pushing the child in the direction of the parent's solution to the problem, which may not be the same as the child's solution (see Figure 8.5).

College students come to my office to talk about their struggles with decisions—choices about their major, post-graduation plans, marriage, relationships with parents and friends. I enjoy helping

Figure 8.5
The Parent's Solution to the Child's Problem May Not
be the Same as the Child's Solution

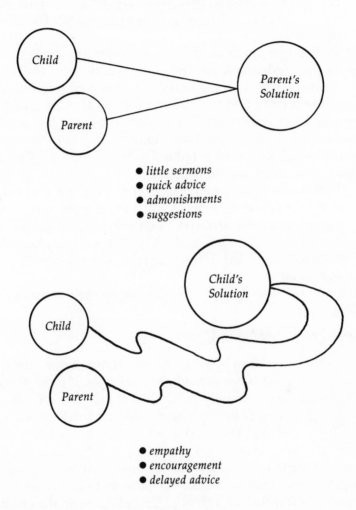

● *little sermons*
● *quick advice*
● *admonishments*
● *suggestions*

● *empathy*
● *encouragement*
● *delayed advice*

them sort through their options and weigh the merits of each, but in most instances I will not tell them what they should do. The choices are theirs to make and the responsibility for the decisions needs to remain with them.

In the same manner, parents at times play the role of counselor to their children. It is one of several hats parenthood requires them to wear. And delivering advice too quickly makes for poor counseling.

Greg remembers with appreciation how his parents responded when he broke up with his girlfriend:

> When I told them, they were interested but they didn't pry, didn't drill me with many questions. Later when I did feel like talking about it, they were attentive and patient, not condescending or throwing advice all around. This was important to me.

With younger children, too, it's important to listen to children express their indecisiveness and confusion without overwhelming them immediately with suggestions. When Neil was eight, he answered the door to find two strangers there. They seemed friendly; they asked him questions about his interests, gave him a pamphlet and then asked for money. Neil found some money and gave it to them, although he wasn't sure he did the right thing. When his dad arrived home, Neil told him about it:

> Right away Dad started yelling at me. He said that I should not have talked to them or given them money. I felt really confused and embarrassed. I started crying and ran out of the house. Later that evening, Dad said he was sorry he yelled at me and told me that if they come back to tell them we aren't interested.

Parents are wise to delay the passing of their wisdom until the timing is right.

Responding to Legitimate Dependency

Sometimes children need to be assisted in some specific way. Listening by itself is not enough. For example, if a preschooler has been trying unsuccessfully to tie her shoes, the remark, "Tying shoestrings can really be frustrating," doesn't get the shoes tied even though it is on target as an active listening response to the situation.

Even in this instance, however, active listening is appropriate. Does she really want help with her shoe laces or does she want to struggle some more? It's easy for parents to make both kinds of mistakes—abandoning a child in time of need, on the one hand, or interfering with the child's attempts to cope, on the other. Unless parents have the wisdom of Solomon, they need to use the listening skills to find out if assistance is wanted.

In discussion groups, I've heard children and parents relate numerous stories about children needing help from their parents, in addition to sensitive listening. Sixteen-year-old Bobbie, for example, came home late one night and discovered that the back door could not be unlocked. Everybody was asleep. She knocked, softly at first and then more insistently, but couldn't arouse anybody. Finally in desperation and tears she dragged the ladder out of the garage and across the lawn and lifted it upright against the house in order to climb to the roof:

> I crawled over to my parents' window and knocked and yelled until finally Mom appeared. She opened the window and I crawled in, shaking and sobbing. Mom held me for awhile and she and Dad told me they were sorry it happened. The next day Dad changed the lock on the back door. He never fixed anything that fast before.

Bobbie's parents listened and also acted in response to a problem she experienced. A similar story was told by Rhonda:

> When I was in elementary school I read a book about ghosts and it scared me so bad I couldn't sleep. I couldn't tell my folks why I was scared since Mom had told me not to read books like that. But I insisted that I was too scared to be alone, so Dad came and stayed with me until I went to sleep. I appreciated the fact that Dad took my fear seriously, although I felt bad that I had done what Mom told me not to do.

Here are additional examples of parents' responses to needs for assistance:

> "OK, I'll pick you up later this afternoon. Call when you are ready to leave."
>
> "Can't find your shoes? Maybe we can find them if I help look."
>
> "Looks like you're hungry. There's leftover pizza in the refrigerator you can have."
>
> "You'd really like one of those, wouldn't you. Well, maybe Santa Claus will bring you one."
>
> "I'm sorry you scraped your knee. Let's have a look at it."
>
> "We're very sorry about your friend's death. We'd like to fly you to the funeral if you want to go."
>
> "If you'd like me to, I will call the coach to explain why you can't be at practice tomorrow."

Granting Wishes in Fantasy

Sometimes children want things they can't have, or would like to change a situation which can't be changed. Parents typically respond to such situations with explanations of why the children can't have what they want. For example:

"Unfortunately, bad hops are part of the game. Maybe next time you'll get the good bounce."

"Kids can really be unkind to each other. You'll have to use your influence with the others to help them stop this."

"We just can't afford the more expensive shoes. But for what you need, these others will be just as good."

"You've got the bug which everybody has been getting. It usually lasts two days."

However, explanations aren't very comforting, even when they are perfectly reasonable. The more parents explain, the more children tend to protest their fate. As an alternative to this, Faber and Mazlish (1980) recommend that parents "give them their wishes in fantasy." For example:

"I wish we could run time backwards so that you could play that last inning over."

"I wish I could wave a magic wand and make your friends all get along with each other."

"I wish that we could afford those expensive shoes you'd really like to have."

"I wish I had a magic formula for making your stomachache disappear."

Granting their wishes in fantasy is a way of acknowledging the child's feelings about the matter. It's another way for parents to show that they are listening and care about what the child is going through, even though they can't solve the problem.

Questions for Thought and Discussion about this Chapter are on page 294.

9. Encouraging Autonomy

Sometimes parental intervention in a child's problem is appropriate, but many times it is not. In fact, one of the most common problems of the families that I know best is the problem of parents doing too much for their children. This seems to happen more often with mothers than with fathers, although I've seen fathers do too much also. (Fathers seem more likely to err on the side of doing too little for their children.)

Many examples come to mind:

Rebecca refuses to feed herself. Her parents still feed her long after she could be doing it herself.

Kyle and Mark, ages four and two, wake up in the middle of the night; their mother gets up to get them a drink, put them back to bed and read them back to sleep as she has done every night for years. When she "complains" about this, she does so with a smile on her face as if she is pleased with herself for being such a good mother.

Tommy, who is small for his age, is still carried to church by his parents at age seven.

When Curt's dad plays ball with the neighborhood kids, he makes sure that Curt is always on the winning team. If Curt and his dad are on the same team, his dad plays just hard enough that they win; if they are on opposite teams, his dad makes sure his team loses so that Curt's wins. If Curt does lose, he cries and pouts; his dad consoles him, usually offering something special to make up for the loss.

Eight-year-old Davie is unable to spend a night away from his parents without emotional trauma.

Billy speaks "baby talk" at home with his mother, but at school is able to speak like the other children in his sixth-grade class. However, he prefers to play with third graders at recess and after dismissal.

Joshua's mother shops for all of his clothes and decides each morning what Josh, at age 14, will wear.

When sixteen-year-old Gina and her parents go shopping for her, she doesn't have a chance to speak to the sales clerks herself because her parents speak for her.

Years ago when long hair bothered parents more than it does today, a newly arrived freshman and his dad visited a barber shop in our college town during orientation weekend. The father introduced himself and then said to the manager of the shop, "This is my son, Kevin, who will be coming here once a month to get his hair cut. I just wanted Kevin to find out where the barber shop is and to meet you."

College students Clark and Ellie announced their engagement a few months ago. They live in campus dormitories, but each weekend Ellie takes their laundry home for her mother to do.

The important question in each of these examples is whether the child is being held back or is on schedule developmentally. Being on schedule requires a gradual and steady increase in independence. The amount of personal responsibility *granted* children, and *expected* of them, needs to keep pace with the physical and intellectual changes which occur throughout childhood and adolescence. Independence, therefore, is not acquired in a dramatic fashion on the eighteenth birthday; it occurs in a gradual way and by the eighteenth birthday is nearly complete.

Figure 9.1 portrays this gradually increasing independence as the climb up a flight of stairs. The only way that children can make the ascent to the happy, productive adulthood which awaits them at the top is to climb the steps themselves. And the only way that parents can help is by helping children acquire the ability to climb stairs. Sometimes they want to get their children to the top by carrying them there or providing an elevator or escalator. But if children are held back and not encouraged to make gradual steps towards independence, the climb ultimately will be so steep that some will falter. Over-responsibility of parents and under-responsibility of children go together.

In some of the examples above, what the parents are doing might not indicate a long-term problem, but in others, a serious problem could be indicated. Perhaps Ellie's mother, for example, offered to do their laundry simply because she wants to help the couple out in this way before they move far away in a few months. Even though Ellie and Clark are quite ready to get married and assume responsibility for themselves, they accept her offer with appreciation.

On the other hand, the father who was taking charge of his college-age son's haircuts surely was having trouble letting his son stay on schedule developmentally.

If children whine, cling, tattle, give up quickly or show the other characteristics of over-dependency listed in Figure 9.2, they probably are behind schedule developmentally because their parents are doing too much for them.

Figure 9.1
Independence and Age of Child

Independence occurs gradually throughout childhood and adolescence and not suddenly at the end of adolescence.

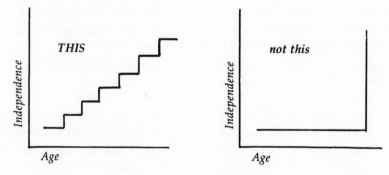

Obviously parents can also do too little for their children. Doing too little is called neglect in the language of the law and is a form of child abuse. As with the other aspects of parenting, the goal is to achieve balance; in this case, balance between doing too much and doing too little for children.

Figure 9.2
Characteristics of Overly-Dependent Children

Children of parents who have encouraged dependency rather than autonomy tend to:
● take and not give
● be afraid of new situations
● blame others for problems which arise
● expect others to make them happy
● whine
● cling
● tattle
● be unable to sustain cooperative play with age-mates
● omit common courtesies
● have difficulty conversing with adults in nonmanipulative manner
● show poor sportsmanship
● drop out of games, activities, projects
● give up quickly

The antidote to over-dependency is to encourage children's autonomy — that is, to help them develop the capacity to solve their own problems. Five means of encouraging autonomy follow.

Expecting Responsible Behavior

Expectations of adults have a powerful effect on the abilities of children. This is the conclusion of a famous study by Robert Rosenthal, a Harvard University psychologist, and Lenore Jacobson, a public school administrator. They told elementary school teachers at the beginning of the school year that certain students in their classes had been identified as "bloomers" and could be expected to make unusually large gains in school achievement during the coming year. At the end of the year, tests revealed that first and second grade children identified as bloomers indeed had made significantly greater gains in intelligence than children not identified as bloomers. What the teachers didn't know, however, is that the bloomers had been randomly selected by the researchers. The differences between the bloomers and nonbloomers existed only in the minds of the teachers (Rosenthal & Jacobson, 1968). The children identified as bloomers were better problem-solvers on the test at the end of the year because of the power of expectancy which had been operating in their lives in subtle ways the previous nine months.

For ethical reasons the researchers did not experiment with the effects of negative expectations; there is ample reason to believe, however, that negative expectations are self-fulfilling in the same way that positive expectations are. The story is told of the mother who left her son alone for a time while she went to the store. As she walked out the door, her instructions were, "And Johnny, whatever you do, don't put a bean in your ear!" She returned to find that he had done exactly that, of course, fulfilling her negative expectations. Parents are more likely to get good behavior if they expect good behavior and act as if they expect their words to be heeded.

I think that children, in general, are capable of more mature behavior than their parents expect. At the same time, I am aware that some children are expected to meet such high standards that they become discouraged and never gain their parents' approval, in spite of high achievement. So I want to avoid the hazards of inappropriately high expectations, too. The level of expectations that I have for my children, therefore, is somewhere between the level that is average and the level that is too high — where expectations are high, but reasonable; demanding, but fair (see Figure 9.3).

Figure 9.3
Levels of Expectations and Characteristics of Children

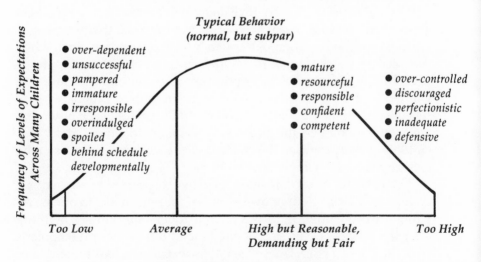

Levels of Expectations of Parents

One cold, snowy morning during Nathan's second grade year, he had to get himself ready for school. Lorna's job required her to leave home very early, and I had an early morning meeting so I was not able to get the children off to school as I usually did. Later that day Nathan's teacher called me to share her amusement about his arrival at school that morning. He wasn't wearing a coat because he hadn't been able to find it. But he had on seven shirts! Needless to say, I was embarrassed about being such a neglectful parent, but I was proud of Nate's resourcefulness.

In speaking of maturity, I am talking about that kind of resourcefulness, not adultlike sophistication. I am not referring to the age when girls begin to wear make-up, for example, or when teens begin to date. I don't mean that parents should hurry their children through childhood to become teenagers, nor that they should push them through adolescence in order to reach adulthood as soon as possible.

I am talking about abilities of children to get along with others (showing friendliness, empathy and trustworthiness) and the ability to achieve (solving problems, pursuing a goal and delaying gratification in the present in order to achieve a more important reward in the future). Children need to develop these traits in order to play and work cooperatively with others, giving as well as getting so that others do not feel used by them. These traits are the opposite of those listed in Figure 9.2.

Parental expectations are revealed when parents talk with others about their children. Years ago Lorna and I noticed that the parents we most admired rarely spoke critically of their children. Even when they disapproved of what their children had done, the disapproval was counterbalanced with optimism and humor. Because we wanted to develop the same kind of positive expectations we saw revealed in these other homes, Lorna and I promised each other that we would minimize the times we complain to others about our children. I also promised the children that I will not tell stories in the college classroom which demean them.

Perhaps the most damaging negative expectations are critical comments which children overhear their parents make to others. As parents were gathering in the church foyer one Sunday morning after the service, Leslie said as she helped put on her preschooler's coat, "Just look at her. Doesn't she look weird? She looks retarded or something." I cringed, wishing that her daughter did not have to be exposed to such comments. Leslie's daughter was normal, but even if she hadn't been, such a comment would have been inappropriate.

Rather than saying negative things in front of children and setting up self-fulfilling, negative expectations, it's possible to do just the opposite of what Leslie did. The power of expectations is put to good use when complimentary things about children are said in conversations which they overhear. Sue did this one morning as she was speaking on the phone with her mother while Jordan was playing nearby: "Grandma, you should have seen Jordan this morning. He walked right into the kindergarten room without any help from me. He is ready for school and I'm so proud of him." We would predict that Jordan walked into the classroom the following morning even more confidently, because he knew his mother expected him to do exactly that.

Another way that parents show that they expect responsible behavior is to treat misbehavior as a mistake. When I was a sixth-grader, I hurt one of my classmates one day by bending his arm behind his back. I can still hear the words and tone of voice of Mrs. Nickel, our teacher: "Well, Philip! You're hurting Roger." She sounded surprised. Immediately I let go, embarrassed to have been seen making such a mistake. Mrs. Nickel expected better things of me than that and I didn't want to disappoint her.

So often the words and tone of voice indicate expectation of the negative: "Not again!" "I've told you a thousand times!" "Don't you ever _____?" "You're always _____." "You never _____."

Parents also use the power of expectations when they place their children in positions of trust. Asking a child to take responsibility for cleaning up the kitchen on a given evening is more likely to encourage cooperation than is ordering the child to do the dishes. Trusting a child of sufficient age to go to the neighborhood convenience store on an errand is more likely to develop confidence than is reluctance to let the child go out of the house alone.

Using Words of Encouragement

Almost everything that children do, their parents can do better because of the natural superiority of adults. Adults are bigger, stronger, smarter, more experienced, more resourceful and so on. The challenge for parents is to help children develop their abilities and their confidence without being overly patronizing on the one hand, or overly corrective on the other.

One of the themes in parenting advice is that praising children, contrary to what parents might think, is not recommended as the best way to encourage. Haim Ginott (1965), for example, wrote:

Praise, like penicillin, must not be administered haphazardly. There are rules and cautions that govern the handling of potent medicines — rules about timing and dosage, cautions about possible allergic reactions. (p. 45)

The most important rule about administering praise, Ginott suggested, is that it deal only with the child's efforts and accomplishments and not with the child's character and personality. A child whose personality is praised following good behavior is uncomfortable in the same way that a child whose character is criticized following misbehavior tends to be defensive. In neither case is it totally deserved.

When a boy cleans up the yard, it is only natural to comment on how hard he has worked, and on how good the yard looks. It is highly unrelated, and inappropriate, to tell him how good he is. (Ginott, 1965, p. 45)

This is why children who are praised sometimes respond with behavior less worthy of praise — they are showing that the praise was not totally honest or deserved, in the same way that children whose character is attacked protest.

Thus, statements which praise the child's character or personality ("You are terrific." "You're a great helper!" "You always do such good work.") are not recommended by Ginott.

To avoid the pitfalls of evaluative praise, Faber and Mazlish (1980), followers of Ginott, recommend that parents describe what they see ("I see a yard which has been neatly raked."), describe what they feel ("It's a pleasure to walk into this yard."), or sum up the child's praiseworthy behavior in a word ("I see a yard that is free of litter and leaves. That's what I call *neatness*.").

Rudolf Dreikurs (1964) and the Systematic Training for Effective Parenting (STEP; Dinkmeyer & McKay, 1976) program which is based on Dreikurs' work, are also cautious about the use of praise. The essential difference between praise and encouragement, in their point of view, is that praise is an attempt to motivate children with external rewards, whereas encouragement attempts to motivate through internal means. Praise places value judgments on the child or the child's behavior for the purposes of social control. Encouragement, according to the STEP program, focuses instead on internal evaluation and contributions.

For example, "You're such a good boy!" is praise, but "I appreciate the way you took care of the trash" is encouragement. "You got an A! That's great!" is praise, but "You worked hard for that A, didn't you" is encouragement. "What a good job you did!" and "I'm so proud of you!" are praise, but "I can see that you're proud of it" is encouragement.

The following suggestions regarding encouragement take into account the recommendations of these authors. The goal of encouraging remarks like these is to recognize the child's effort, contribution and feelings of confidence and satisfaction, and to avoid evaluative praise.

Acceptance of child's level of performance

"I enjoyed watching your game today."
"I enjoyed working with you in the kitchen this morning."

Appreciation of child's contribution

"I'll need your help in the yard on Saturday."
"Thanks. I appreciate your help."
"When you get your job finished, let's go get something to drink."
"Let's trade jobs. I'll clean your room if you clean the car."
"Let's do it together."
"Can I count on you to take care of it?"

Support of child's effort

"Look at the progress you've made!"
"That's quite an improvement."
"It's coming along nicely, isn't it?"
"Too bad it didn't work out. Maybe next time it will."
"You worked hard on that."
"I'm impressed by the way you worked at the project."
"I'm proud of the way you stuck with it."
"I'll bet you learned a lot anyway."

Confidence in child's ability to solve problem

"Would you like to try it?"
"You'll figure it out."
"I think you can do it."
"I have confidence in your judgment."
"Let me know if you need my help."
"You'll learn. It just takes some practice."

Interest in child's level of satisfaction

"It looks like you enjoyed doing this."

"How do you think it went?"

"Sounds like you're not quite satisfied with the results."

"Did you reach your goal?"

"Were you very disappointed?"

All of these encouraging remarks are in contrast to the following discouraging words.

Words that discourage

"You don't know how."

"Wait until you're older."

"You might get hurt."

"Let me do it."

"What a mess!"

"You're doing it wrong."

"You always break things."

"You're too slow."

"Do I have to do it myself?"

"You should have known better."

Some parents think the suggestions about encouragement covered in this section are hardly worth worrying about. Since genuine support is revealed more by tone of voice than choice of words, they argue that it is better to be encouraging naturally than to be encouraging "correctly."

To some extent I agree with these parents. It is important for parents to be positive and supportive, rather than negative and critical. "You can't take the dents out of the milk can by kicking it from the outside" is a Pennsylvania Dutch saying which captures the issue. Any attempt to be positive is better than none at all.

But it is better yet to be positive in the most effective manner. That's why the suggestions in this section are offered. Put them to the test and let your experience help you decide if the ideas are worth following.

Equipping Children for Problem Solving

Parents facilitate their children's movement towards independence by preparing them ahead of time to handle situations in a resourceful, responsible manner. Some of the many ways of doing this are listed here, with the hope that individual households will expand or adapt the list for their own use.

Train children to use the telephone by teaching them to:

- answer the phone
- take messages
- dial
- find frequently called numbers
- call certain neighbors or relatives if they need help
- call long distance
- memorize and use the family's credit card number
- call collect
- call 911 for emergencies
- memorize the address of the home and places of employment of the parents

Help children to manage time by:

- Using the television schedule, noon whistle, traffic pattern, hands of a clock or oven timer with young children as signals for certain activities.
- Teaching them to tell time as soon as they are capable.
- Providing them with their own watches or clocks.
- Having them take responsibility for getting themselves up by using an alarm clock.
- Keeping a family calendar which all members use to mark upcoming events.
- Previewing the activities of the coming week, so that all members are informed about schedules and duties and can plan accordingly.
- Going over household duties and dividing them in advance. (Each of our three children was assigned two days of kitchen duty; on Sunday, everybody was to help. We followed the same weekly pattern for months, to minimize surprises and protests.)
- Planning meals — going over the schedule of activities and mealtimes, kitchen duties and special grocery requests.
- Using a message center. Keep a supply of scratch pads and pens and a consistent location for messages. When leaving, all members leave message about destination and time of return.
- Calling home when delayed. Parents, too.

Prevent household problems by:

- Hiding a house key or providing house keys for book bags.
- Teaching children to use the appliances.
- Installing hooks and shelves low enough to be reached easily.
- Providing hampers for each bedroom and bathroom so that dirty clothes don't end up on the floor.
- Providing adequate containers and labels for storage.
- Designating certain spaces in the yard, garage or basement for messes.
- Providing access to tools and utensils which can be used by children.
- Using locks, high shelves and warnings for tools which are not to be used.
- Providing a safe stool for climbing.
- Discussing procedures to follow in case of fire or tornado.

Involve children more responsibly in the family finances by:

- Giving an allowance and being clear about what kinds of expenses the child is expected to pay for with the allowance.
- Asking the children to help make a choice between two options, if there is not money for both.
- Using a "pot" to save money for a favorite, but expensive, family activity, and making deposits after household goals or tasks are met (for example, each time the weekly cleaning gets done).

Extending Courtesy to Children

In order for children to face their problems with self-assurance, they need assurance from their parents that they are adequate individuals worthy of respect. Children acquire self-respect by being treated in a respectful manner. This is important for all ages, but especially during adolescence when self-worth is a constant concern.

Children feel respected as persons when their parents speak to them in a normal tone of voice and establish eye contact and a close but comfortable distance for conversation. With infants, adults naturally speak in a higher tone of voice, emphasize inflection and use a simple vocabulary. This is called "baby talk." What is appropriate with infants, however, is not appropriate with older children. Parents don't need to talk in the condescending manner or restrict their vocabulary as much as they typically do. Young children are capable of comprehending far more language than they can produce themselves.

Children feel respected as individuals when their parents converse with them as they would with others, expanding the conversation with opinions and explanations rather than abbreviating it with curtness.

Children feel respected as persons when their parents extend to them the courtesies offered to other friends: "Good morning," "Please," "Thank you," "Goodbye," "Good night" and so on.

Children feel worthy of respect when their parents keep the promises they make to their children.

Children feel valued when their parents treat them cordially in public: greeting them in a friendly manner in the midst of onlookers; responding to children's requests, made in front of friends, in a supportive rather than antagonistic way; being slow to criticize and quick to compliment their children in conversations with other adults; and holding in confidence those matters which were told to them confidentially.

Children receive permission to differentiate themselves from their parents when parents refrain from reading their children's mail, rummaging through their drawers or entering their rooms without knocking.

Children gain in self-respect when parents control the urge to laugh at the humorous things they say without intending to be funny; when parents abstain from sarcasm and ridicule, which damage self-worth; and when parents resist the temptation to punch holes of realism into the balloons of their children's hopes.

In late childhood Brenda developed an interest in interior design and spent long hours creating floor plans. Especially important in her plans was space to be quietly alone because the house her family lived in was small and Brenda desired more privacy than she had. "When I would tell Mom about my interest in this career and my ideas about house designs," Brenda remembered, "she would laugh it off. That hurt, because it was important to me."

When Steve was an early adolescent he dreamed of getting a certain kind of car when he was 16. His parents told him he would never be able to affort it:

As it ended up I didn't get any car when I was 16. When I was 17 I got an old red VW—which became the car of my dreams. Even though I wasn't very realistic when I was younger about the kind of car I would be able to buy, it would have been nice if my folks had allowed me to hope. Part of the fun in obtaining something is to dream and plan, but my folks were just too realistic.

Following are other examples of comments which take away hope:

"You'll never get a playhouse built that way!"

"You plan to earn a letter in tennis? But you're just a freshman."

"Kids today just don't learn to cook like they did in my day."

"Are you sure you want to take guitar lessons? It takes a lot of practice to be any good."

Children's dreams deserve to be treated as gingerly as the aspirations revealed by any one friend to another. Since unrealistic plans tend to be self-correcting, parents don't need to worry too much about making the corrections.

Exercising Caution in Rescuing Children

Doing too much for children occurs for the same reason that fighting with children occurs — because of lack of differentiation of parents and children as separate persons. When a parent and child are fused as one individual, they are highly reactive to each other because each is treated as an extension of self. Reactivity shows up in benevolent ways, as in the case of overly-involved parents who do too much for their children, as well as in malevolent ways as in the case of parents who fight with their children. The control of each other's behavior and feelings and beliefs becomes the underlying issue in all of the interactions of a fused pair.

Fusion is a problem which some children outgrow. Eventually they decide that they have lived in the shadow of a controlling parent long enough and they emerge from the shadow to declare their own independent personhood. Since an over-involved parent is unlikely to relinquish control willingly, the child's declaration of self involves a painful tearing away. In the case of the college student whose father was taking responsibility for his haircuts, the son rebelled. By the end of his second year of college, he had let his hair grow long, had grown a beard as well and left the religious denomination of his parents to join a small sect.

Unfortunately, there are many cases where the problems of an over-close parent and child are not solved by time alone. Their attempts to manipulate each other are not struggles to separate themselves, but just the opposite—struggles to sustain the systemic pattern of their fused relationship. "See? You can't take care of yourself. I don't know what you'd do without me. Why did I have to get stuck with a kid that won't grow up?" the over-responsible parent complains following another failure by the child. The under-responsible child says, "See? It's your fault. I told you it wouldn't work." And the cycle of failure-rescue-failure-rescue goes on.

For parents, the way to get out of the rut of over-responsibility is to become more differentiated themselves. Then as parents gain freedom from children, children are enabled to gain freedom themselves. Parents become differentiated from their children by treating them with dignity and affection, but as separate persons—persons with their own wishes, feelings, preferences and responsibilities. When a child experiences a problem, a differentiated parent responds with concern and interest, but doesn't necessarily get involved in the problem since parent and child are not yoked to the same set of problems or to the same set of emotions.

This doesn't mean that parents are to become distant from their children or apathetic to the parent-child relationship. On the contrary, differentiated parents are able to remain close emotionally to their children, but avoid the web of manipulation which entangles over-controlling parents and over-controlled children.

It's impossible to prescribe certain actions for parents to avoid being over-responsible, since the *pattern* of behavior is what is important. For example, suppose a child calls home from school to say that she left her books at home and to ask the parent to bring them. Should the parent take them? It depends on the pattern of behavior. If the daughter is not usually forgetful like this and if the parent can accommodate the request, it would be appropriate to say, "I'm sorry you forgot them. I'll bring them as soon as I can get away." People who care about each other make sacrifices for each other's well-being. On the other hand, if forgetfulness is a pattern it would be more appropriate for the parent to say, "That's too bad you forgot your books. When you get home, they will be right where you left them."

Children can be skillful about getting parents to take responsibility for their problems. Complaining of being bored is an example of this. Boredom is a feeling generated internally and is under internal control; it is not imposed from the outside. Although parents might choose to offer suggestions, they take on an impossible task if they assume responsibility for the relief of boredom.

Another way that children get parents to take responsibility for them is by tattling. Often the problem is made worse when adults intervene, as in the following incident. Sandy was upset because a few of her sixth grade classmates refused to play with her:

I told the teacher about my problem and she made out a schedule that told who could play with whom. I felt degraded. Her "solution" didn't help. It seemed to make matters worse, because there were many hurt feelings and a lot of anger.

It's easy to see that the sixth grade teacher used poor judgment in her attempt to solve Sandy's problem, yet that is exactly the sort of thing that parents frequently do. Instead of finding ways to help children deal with their problems more autonomously, they tend to solve the problems for the children, which keeps them dependent and seldom produces satisfactory results.

Children who tattle regularly have parents who encourage their dependency. The mother in the following example stopped the tattling and encouraged her daughter's autonomy by helping her respond to a sibling problem in a different manner:

When my brothers fought I would get upset, thinking that one of them surely would kill the other. "Mom!" I'd scream, "The boys are fighting again." She usually came and settled the argument. Finally one day she told me to ignore them and advised them to settle their own arguments. This made me feel less responsible for them. After all, if she wasn't going to worry about them there was no point in my telling her about their fights. So I decided I wouldn't worry about them either. Surprisingly, they didn't fight as much after that.

I don't mean to suggest that parents should always ignore tattling. I am referring to a pattern of tattling, not necessarily to a single incident. There are times when reporting what another child has done is the responsible thing for a child to do and when acting swiftly on that information is the appropriate parental response.

Another way that parents show respect for the struggles of children is by helping children explore their alternatives in a problem situation. The following questions are useful for doing this:

"Have you thought of what you might do?"

"Are you faced with a decision about this?"

"What have you decided to do?"

"Would you like to look at some ideas about this?"

"Which plan appeals to you the most?"

"What would happen if you _____?"

"Are there other people you could talk to for information or advice about this?"

"Sometimes when I'm in a similar situation, I _____."

"What would happen if you did nothing?"

"Is there any way to correct the mistake?"

Nancy's father helped her explore her alternatives following a mistake she made while touring with a singing group during her fifteenth summer. Doing some laundry on one stop she absentmindedly poured bleach into the load which contained her navy colored uniform. She realized immediately what she had done, but instead of admitting that she had made the mistake herself she blamed the damage on some boys who were playing nearby. Later she felt so guilty about her deception that she cried into her pillow at night, unable to sleep.

> Even after we had been home from tour for some time I still couldn't get it out of my mind. Finally I told my father about it. I was sobbing so hard I could hardly get it out. He just sat in his recliner and listened — I think he knew what had happened before I told him. I told him that I had asked God to forgive me, but I still felt guilty. He shared with me what he believed about forgiveness — that I probably needed to acknowledge it to the others too to feel forgiven. I couldn't see myself getting up in front of the group, so he helped me think about who needed to know and I told them.

Parents show respect for a child's struggles when they allow room for imperfection. Darlene made a mistake one day while baking a batch of cookies:

> The recipe called for a half a teaspoon of salt, but I put in half a cup instead. I knew there was no way I could undo what I had already done, so I told my mother, hoping she would not get angry. She surprised me with her response: "Well, I guess we can't use that batter! Throw it out and start from the beginning." She still believed that I could do it right. I was glad to have another chance to prove to her that I could — and I did!

Responses like this one help children acquire, in the words of the STEP program, "the courage to be imperfect" (Dinkmeyer & McKay, 1976, p. 109).

Parents show respect for a child's struggles when they maintain attitudes of patience and optimism, knowing that many of the problems of children work themselves out in time. For example, certain kinds of fears are predictable for the preschool years and then they fade. In late childhood and early adolescence, problems related to status among peers are common; worries about peer acceptance tend to diminish by late adolescence, however, when they are subdued by greater self-acceptance. As Sandy reflected on the peer problem she had experienced earlier, she said:

> As I look back, I laugh at myself and see how silly the whole ordeal was. I also see how much I've grown because of the situation. I hope that when I'm a parent I will be able to identify with the children and understand the problems — and triumphs — they go through.

Patience and optimism allow the parent to support the child's movement towards greater autonomy, without overreacting in the moment a problem strikes.

Questions for Thought and Discussion about this Chapter are on page 296.

Part IV
The Parent's Problem Area

Saturday morning at Joanie's house is cleaning time. Her job is to dust the living room, but instead of getting it done, she sits and watches cartoons. Her mother reminds her of the job and then a little later reminds her again. Joanie doesn't move. Her mother's reminding turns to nagging and then scolding: "You're old enough to help clean this house. I don't know what that school teaches you that you just sit around all the time!" Still Joanie doesn't move. Finally her mother turns the TV off, makes another speech and stomps out of the room. Joanie finally begins to dust, grumbling under her breath and mocking her mother.

Week after week this scene is replayed as if it were on videotape. Other households are drawn into the repetition of a similar drama without a happy ending. Even though the pattern is not satisfying to either parent or child, they seem to be unable to break it. The result is that children become sullen about the issues which precipitate the cycle. Parents become resentful of their children's lack of cooperation and long for a more pleasant and efficient way to get their children to cooperate.

The chapters of Part IV cover a sequence of steps to use to alter the pattern. The steps will not necessarily make the job of parenting any easier or more pleasant, but the steps will help parents to become free from their usual reactions and to gain the initiative in interactions with their children. As parents develop the skills needed at each level, they will become more powerful persons who are capable of having a greater impact in their children's lives. This will enable them to have a greater sense of control over their own lives.

Mr. Miller, one of my junior high teachers, was a man of personal power. He delighted us with his humor and captivated us with his stories. We were pleased that he treated us like adolescents rather than children, and we in turn wanted to please him. Occasionally he got angry at us, and we hated that experience. When he was mad, you knew it; he expressed it quickly and forcefully.

During the first week of classes, Mr. Miller came to the locker room where we boys were hurrying through our showers. We were required by school policy to take showers after gym class, but had been in the habit of getting just wet enough that we could say we'd showered. Mr. Miller saw what was happening and said, "Whoa! Get back in there! You guys need a shower, and you haven't had one yet." Then he undressed, got in the showers with us and gave us a lesson in lathering our bodies thoroughly with soap. He continued to shower with us for the next few weeks, soaping himself thoroughly, singing, laughing and telling jokes. Before long we were doing the same. Because of the concern today with sexual abuses of children, this incident may raise questions about Mr. Miller's judgment. But 30 years ago, pubescent modesty was not easily shed and we appreciated his help.

Mr. Miller was demanding in the classroom, too. He expected all students to produce, although he did not treat us all alike. He was gentle with some, and with others he was tough, challenging them with questions or goading them to action. He demanded that those with the greatest academic ability work the hardest of all.

I didn't like this at first and dug in my heels. In prior years I had gotten good grades with little effort. But he turned a deaf ear to my complaints about the unfairness of his grading system, so I dug into the books. He taught social studies through current events and that year I began to read the newspaper every day. His observations about human behavior inclined me towards my eventual field of study, psychology. Mr. Miller was a powerful person, and I'm grateful for the impact he had on my life.

Parents need to be powerful people in their children's lives, just as Mr. Miller was in mine. By powerful, I don't mean autocratic, dictatorial or authoritarian. By powerful, I mean capable of effecting change in their children's behavior, thought and feelings. The kind of power I am talking about induces change by generating respect in children, not fear.

Powerful parents influence children by explaining and reasoning. When powerful parents speak, their children listen.

Powerful parents express a variety of emotions, including both pleasure and displeasure. They are honest and spontaneous, and when they feel strongly, they can express feelings strongly. Their children have learned to be considerate of their feelings and modify their behavior accordingly.

Powerful parents make requests which children heed. The requests sometimes are made as subtle suggestions, sometimes as clearly stated expectations and sometimes as assertive demands.

When children don't respond to reason, disregard their parents' feelings or defy parental demands, powerful parents stop talking and take action. They use punishment effectively and appropriately. Sometimes they allow children to suffer the natural consequences of their behavior, and sometimes they devise logical consequences to reduce misbehavior.

Powerful parents are not paralyzed by fear of their children's displeasure. When necessary they are able to disengage from emotional appeals and stand firmly in the face of complaints.

The skills of the Parent's Problem Area are what people commonly have in mind when they talk about discipline. They use the word discipline to mean correction or even punishment. But these three words do not mean the same thing, and in my classes I do not let students use them interchangeably.

Punishment is just one part of correction, which is one part of discipline. Suppose that I decide to punish my daughter by taking away a privilege. It's true that I am taking away the privilege to "discipline" her, which is how most people use the word. But it's also true that I discipline her when I talk with her about how the day has gone and reassure her of my love. Discipline is the sum of all the things I do to help my daughter become the kind of person I want her to be. Discipline takes place in all four areas and not just the situations in which the child's behavior is a problem to the parent.

Correction is more limited than discipline. It refers to the use of the skills of the Parent's Problem Area to change the behavior of the child which is offensive to the parent. Punishment is even more limited; it is one of the means of correcting the child.

Parents need to be powerful persons in their children's lives, powerful enough to make the corrections which all children need from time to time. Without this, their parenting skills will be out of balance and everybody suffers because of it. Parents become drained emotionally when their attempts to correct a situation they feel responsible for are futile. Uncontrolled children annoy other people by their misbehavior. And the children themselves are unhappy because they create an unfriendly world to live in and because they don't have the security of being in the care of someone more powerful than they.

Questions for Thought and Discussion about this Chapter are on page 298.

10. Providing Information: Facts and Feelings

A young mother and her four-year-old son were in the waiting room of a medical clinic. She ordered him to do one thing after another: "Jimmy, sit down!" "Jimmy, be quiet!" "Stop running around!" She threatened to punish him if he didn't stop, but he ignored her threats and continued running about. She did nothing. At one point she said, "Now I told you to stop running into the hall!" and he responded in the same tone of voice, "Now I told you I don't want to stop!"

After a half hour of this, Jimmy's name was called and the two of them entered the X-ray lab. They emerged 15 minutes later with a visibly distraught technician. Jimmy was holding two suckers. His mother said laughingly to no one in particular, "Wouldn't you know? He got two suckers and every other kid would go in there and get one, but he conned them out of two. That's my Jimmy!"

A short time later a mother with four preschool children arrived. She seated them near her and explained, "We will have to wait here until the doctor is ready to examine David." They remained in their seats, looked for things to do, visited among themselves and asked questions. The mother gave them instructions, suggested that they look at books and magazines, initiated a word game with them and explained what was happening. One of the children asked, "Can we all see the doctor?" and the mother replied, "We can all go in with David to see the doctor, but the room will be very small. Since the doctor is going to examine David, we'll let him sit on the special chair and the rest of us will wait quietly. If the examining room is too small for you to wait quietly, you can come back here to the waiting room."

This information evidently satisfied them and they went on entertaining themselves for more than an hour. During this time they were not quiet, but their behavior was appropriate. Other people in the waiting area watched with amused respect and from time to time made small talk with the children.

If you were to ask the first mother about the control of her son, I am sure she would say she works very hard at it and does about as well as could be expected with such a difficult child. She would be right in saying that she works hard at it, but her effort is like that of a poor swimmer who churns the water without going anywhere. Her exhaustive battles with her son have more to do with her style of interaction with him than with his nature. The other mother is like a swimmer who glides through the water with powerful and less fatiguing strokes. The management of her children is efficient.

Using Facts and Reasons

The two mothers illustrate the differences in the way parents use language to guide their children's behavior. The first mother relies on commands to control her child, and although her words are plentiful, she conveys little information. The second mother talks informatively with her children and issues fewer commands.

Parents who talk informatively provide enough information about the situation so that children understand what is expected and why. This seems simple, and yet many times children are corrected for doing something they didn't know was wrong. Parents skip right over the information gap and punish them without considering the importance of information to the child's internal control of behavior.

Many of the memories which children retain have to do with being punished for reasons they didn't understand. Sometimes it has to do with sexuality, as in the following story:

> The neighbor girl and I were alone in a tent in our back yard and we decided to play "doctor." My mother discovered our activity and immediately sent me to the room in the attic for punishment. We had been curious about our bodies, but at that point knew nothing about sex. I wish my mother had explained the facts of life, but she didn't then or any other time. I learned from my friends.

Because parents are uncomfortable talking about sexuality, they don't ascertain what children understand about sex or help them to understand more adequately.

Another illustration is supplied by the child who piled rocks in a small stream in the back of their property. She got in trouble with her parents because the landlord saw what she had done and complained. When she told this story, she still didn't understand why it was a bad thing to do.

A teenager recounted an event that happened soon after her family returned from another country:

> Mom told me, "I forgot to give Grandma one of her gifts, this lipstick. Take it to her house. Don't give it to anybody else and be careful with it." I went to Grandmother's house, but she wasn't there so I waited for her to return. Finally I asked my uncle to give the lipstick to her. He said he would so I went home. When I told my mother she was furious. She slapped me and sent me back to get the lipstick. When I got home again she broke the lipstick in two and threw the pieces out the window. I never could understand this.

Why her mother reacted as she did remains a puzzle to this day. The story needs an explanation because we adults are accustomed to explanations. But for children in households where parents don't explain, puzzles like this are a daily occurrence.

One of the earliest memories of a man who is now in his thirties is of a time he nearly suffocated his baby brother:

> We had just awakened and the baby was crying. My mother asked me to come and play with him while she prepared a bottle. I stood by the crib and did my best to quiet him but he kept crying. Finally I covered his mouth with my hands. Mom returned to the room, yelled at me and then gave me a spanking I've never forgotten. This was the first lesson I remember learning: never cover someone's mouth to keep them from crying.

It's understandable that in this situation the mother would have yelled and spanked because of her concern for the safety of the baby. But explaining why she was concerned was even more important.

British social scientist Basil Bernstein (1971–75) studied the two styles of language represented by the mothers in the waiting room. Parents like the first mother use what Bernstein calls a restricted code (see Figure 10.1). They use language to control. They do this by issuing commands and emphasizing the commands with voice inflection, physical gesture and threat. They tend to justify the commands with their authority as parents.

Figure 10.1
Restricted and Elaborated Styles of Language

Restricted Style	Elaborated Style
Language used to control ("Sit down.") or express emotion ("I've had it.").	Language used to reason or convey information ("We'll have to wait until they are ready for us.").
Appeals based on position of authority ("Because I'm your Mom and I said so.").	Appeals based on personal considerations ("Because they have gotten behind schedule and are working as fast as they can to catch up.").
Sentences strung together by conjunctions and without pauses.	Sentences separated by pauses.
Short questions or statements with tags at end (". . . , aren't you?") which are rhetorical and not meant to be answered.	Longer questions which are conversational.
Voice inflection and physical gestures emphasized.	Use of subtlety in tone and gesture.
Generalized statements.	More precise statements.
Use of idioms, cliches.	Use of a variety of adjectives and adverbs to qualify.
More use of personal pronouns (especially "you" and "they").	More use of impersonal pronouns ("one," "it").
Limited vocabulary.	Expansive vocabulary.

Based on Class, Codes, and Control (3 vols.) by Basil Bernstein, 1971–75. London: Routledge and Kegan Paul.

Parents like the second mother use what Bernstein calls an elaborated code. For them, language is used to reason and convey information. Their speech is more complex in grammar and vocabulary and contains subtle emphases in tone of voice and gesture. Appeals are based on pertinent information, rather than on the authority of parents.

The differences in the results of the two language styles are striking. Children raised with the restricted code develop a "keep out of trouble" orientation to life. They are more pessimistic about their fate, and, in fact, turn out to be less successful academically and vocationally. Children raised with the elaborated language code develop greater capacity for conceptualizing and solving problems and acquire a sense of internal control over their lives. Children of the first style learn to churn water and become resigned to not getting anywhere. Children of the second style learn to swim.

It should not be surprising that parents who use language to control tend to have children who use language in the same way. Socially aggressive children and their parents train each other in patterns of interaction which Gerald Patterson (1984) calls fight cycles. In a fight cycle, one family member starts a fight by issuing a command, another counterattacks and then the first person continues it. For example, a mother might suddenly say to a child watching television, "You're wasting time. Go do your homework." The child being attacked may counter with something like, "Leave me alone. Why don't you go cook supper?" Then the parent is likely to issue another command in defense of her parental authority. She may turn off the television and yell at her son, "Don't you talk to me that way! Go do your homework!"

Patterson has successfully trained parents to break the habit of fight cycles by using language in more rewarding ways. When they do, parents make dramatic gains in the social control of their children. They learn to give fewer orders, but interact so that when they do give an order, it is heeded.

Reasoning is important at every age of the child from young to old, either by itself or in combination with some other technique. Clifford (1959) found that some methods of control, like spanking, are used less as children get older. Other methods, like taking away privileges are used more as children get older. Reasoning, however, was the most preferred method for each age he studied.

Like other techniques, reasoning can be used too little or too much. Parents who emphasize obedience tend to overlook the importance of information. For children to develop internal control of their behavior, they need information, as Alta Mae Erb, a teacher in the area of early childhood education, wrote years ago:

> To many people the first association of the word discipline is that of obedience to some spoken command which the child springs promptly to obey. If he should ask, "Why?" the parent would answer, "Because I told you so" . . . . [But] the child obeys because he must, not because he has an inner

desire to obey. . . . Back of the command there must be a
purpose which the child is able to understand and which will
lead him to act of his own free will. . . . His will is not an
obstacle to obedience but an asset. True obedience must
come from within. (Erb, 1944, p. 108)

On the other hand, reasoning is used too much when parents rely
exclusively on it to solve problems in the Parent's Problem Area.
Even adults do not always respond to reason, and children are more
limited than adults in their ability to resist temptation, delay gratification and exercise good judgment. Reasoning is used too much
when it stops being informative and becomes argumentative. At that
point, parents need to supplement reasoning with other techniques
of the Parent's Problem Area. Reasoning is an important first step,
but it is just that — the first step.

Expressing Feelings

The second step in the sequence of methods in the Parent's
Problem Area is to provide emotional feedback. Unlike the first step,
emotional feedback statements are not necessarily calm, informative
statements. They are messages conveyed verbally and nonverbally
in those moments when children learn that their parents, too, have
feelings and become offended.

A few months after leaving home, a college student became
reflective about his relationship with his parents. He sent a letter to
them which contained the following paragraph:

I remember pulling the chair out from under you before
breakfast one morning, Mom. It started as a game, but I must
have really hurt your feelings. You started crying, I started
crying, and soon our whole family was sitting around the
table crying. I don't know the significance of what happened, and we never really talked about it, but it is one thing
that sticks out in my mind.

The significance of that moment is that the family was made
aware of their emotional importance to each other. They could hurt
each other easily because of their closeness. And when one member
was hurting, the others shared that hurt empathically.

In another letter to a parent, a college student wrote about a
moment in which she became more aware of the impact she had on
her mother. She gave me permission to use this portion:

Remember the time we had that horrible argument? You
were so angry about something I did that you started crying

and walked out of the house. I watched you get your hoe and work in the garden, which was your way of dealing with tension, I guess. Later you went to town and left a note for me on the kitchen table. I read that note even though at the time I said I didn't. It was your apology for being somewhat harsh with me. It also explained that you were trying your best to be a good parent and that you hoped we could grow closer to each other. That was the first time I realized you had feelings and your feelings could be hurt just as easily as anyone else's.

Discipline includes emotional training. Children need to learn to hurt when others hurt, to be sorry when they have caused the hurt, and to care enough about others to help heal hurts or to alter their behavior to prevent hurts. Beth, the child in the following story, is one who learned this very well:

After I broke the spring I knew I was in trouble. Dad wasn't home yet, so I went to my room and wrote him a letter explaining what happened. One of the pages read, "I am very, very, very . . . (I continued with the word 'very' to the bottom of the page) . . . sorry!" Then I sent myself to bed. When Dad came home, everyone told him what happened. He came into my room, read the letter and sat down on my bed to hug and kiss me. I really did feel bad about breaking the spring and I was relieved that he was not mad, as I thought he would be.

To do what she did requires the capacity to empathize. The seeds of empathy are planted in the first few months of life as parents respond to infants with pleasure or displeasure. Empathy grows throughout childhood, if children are fed information about how others are affected emotionally by their behavior. Finally, empathy blooms with the child's consideration of the feelings of others and bears the fruit of behavior which relieves their distress.

The importance of empathy to the child's social development was demonstrated in an Empathy Training Project conducted in public elementary schools of Los Angeles. In some of the activities of this project, children were asked to imagine the preferences of different people (e.g., "What birthday present would make each member of your family happiest?"). They listened to stories and then recounted them from the point of view of each character in the story. They were trained in the identification of different emotions in photographs, in tape recordings of affective conversations and in videotapes of emotional situations.

After the training period was over, the children were observed to determine the effect of the training. Those who received empathy training were less aggressive and more cooperative compared with children who hadn't received the training (Feshbach, 1985).

Children ordinarily don't receive formal training in empathy. However, most parent education programs teach parents to provide emotional feedback. The Parent Effectiveness Training (P.E.T.) program teaches a technique called the "I-message" to enable parents to send feeling messages in a sound manner. The I-message is like the active listening communication process (see Chapter 8), except that now, in the Parent's Problem Area, the parent is the sender of the message and the child is the receiver.

The I-message is sent when the parent experiences a feeling (which is an internal, subjective, private state) and wants to communicate a message about that experience. The message is encoded with verbal and nonverbal signals. The child witnesses the encoded message and decodes it to understand what the parent is experiencing (see Figure 10.2).

Figure 10.2
The Parent as Sender and Child as Receiver of Message

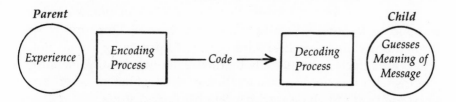

Adapted from Parent Effectiveness Training (p. 117) by Thomas Gordon, 1970. New York: Peter H. Wyden. Copyright 1970 by David McKay Co., a Division of Random House, Inc. Adapted by permission.

Imagine a young child playing on a tractor. He turns the steering wheel back and forth, moves various levers and makes tractor noises. Eventually he pushes in the clutch and since the tractor is parked on a slight incline, it begins to roll. Realizing that the tractor is moving, the child frantically pushes pedals and pulls levers until the clutch is disengaged once again and the tractor jerks to a stop a few feet from where it began rolling. The boy's father notices this from the other side of the barnyard, yells and runs towards the tractor, arriving after it had stopped rolling.

The father was badly frightened by this and relieved that the incident ended harmlessly. When he reached his son he could have said, "I was so scared when I saw the tractor start to roll and I'm really glad you're okay." The son would have decoded this message and understood that his dad was scared, just as he was, and was glad he wasn't injured (see Figure 10.3).

Figure 10.3
The I-Message Communication Process

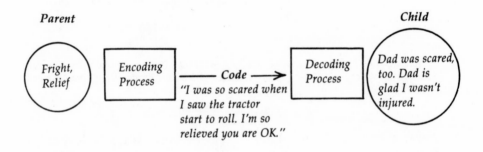

Adapted from Parent Effectiveness Training (p. 117) by Thomas Gordon, 1970. New York: Peter H. Wyden. Copyright 1970 by David McKay Co., a Division of Random House, Inc. Adapted by permission.

What the father actually said was similar to the way parents usually respond in situations like this. They feel disapproval and anger about what the child has done, and these secondary reactions get mixed up with or even replace the primary reactions in the encoding process. The child then decodes the message to be about disapproval and anger and responds to that, missing the more revealing initial feelings (see Figure 10.4).

Obviously a parent will be disapproving of the child's behavior in situations like this and probably will say something like "I told you

Figure 10.4
The You-Message

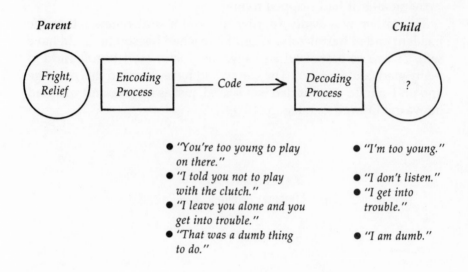

Parent   **Child**

| Fright, Relief | Encoding Process | —— Code ⟶ | Decoding Process | ? |

- "You're too young to play on there."
- "I told you not to play with the clutch."
- "I leave you alone and you get into trouble."
- "That was a dumb thing to do."

- "I'm too young."
- "I don't listen."
- "I get into trouble."
- "I am dumb."

Adapted from Parent Effectiveness Training *(p. 117) by Thomas Gordon, 1970. New York: Peter H. Wyden. Copyright 1970 by David McKay Co., a Division of Random House, Inc. Adapted by permission.*

never to play with the clutch," "I hope you learned a lesson" or "Don't ever do that again!" However, when parents use only that kind of statement, the complete message of the parent has not been transmitted. Children need to hear about parental fears, hurts and disappointments, too, if they are to fully understand the impact they have on their parents. Ironically, the I-message which is omitted often is a much more powerful motivator of behavior change than parents realize.

In the P.E.T. program, the message which focuses on disapproval is called a "You-message" (Gordon, 1970, p. 115), because it often literally begins with "You . . .":

"You ought to know better."
"You're being very thoughtless."
"(You) clean up that mess."
"Can't you put anything away after you finish with it?"
"You can't be counted on."
"You're acting like a big baby."

You-messages are negative evaluations, and children, like all persons, tend to respond defensively to negative evaluations. After all, evaluations are open to debate because no one evaluation is the whole story. This is why You-messages are not very effective in engaging the child's cooperation. You-messages elicit defensiveness and call children's attention to themselves when they misbehave, rather than to the ones who were affected by their misbehavior.

I-messages, on the other hand, call the child's attention to how others are affected by the misbehavior. If the I-message honestly portrays the inner state of the parent, there is nothing for the child to argue about since a feeling is not open to debate. Feelings of parents may make children uncomfortable, but they are not right or wrong. Feelings simply come and go. Furthermore, I-messages are less likely to elicit defensiveness because they do not focus attention on the shortcomings of the child as directly as You-messages do.

In P.E.T., I-messages are given that name because they usually begin with or contain "I." A simple, three-part formula is useful in constructing I-messages:

"When you _____(state the behavior)_____

I feel _____(name the feeling)_____

because _____(state the results of the behavior)_____."

Consider the following examples:

"When you make so much noise while I'm on the phone, I get annoyed because I can't hear."

"When you go to somebody's house after school without discussing it with me, I am bothered because I don't know where you are and because I haven't given my approval."

"When you tracked mud into the back room, I was furious because I had just cleaned it."

"When you enter without knocking I feel invaded, because I come into this room to have some time alone."

"When you stay up late watching movies with your friends I worry that you will get sick again or be too tired to keep our plans for Sunday."

The three parts of the formula are not always included in an I-message. Sometimes parts of it are assumed or just not necessary, as in the following examples:

"I'm too tired to play with you right now."

"I've got a headache and can't take much more of your fighting with each other!"

"I was embarrassed by the way you acted when Mrs. Jantz was here."

"I'm bothered that the lawn still hasn't been mowed after you promised to do it by Saturday evening. I don't have time to do it myself, and I would like to be able to count on your help."

"I feel exploited when others leave their kitchen mess for me to clean up."

How much better the following situation would have been handled if the mother had been able to use I-messages with the 16-year-old telling this story:

I've been dating a guy my mom is leery about, although she can't seem to put her finger on what it is that bothers her. The other night we were watching a late night movie. Mom got out of bed and came into the family room. We were startled and the guy jumped straight up from the couch. It was obvious that Mom thought we had been making out because of this reaction. He and I started laughing and that only made matters worse. I went into the kitchen to try to talk to her. It made me mad and embarrassed that she assumed that something sexual was going on, especially since she never talks with me about guys or sex. Little does she know that I've not let this guy do much more than hold my hand.

The mother was worried about her daughter's vulnerability to sexual involvement and its aftermath, and felt shut out of her daughter's relationships. Yet she was not able to express these concerns in a way which reduced the distance and mistrust between them.

To develop socially, children need information about the feelings of other people, too, besides their parents. However, many times children cause other people to be distressed and receive no feedback about it. Passersby, neighbors or other relatives are not apt to provide it. A recent letter to Ann Landers illustrates this:

A kid who appeared to be about seven years old kicked the back of my seat all the way from Cleveland to New York. When I asked the flight attendant to ask him to stop, she said, "Sorry, I've got 57 meals to serve. You ask him" ("The Saga," 1988).

The flight attendant was right in that the situation would have been managed more easily if the offended passenger had sent the message. But both seemed reluctant to do it and that is typical.

When my children behave badly with others, I am bothered

because I want my children to become considerate of others in general, not just those with whom they have emotional ties. I want them to develop a sense of responsibility for living interdependently with their fellow human beings. Part of my job as parent is to point out to my children how other people are affected by their behavior. So there are times when I serve as mediator between my children and the world, sending messages for others by proxy:

> "Mrs. Sommerfeld must feel terrible about what happened to her flower bed."

> "That man behind you was really upset when you cut into line."

> "If I were the coach, I wouldn't put up with that."

> "Here it is two weeks after your birthday and you still haven't written any thank you notes. I'm sure your grandparents are disappointed."

> "Did you notice Shari's face? You really hurt her feelings when you said that."

This kind of explicit teaching by parents in situations of child-caused distress was studied by researchers at the National Institute of Mental Health (Zahn-Waxler, Radke-Yarrow, & King, 1979). They observed mothers and young children over several months and found that children whose mothers frequently explained how others were affected by their behavior scored higher on measures of altruism (cooperation and helpfulness) than children whose mothers did not explain.

Children's scores on cooperation and helpfulness were especially high "whenever the basic cognitive message was embellished with mothers' intensity of feelings, judgmental reactions, principles of convictions and disappointments" (p. 325). This type of message "is not calmly dispensed reasoning, carefully designed to enlighten the child: it is emotionally imposed, sometimes harshly and often forcefully" (p. 327).

Like all other parenting techniques, feeling messages can be used too little or too much. Once again, balance is the goal. Too little emphasis on the feelings of others stunts the growth of children's capacity to experience guilt. Unless children are trained to feel bad when their behavior hurts others, they become self-centered and mean. In the extreme they become sociopaths who lie, cheat or steal without remorse.

A limitation of the I-message technique, which causes it to be used too little, is that parents find it difficult to employ. This is not because the conceptual difference between the You-message and the I-message is so hard to understand. Neither is it because of lack of opportunity to practice. Everyday life with a spouse, roommate, child, business associate or teacher provides ample opportunity. When people live and work together, they do things which bother each other.

The I-message is hard to put into practice because it is confrontational, and conflict with another person generates discomfort. Even when it is designed to be nonthreatening, it stirs the most basic human concern: Does this person care about me?

At a recent concert I was seated next to a woman who was chewing gum. She cracked it almost constantly and I became annoyed. I wanted to say, "I am trying to listen to the music and gum chewing bothers me." I didn't, however; I chose to say nothing. But it continued to bother me and I went home and grumbled. Had I sent an I-message, she probably would have been embarrassed, apologized and taken care of her gum. But I don't know that. She might have gotten angry, told me she didn't care if I was bothered or not and put another piece in her mouth.

I-messages are scary because the sender is in a vulnerable position: "This is how I'm feeling about something. I hope you care enough about me that you take this into account." The person receiving the I-message might say, "No, I don't care about you that much."

Another limitation of the I-message technique is that it's effectiveness requires the desire to maintain the relationship. The woman seated beside me at the concert was a stranger and had no reason to value our relationship. Chances are we never would have seen each other again. If she had chosen to disregard my feelings, had I made them known, little would have been lost other than the indignity suffered by two human beings in that moment of conflict.

Unfortunately, there are children who don't value their relationships with their parents. With them, I-messages don't work well, so parents use them less and less to protect their feelings. This is why the I-message, as important as it is, needs back-up help. By itself, it is not sufficient for handling the Parent's Problem Area.

This became clear to me in the early 1970s through the experience of a participant in a parenting group I was leading. The group met weekly and between sessions practiced the skills which were covered. The week after the I-message technique was introduced, one of the fathers in the group reported that it hadn't worked very well for him. After role playing the situation, which involved the son's piano practice time, the group suggested that he try again, expressing his feelings more strongly.

He came back in more distress the next week, because he had expressed really strong feelings and his son still wasn't practicing regularly. And he reported that he had felt so sick about the way he unloaded on the son that he threw up afterwards. I knew the father well enough by this time that I was convinced that he had given the technique a fair trial. His experience raised the question of what happens when parents rely too much on the I-message.

The I-message technique can prevent children from differentiating their emotions from their parents' (the third limitation). When parents overemphasize the responsibility children should take for the feelings of others, children have trouble differentiating themselves as individuals with their own feelings and preferences. This can induce guilt by manipulating children's emotions, as in the following examples, and confuses children about their responsibility for their own feelings:

"If you don't give your Grandpa a kiss, he'll be offended."

"Your mother has been sick with worry about you."

"If you don't come home for Christmas we'll be terribly disappointed. I don't see how we can have Christmas without you."

"I am really bothered that we pay for piano lessons and want so badly for you to learn to play but you never practice!"

Parents who are highly reactive to their children turn over control of their emotions to their children. This places the parents in a weak (as well as emotionally unhealthy) position. Parents are in a more powerful position when they retain responsibility for their feelings.

The fourth limitation of the I-message technique is that it needs to be used in combination with other methods, especially requests, to be most effective. I think parents have gotten bad advice about this. In P.E.T., Thomas Gordon argues against sending a "solution" with the I-message:

Have you ever been just about ready to do something considerate for a person (or initiate some change in your behavior to meet a person's needs) when all of a sudden that person directs you, exhorts you or advises you to do exactly what you were going to do on your own? . . . When people do this to you, they are "sending a solution." This is precisely what parents often do with children. They do not wait for the

child to initiate considerate behavior; they tell him what he
must or *should* or *ought* to do. (Gordon, 1970, p. 109–110)
Gordon recommends that parents omit the solution and send only
the feeling message, trusting children to modify their own behavior
in a manner which solves the parent's problem. Another program
which teaches the I-message technique claims, ". . . [the I-message]
should carry with it no expectation that the child will act differently
because of what you [the parent] said" (Abidin, 1982, p. 25).

This is poor advice for several reasons. First, the I-message *is* a
Parent's Problem Area method for changing the behavior of the
child. Parents need to be clear in their own minds about this and not
pretend the purpose is otherwise. Second, children need to know
what is expected of them. To expect them to guess the preferred
solution is unfair. Children can't say "yes," "no," "maybe" or
"later" to an unspoken request. Third, when parents withhold
information about what they want, they remain offended and angry
enough to manipulate the solution to their satisfaction. It is hard for
children to respond in a non-manipulative manner themselves if
parents remain hurt.

When parents react strongly to children and expect that their
reactions will take care of problems in the Parent's Problem Area,
they will be disappointed. What will happen is that the parent-child
relationship will become emotionally tangled. Children will be made
to feel obligated to fix the feelings of parents, but that is something
they cannot do. What they can do is negotiate changes in the
behaviors which are bothersome.

The I-message needs to be followed by a request. This is why the
technique of sending feeling messages is just one step in the Facts-
Feelings-Demands-Consequences progression of techniques for the
Parent's Problem Area (see page 184). If a child doesn't respond to
facts and reason and disregards the feelings of parents, then it's time
to make an assertive demand, which is step three.

In spite of its limitations, the I-message technique is an important
tool for parents. Many situations in the Parent's Problem Area can be
handled quickly and simply with honest feedback. Affective (referring to the emotions) discipline is effective.

Questions for Thought and Discussion about this Chapter are on page 299.

11. Taking Charge: Demands and Consequences

For family members to take care of household chores, pursue lifestyle goals, and treat each other fairly, a sense of order is required. Parents have the job of providing the order that the family needs. Parents are in charge of families.

Unfortunately, many parents feel helpless about carrying out their charge effectively. They have excuses about why their personal responsibility is limited (see Figure 11.1). Although the excuses contain truth, excuses deny the role that parents have in putting an end to the misbehavior of children. It can be easier for parents to excuse the misbehavior, than to take responsibility for changing it.

Another way parents show their reluctance to take charge is by blaming children for their misbehavior. Again, this may be based on truth, since children *are* blameworthy. But blaming them does not necessarily alter the misbehavior.

The parent-child relationship is dynamic, somewhat like a seesaw ride. When parents are reluctant to take charge of the relationship, they sit too close to the fulcrum and get stuck in the upper position. They feel helpless then, because children have enough leverage in the relationship to hold them there. Parents scold, nag, threaten and plead to get their children to move. To regain control, parents simply have to take responsibility for the way their own positions affect the balance of power (see Figure 11.2).

Figure 11.1
Parental Excuses for Misbehavior of Children

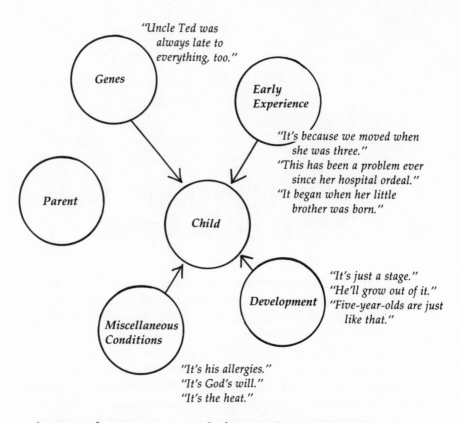

Anger and resentment result from techniques that don't work well. When parents feel like complaining, they would be wise to ask themselves what they could do differently to take charge of the situation. They possess ample power to regain control of the balance, since children are dependent on them. Dependence makes children lighter than parents in the parent-child balance of power.

When parents take charge of the family, they really are taking charge of themselves. They take charge by developing firmness, and the firmness comes from within themselves, from their sense of self. It does not come about by becoming increasingly coercive with children.

To be firm, parents need to be self-assertive enough to be able to make demands of their children and to refuse to indulge every demand children make of them. Firmness also requires that parents

Figure 11.2
Parents Take Charge by Changing Themselves

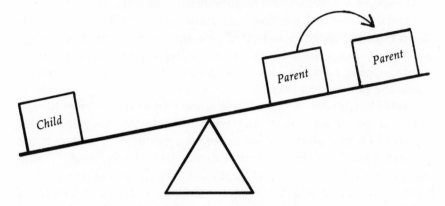

establish rules for their children and follow through with consequences for breaking the rules.

Assertive demands and logical consequences are covered in this
chapter. They are the third and fourth steps in the Facts-Feelings-
Demands-Consequences sequence of strategies for the Parent's
Problem Area. The full sequence is illustrated at the chapter's end.

Making Assertive Demands and Denials

A young couple and their two-year-old son were sitting on their
front porch one summer evening. Christopher, the son, slowly
scooted his way down the steps, got to the bottom and turned
around to look at them. "No, no, Christopher. Stay here," one of
them said. They kept their eyes on him, taking pleasure in watching
him. Christopher edged down the sidewalk leading from the porch
to the street, looking over his shoulder. "Don't do that, Christopher.
Come back," they called to him still visiting amiably. He moved
closer and closer to the street until finally the mother got up and
retrieved him. She carried him back to the porch and tossed him
affectionately in her arms.

Christopher descended the porch steps once again and made his
way down the sidewalk, more quickly this time. He sneaked glances
over his shoulder to see if they were watching. They called to him as
before, "Don't do that, Christopher. Come back." This time the
father brought him back. He shook Christopher playfully as he
carried him back, as the boy's mother had done.

This continued. By the fourth or fifth time, Christopher ran down the sidewalk without looking back. His dad ran after him, brought him back, spanked him and set him down. The pattern was repeated several more times. Each time the parents ordered Christopher not to do it, but their laughter indicated pleasure in the summer evening's activity. It finally ended when Christopher began crying. From my vantage point, I assumed he cried because of his confusion about the game the family was playing.

Children continue to misbehave when parental responses to misbehavior are ambiguous, as they were in this incident. Children also continue to misbehave when parental responses to requests are unclear, like the Family Circus cartoon parent who said, "I said maybe, and that's final!" Messages like this invite children to cry, pout, get angry, procrastinate, ignore their parents or compare them unfavorably with other parents. All parents face these tactics at times, of course, but some parents face them more than others, depending on their style of making and turning down requests.

Parents whose children make frequent use of these tactics will find assertiveness training beneficial. By becoming more assertive, parents will be clearer about what they want their children to do, hold a position more firmly and reduce contentious and manipulative interactions with their children.[1]

Through assertiveness training, parents learn to recognize three interaction styles: a meek (unassertive) style; an intimidating (aggressive) style; and a direct, firm (assertive) style. Unassertive parents seem uncertain, confused or apologetic about their position. They give away power to their children and lose or prolong the struggles which ensue. Aggressive parents threaten, argue, cajole, bribe or punish in an attempt to overcome conflict and gain compli-

---

[1] The assertiveness movement grew out of the behavioral branch of psychology, and began to have a major impact in counseling with the publication of *Your Perfect Right: A Guide to Assertive Behavior*, by Robert Alberti and Michael Emmons, in 1970. Their book sold widely and set the vocabulary which continues to be used today.

In the beginning, assertiveness training was used primarily with women's groups. Its appeal was broad, however, and the book by Manuel Smith (1975), *When I Say No, I Feel Guilty*, which introduced the techniques of assertiveness therapy to the general public, became a best seller. Assertiveness was applied to many different areas, including pastoral care (Augsburger, 1979) and personal development for laypersons (Sanders & Malony, 1985).

By 1977, assertiveness training had reached parent education with the publication of *How to Get Your Children to Do What You Want Them to Do* by Paul Wood and Bernard Schwartz. Wood and Schwartz and also Lee Canter made films about assertiveness for use in parent education.

The best of the materials for parents, in my opinion, is the book by Melvin Silberman and Susan Wheelan (1980), *How to Discipline Without Feeling Guilty*. These authors place the assertive style of interacting with children in the broader perspective of the family system.

ance. They take power from their children, which enables them to win the struggles but leaves the children frightened and weak.

Assertive parents state their position directly, hold to it firmly and refuse to participate in power struggles. Assertive parents are more likely than parents of the other two styles to get the behavior they want without damaging the self-respect of themselves or their children.

The goal of assertiveness training for parents is to teach them to be firm when the situation calls for firmness. Firmness requires the ability to clarify a position, a willingness to tolerate conflict and an assertive appearance.

Clarification of Position

Firmness has to do with the ability of the parent to clarify a personal position, not with the ability to persuade the child. In fact, when parents *stop* trying to persuade, they typically discover firmness within themselves they didn't know was there.

Assertive parents state what they want in a direct manner, taking ownership for their preferences and wishes. Silberman and Wheelan (1980) suggest that parents use the following phrases to clarify their positions:

"I will not . . ." ("I will not allow you to run into the street!")

"I want . . ." ("I want the lawn mowed by 5 o'clock.")

"I'd like you to . . ." ("I'd like you to be in early tonight.")

"I expect . . ." ("I expect you to come home immediately after school or to call me to discuss your plans.")

"The rule is . . ." ("The rule is that you must take your bath before I read a story.")

"It is time to . . ." ("It is time to eat.")

"I like it when . . ." ("I like it when you let me nap for a few minutes.")

"I do not like it when . . ." ("I do not like it when you interrupt me when I'm on the phone.")

"I need . . ." ("I need your help on Saturday to get ready for our guests.")

"I'm willing to . . ." ("I'm willing to take you shopping on Friday, but not tomorrow.")

Manuel Smith (1975), one of the pioneers of assertiveness training, recommends a technique called "broken record" for taking a position and holding to it in conversation. It consists of persistently repeating the position statements illustrated above without getting angry, irritated or loud. At the same time, side issues brought up by the child are ignored.

Parent: It's time to eat now.

Child: The show is just about over.

Parent: It's time to eat now.

Child: I'll be there in a little bit.

Parent (standing in front of child and speaking in a firm but not menacing tone of voice): It's time to eat now.

To remind children of parental expectations without nagging, Faber and Mazlish (1980) suggest that parents use notes and single words. For example (p. 65), a father left the following note on the bathroom mirror to remind his daughter to clean hairs from the sink drain:

Help!

Hairs in my drain give me a pain.

Glug,

your stopped up sink.

One-word reminders assertively delivered are better than long, nagging reminders which are filled with You-messages. For example:

"Kids, pajamas!"

"Your coat!"

"Homework!"

"The dog!"

All of these examples are straightforward statements about parental expectations and preferences. Since parents are in charge of their preferences, the statements are made without apology and without fear of conflict. Agreement is not required.

Unassertive parents are less direct. They plead or beat around the bush, and they tend to ask rhetorical questions like the following:

"Don't you think . . . ?" ("Don't you think the lawn needs mowing?")

"Why don't you . . . ?" ("Why don't you come in early tonight?")

"Would you like to . . . ?" ("Would you like to take your bath now?")

"How about . . . ?" ("How about helping me get ready for our guests this Saturday?")

"Don't you want . . . ?" ("Don't you want to eat now?")

Unassertive parents use rhetorical questions like these to soften requests. Getting what they want with indirect requests feels kinder.

The problem with these questions, however, is that they don't work well. They imply that the desired behavior is optional, so children sometimes choose not to comply. What was intended to be kindness turns into unpleasant argument and manipulation. Questions offering a choice work well only when both responses are acceptable:

"Would you like to clean up the toys first or take your bath first?"

"Would you prefer to fold the clothes before we eat or after?"

Aggressive parents give orders and then use personal attack and threats of punishment to intimidate children into compliance:

"Don't ask questions, just do it!"

"Because I said so!"

"That's ridiculous!"

"Right now! Move!"

"If you do that one more time, you'll be sorry!"

"Don't be so dumb!"

If children comply with the orders, aggressive parents feel personally victorious; if children defy the orders, aggressive parents feel personally threatened or defeated.

Assertive parents, in contrast, demand a change in behavior, but do it in a way which does not emphasize feelings of victory or defeat. This is possible because they are able to tolerate conflict.

Acceptance of Conflict

Unassertive parents are afraid of conflict and anger (see Figure 11.3). They give in quickly or deny conflict is taking place to avoid the child's displeasure. Aggressive parents, too, are uncomfortable with conflict. But they are not afraid of anger and use it to teach the child not to raise that particular issue again.

Assertive parents accept some conflict in the parent-child relationship as inevitable and can tolerate it. They want their children to comply with their requests, but don't expect children to agree with them all of the time. Therefore, they don't feel a need to win an argument.

When children argue with parents, it's difficult for parents to refrain from countering with arguments of their own. Social training compels them to respond to reason with reason, just as they feel compelled to answer the ringing telephone or doorbell. Assertive parents, however, do not answer questions or give reasons out of obligation. They move in and out of debate at their choice.

Reasoning is important, of course. It's the first step in responding

Figure 11.3
Unassertive, Assertive and Aggressive Styles of
Making and Denying Requests

Unassertive Style	Assertive Style	Aggressive Style
Pouts, reveals hurt feelings but doesn't make requests	Reveals feelings and makes requests	Makes demands but doesn't reveal feelings
Expects child to make parent happy	Expects child to comply with request but not necessarily agree	Expects child to acquiesce
Uncomfortable with conflict; avoids it	Accepts conflict as inevitable; is willing to live with it	Uncomfortable with conflict; seeks to put an end to it
Afraid of anger	Controls anger; not needed to take position	Uses anger to teach child to not raise issue again
Gives in easily to argument	States position briefly; listens to child's point but refuses to argue	Tries to persuade, win argument
Indecisive	Firm	Belligerent
Ambiguous about issue	Clear about issue, persistent	Brings in other issues
Allows self to be treated unfairly by child	Refuses to participate in unfair treatment of self by child	Objects to child's requests with ridicule, sarcasm, putdowns

to problems in the Parent's Problem Area. But when reasoning stops being informative and becomes argumentative, it's time to stop reasoning. Otherwise, parents become trapped by their own reason-ableness, as in the following example:

    Child: We're going to get together at Matt's house tonight and
        watch some movies.

    Parent: More than one movie? That's going to get awfully late, isn't it?

Child: We'll probably be there until about 1:00.

Parent: But you were out late last night. You need your sleep.

Child: I can sleep tomorrow afternoon.

Parent: But that's not the same as getting to bed at a decent time.

Child: It doesn't seem to bother me. I haven't been sick for a long time.

Parent: Well, how about 12:00?

Child: That's right in the middle of the second movie!

Parent: You can watch the rest of it at another time.

Child: Sure! That would be a lot of fun, watching a movie by myself. You just don't want me to have any fun.

Parent: How can you say that when I just let you go with your friends last night?

Arguments like this can go on and on. For every argument there will be a counter-argument. The parent is seeking to persuade, and the child is unlikely to be persuaded.

Assertive parents don't need to argue that their positions are the most fair, rational, logical or desirable positions to take. They are able to respond to queries by acknowledging that their positions may be for their own convenience or to satisfy a worry or because of personal preference:

"Because I worry about things like that."

"I know not everybody feels this way, but that's the way I feel."

"Because I want you to."

"Because I said so. I know that doesn't sound like a very good reason, but for now it's reason enough."

One means of withdrawing from an argument is to concede that the child has a point or may be right. Manuel Smith calls this "fogging," because it resembles a fog bank:

[A fog bank] is very persistent. We cannot clearly see through it. It offers no resistance to our penetration. It does not fight back. It has no hard striking surfaces from which a rock we throw at it can ricochet back at us, enabling us to pick it up and throw it at the fog once more. We can throw an object right through it, and it is unaffected. Inevitably, we give up trying to alter the persistent, independent, nonmanipulable fog and leave it alone. (Smith, 1975, p. 97)

Smith recommends such phrases as the following to disengage from an argument by fogging:

"You are/probably are/could be/may be right."

"I see what you mean."

"You've got a point."

"Perhaps so."

"That could be."

"I realize you see it differently."

"I'd probably feel that way, too, if I were you."

The following dialogue illustrates the use of the fogging and broken record techniques to withdraw from an argument without giving up the position:

> Child: We're going to get together at Matt's house tonight and watch some movies.
>
> Parent: I realize you've made plans, but I want you to be home by eleven tonight. [position stated]
>
> Child: Eleven! But we don't have school tomorrow.
>
> Parent: That's true. [fogging]
>
> Child: I can sleep tomorrow afternoon.
>
> Parent: Yes, you probably can. [fogging]
>
> Child: Everybody else gets to stay out late tonight.
>
> Parent: That may be, but I want you in by eleven. [fogging and broken record]
>
> Child: You just don't want me to have any fun.
>
> Parent: I'm sure it looks that way. But I want you to be home by eleven tonight. [fogging and broken record]

Assertive parents are willing to take a position even though it makes them unpopular with their children. They withdraw from arguments because they do not demand agreement with their attitude about the issue. What they demand is compliance with a request to do or not do some particular behavior.

Assertive Appearance

Four-year-old Ricky approaches his little sister who is in a stroller, greets her, leans over and kisses her. But while he is kissing her, he reaches under the blanket and pinches her. She begins to cry. Since this has happened before, his mother is aware that Ricky has something to do with her crying. She consoles the baby, and then says to Ricky in a soft, syrupy voice, "Now, Ricky, we mustn't make baby cry. We must play nicely with baby, OK?" Ricky looks at her in silence. Before long, it happens again and Ricky's mother wonders to herself what she should do to help Ricky get over this "sibling rivalry."

The problem isn't simply sibling rivalry. The problem is that Ricky's mother hasn't convinced him that he should stop doing what he is doing. Visualize a parent and child at the moment that the child realizes it's time to get serious about what the parent wants. The signals are different for different parents but commonly include a slightly raised voice, hands on hips, use of the child's full name, finger waving, a certain look in the eye and so on. These nonverbal signals are as important as the words themselves.

If Ricky's mother were more assertive about putting an end to Ricky's misbehavior, she would show that she is concerned for the baby and is upset about what he did. She would probably get down at his level, look directly in his face and say in a raised, serious tone of voice, "Stop that, Ricky! I will not let you hurt the baby!"

Messages delivered assertively have several nonverbal characteristics (see Figure 11.4). They are made with good eye contact, which indicates sincerity and self-confidence. Lack of eye contact indicates anxiety and lack of confidence. At the other extreme are parents who intimidate by glaring.

An assertive message is delivered close enough that the speaker cannot be ignored. The most assertive position for parents of young children is with the parent's body lowered or bent to permit frontal gaze, directly in front of the child and an arm's length away, with one hand gently grasping the child's shoulder. With adolescents the best position is one which rivets attention to the interpersonal engagement, but does not invade the teenager's personal space. If the parent is seated, the posture is forward leaning, rather than backward slouching; arms and legs are uncrossed to indicate openness. If the parent is standing, head and shoulders are up and weight is on both feet to project confidence.

Facial expressions and tone of voice fit the words of an assertive message. If the message is to be taken seriously, then the face needs to be serious, without smiles or twinkles of the eyes. The tone of voice needs to be firm and controlled and not weak, apologetic, syrupy or belligerent. Physical gestures which accompany the words are comfortable rather than nervous and emphatic but not threatening.

Like all other techniques of parenting, assertive requests can be used too much or too little. The proper balance is maintained by selecting the situations which are worth a strong parental stance. In the first situation below, a strong parental stance probably is *not* needed:

Figure 11.4
Nonverbal Differences Among Unassertive, Assertive
and Aggressive Messages

Unassertive Style	Assertive Style	Aggressive Style
Voice soft, apologetic, syrupy	Voice firm, controlled	Voice too loud, belligerent
Questions	Statements	Exclamations
Shifting or averted gaze	Open, direct eye contact	Glaring
Pleading, timid, fearful facial expressions	Engaged, serious but relaxed facial expressions	Tense, impassive or threatening facial expressions
Distant position, shifting posture, fidgeting hands	Respectful distance; if sitting, forward leaning, rather than backward slouching; if standing, upright, balanced position	Position too close, body rigid or arms, legs crossed; hands clenched, finger pointing
Not touching	Engaging touch, gentle grasp, holding to calm, restrain or comfort	Grabbing, poking, squeezing
Silence used to pout or withdraw in fear	Silence used to calm or wait	Silence used to punish

I was a picky eater when I was little, and one of the things I didn't like very well was egg. Mom was the kind who made us clean up our plates, so she made me sit in the corner until I was finished. Many times I was still eating cold eggs at 11:00 in the morning. Yuck!

The next situation, however, is much more important and a strong parental stance *is* needed.

When I was younger I had a curvature of the spine. The doctor said I was to wear a body brace for three years. I hated it! I fought with my parents about it. I cried and begged to get out of it. I refused to eat for 13 days and lost 14 pounds. But my parents stuck to their guns. I really admire them now for the way they supported me by being tough.

Being able to be assertive is important, but knowing when to be assertive is equally important. The important question is whether or not balance among the four areas of the "Balanced Parenting Model" is maintained. When parents use their assertiveness excessively, the parent-child relationship is like a tire with a bulge at the Parent's Problem Area. When parents are at the other extreme, unable to take a position of strength, the relationship is like a tire which is flat at the Parent's Problem Area. But for those with balanced parenting skills who use assertiveness judiciously, the relationship rolls along smoothly.

Parents who use their assertiveness most effectively are neither tyrants nor pushovers. They are sensitive and caring, and also firm when they need to be.

If a child doesn't respond to facts and reasons, disregards the feelings of parents and ignores demands, then it's time for parents to withdraw emotionally from the struggle and use consequences to clarify the choices the child has. We turn next to the fourth step in the Facts-Feelings-Demands-Consequences plan for the Parent's Problem Area.

Setting Consequences

John Rosemond, newspaper columnist who writes about parenting, suggests that parents who have trouble maintaining control of their children may be somewhat like basketball referees who do a poor job of officiating. Imagine a basketball game in which a referee gathers the players around him before the game begins. "You all know the rules?" he asks. "Good," he says, after they nod their heads. "And do you all promise to play by the rules?" Again they nod affirmatively. "Then let's get started."

Shortly after the opening tip-off, one player fouls another. The ref blows his whistle. "That was a foul. You just promised to keep the rules. Have you forgotten already? Now, don't do it again, OK?"

The ball is put into play again, and soon a player travels. The ref whistles the action to a stop and says, "That's traveling! Maybe your coach lets you get by with that in practice, but you can't do that in a game!"

Another foul is committed. "You did it again! How many times do I have to tell you?"

Play continues in this fashion with the referee stopping play each time an infraction is committed. He scolds, nags, threatens, encourages, ridicules and pleads:

"Who started the pushing?"

"Did you do that on purpose?"

"I'll let it go this time, but don't do it again!"

"Come on, guys, you can do better than this!"

"I can't turn my back for one minute without you guys pushing each other!"

"You guys don't have any respect for me or the rules!"

"I'm getting fed up with this!"

"I've had it!"

In a game officiated like this the referee would become increasingly frustrated and angry, and the game itself would get more and more out of control. Fortunately, referees don't officiate in this manner. They do not respond to infractions as though violations were personal affronts, nor do they malign the players. They take charge of the game by enforcing the rules quickly, firmly and impersonally. When players commit infractions, referees employ consequences: the offending team loses possession of the ball, fouled players are awarded free throws, and players who foul too often or too roughly are put out of the game.

Consequences are as important in the home as they are on the basketball court. Yet many parents have trouble taking effective action. They nag, scold and complain, but that's all:

> My mom and I are always bickering at each other. She worries about me so much that she is always nagging me, which really gets on my nerves. For example, if I come in late, she gets mad and yells at me, and we stay up arguing about it. I tell her I'm sorry and won't do it again, but the only reason I say that is to get her to stop nagging me about it.
>
> When she is upset, she'll say I'm grounded for two weeks or something like that. But after she calms down she feels sorry about all the things she has said and lets me off the hook. I think if she would stick to her punishment, things wouldn't have gone as far as they have gone, and we'd feel better towards each other.

As this teenager understands, households become increasingly turbulent when parents are unable to use consequences effectively.

The Systematic Training for Effective Parenting (STEP) program contributes significantly to the skills of the Parent's Problem Area through its emphasis on consequences. In the STEP program, parents are taught to allow children to bear the results of their misbehavior, and thereby develop responsibility in their children and avoid emotionally charged power struggles.

Rudolf Dreikurs, one of the pioneers of parent education groups[2], described two types of consequences — natural and logical (Dreikurs & Soltz, 1964). A natural consequence is the unavoidable result of some action. For example, if Marla leaves her bike on the front lawn, it may become rusted or be stolen. If Sandy goes to bed late, she will be tired the next day. If Joel misplaces his shoes, he won't be able to find them when he needs them. If Bobby doesn't take a bath, others will not want to be around him because of the odor.

In such cases, parents might decide to forgo doing anything to alter the misbehavior, since children will learn from the natural results of what they do and adjust their behavior accordingly. Non-intervention, therefore, is a useful technique if parents can tolerate the misbehavior and wait for self-correction to take place.

Many types of misbehavior, however, cannot be tolerated. For example, Marla's parents probably are not willing to wait until her bike is rusted or stolen for the lesson about putting bikes away to be learned. They do not want the expense of replacing a bicycle.

---

[2] Rudolf Dreikurs based his ideas about parenting on the work of the personality theorist Alfred Adler, a contemporary of Freud. Thus the branch of parent education which is based on Dreikur's work is called Adlerian.

Adler thought that misbehavior (or neurosis, in general) arose as overcompensation for childhood inferiorities. Adlerian childrearing (or therapy) helps individuals to give up perfectionism and other crippling perceptions of self. Individuals are encouraged to pursue lifestyle goals which are more realistic and socially responsible. Another contribution of Adler was his emphasis on birth order and sibling relationships in personality development.

Dreikurs' book *Children: The Challenge* (which he co-authored with Virginia Soltz, 1964) sold widely and established his influence in parent education. He recommended that parents recognize the goals of misbehavior, use natural and logical consequences, avoid power struggles, offer encouragement and establish a home atmosphere of mutual respect. Dreikurs pioneered the use of parent discussion groups.

Donald Dinkmeyer co-authored with Dreikurs a book about encouragement (Dinkmeyer & Dreikurs, 1963), and later co-authored with Gary McKay the STEP *Parent's Handbook* (Dinkmeyer & McKay, 1976). Approximately one million copies of the *Parent's Handbook* have been sold and sales continue to be lively. It has been published in three other languages and translated (but not yet published) in several more (L. Velde, personal communication, June 7, 1988).

The content of the STEP program comes primarily from Adler and Dreikurs, but incorporates the concepts of problem ownership, active (or reflective) listening and I-messages from the Parent Effectiveness Training program as well.

However, it is not the content of the STEP program which accounts for its enormous contribution to parent education. Its success is due primarily, in my opinion, to the appeal of the *Parent's Handbook*. The *Handbook* is inexpensive, colorful and brief and contains practice sets, discussion questions and posters. The program also has been promoted very successfully by its publisher.

Sandy's parents are not willing to leave the bedtime decision to her discretion; she is too young and impulsive to exercise good judgment. Furthermore, they want some time together without her and they don't want to spend the following day with a girl who fusses because she is tired.

When parents cannot wait to let natural consequences take their course, intervention is required. The intervention is in the form of artificial consequences established by the parents. Although the consequences are contrived, Dreikurs recommends that they be logically related to the misbehavior.

Logical consequences can be used when the misbehavior is an isolated incident. More importantly, however, they are useful when the misbehavior is a habit. After other methods of altering the habit have been used unsuccessfully, logical consequences are announced in the following way:

"The rule is that you must _____ by/when _____.

If you choose not to, _____."

The announcement is made in a matter-of-fact tone of voice, without scolding, sarcasm or anger. The parent then leaves the responsibility for the decision with the child and accepts the child's decision. If the child does not keep the rule, the parent follows through with the consequence of the choice, while saying:

"I see that you have chosen _____.

You may choose/try again _____."

In previous attempts to solve the bicycle problem, for example, Marla's parents provided information. They explained that bikes remain in better condition if garaged at night, and they expressed worry about theft. This information did not change her behavior, however. She still was in the habit of leaving her bike on the front lawn, in spite of their reminders to put it away. Her parents became increasingly upset about the problem and began to scold and nag.

Finally, Marla's parents decided to stop nagging and take action. For a consequence logically related to the misbehavior, they decided to make the bicycle unavailable to her. They rejected such options as grounding her or docking her allowance, since these were not as closely related to the misbehavior.

When Marla's parents decided to take action, they withdrew from the power struggle which the bicycle issue had become. They announced the new rule matter-of-factly, without lecture or persuasion: "The rule is that you must put your bicycle in the garage when you come home. If you choose to leave it out, we will put it away before we go to bed. If we put it away, the bicycle will stay in the garage for two days."

In the days which followed, they did not remind her of the rule. But the next time Marla left the bike out, her dad unemotionally wheeled it into the garage, put a lock on it and then told her, "I see that you have chosen to not use your bicycle. You may choose again in two days."

For the two-day period, Marla was inconvenienced without the bicycle and protested the rule. She claimed she just forgot, promised to not do it again, charged her parents with being unfair and mean, sulked and cried. Her parents refused to be drawn into an argument about the situation, treating it as a decision she had made. The consequences of the decision were hers to bear. Marla's parents did not gloat in her predicament, but neither did they rescue her. They kindly and firmly followed through with what they said would happen if the bicycle was left out.

If Marla had had trouble complying with the request even with the consequences, her parents could have escalated the consequences by increasing the time the bicycle was impounded. This wasn't necessary, however, because the bad habit was broken fairly quickly. She suffered the consequences of leaving her bike out only two or three times.

The goal in using logical consequences is to arrange the circumstances so that children bear more responsibility for their misconduct. This happens when parents stop covering for them and instead provide incentive for behaving in more socially responsible ways. Figure 11.5 provides examples of problems and the logical consequences which parents have used to solve them. Other examples follow.

A fourth grader wanted to sit with her friends in church and begged to do so until her parents consented. A few Sundays later she and a friend were sitting in church eating candy and making noise. As she told the story:

> I did not think about my folks sitting a few pews away. They saw what was going on. When we got home I was in trouble for talking, laughing and eating in church. Also for running to the store between Sunday school and the worship service to buy the candy. I had to sit with them until they let me try it again a few weeks later.

Another example is provided by a young teenager who went through a period when she was rebellious:

Figure 11.5
Examples of Problems and Logical Consequences

Problem	Logical Consequences
Leaving clothes on floor	"You are to put your clothes in the hamper. If you choose to leave them on the floor, they will not be washed because I will wash only what is in the hamper."
Procrastination in getting ready for bed	"You are to be ready for bed by 8:30. If you choose to take longer than that, I will not read to you or tuck you in."
Coming late to meal	"You are to be on time for meals. If you choose to be late, you will miss your meal and may not eat until the next meal."
Forgetting to take out trash	"You are to take out the trash each day. If you choose not to, I will do it for you. You will be charged a fee for my service. The fee will be subtracted from your allowance."
Intolerable table manners	"You are to wash your hands (or use a fork, or chew with mouth closed, etc.). If you choose not to, we will set a place for you at another table."
Begging for candy at store	"You are not to whine and beg for candy. If you choose to, you will not go shopping with me the next time I go (or will lose privilege of preparing shopping list)."
Taking too long to get ready	"You are to be ready by 8:15. If you are not ready, you will be left (or will be taken without being ready)."
Using tools and not putting them away	"You are to put away any tools you use. If you choose to leave them out, the tools will be locked."
Tracking in mud	"You are to take off your muddy shoes in the back room. If you wear them into the kitchen, you will have responsibility for cleaning the kitchen floor for two weeks."
Making bothersome noises while others are watching TV	"You may settle down and watch the program with us or leave the room. You decide."

Infant (crawler) playing with cords and plugs	Child is placed in playpen for short while. Repeat, as necessary.
Dawdling at table	Parent clears off table, removes food.
Coming in late (teenager)	"Next weekend you will need to be in earlier."
Neglecting to take care of kitchen messes (teenager)	"You are to clean up your messes in the kitchen. If you do not, you will take over kitchen duty from the one who cleaned up your mess" (or will lose kitchen privileges; or will not receive food services by family).
Neglecting assigned tasks to watch TV	"If you choose to watch TV before this is completed, the TV will be off limits for two days."
Wandering out of yard (young child)	"The rule is that you must stay in the yard. Since you do not feel like staying in the yard, you must come inside. You may try again later when you feel like staying in the yard."

When I was eleven, I never did anything my parents told me to do. Finally they got so fed up with me that they locked the door one night when I was late coming home. I figured they just hadn't heard the door bell, so I went to the neighbors to call. Dad answered the phone and said that since I wasn't helping out and being part of the family, I wasn't going to be allowed in the house. Well, that scared me. I realized what a jerk I'd been and apologized. I think they felt like they had tried everything else. They finally got through to me with this plan. It worked! Boy, did it work!!

What these parents did was risky because the consequence was severe. But in this case, it worked. Their child was jolted into better conduct.

A dairy farm family had a problem with the children's procrastination at milking time. The evening mealtime was 5:00, after which the child with milking duties was to change from school clothes to work clothes and report to the milk barn:

We preferred to read, nap or just poke around—anything but work. Finally, Mom and Dad enacted a plan. The one of us who was scheduled to go to the barn had to be there before the milker pump sounded or wages were deducted.

That solved the problem because the money mattered to us. The penalty was logically related to the misbehavior because dairy farming was the family's occupation, and the parents depended on the children to help get the milking done.

Procrastination before school was a problem with a first grader. He was so slow in getting ready for school that he missed the bus a few times. His parents got tired of this and finally told him that he would be put out the door when the bus was due, whether or not he was ready to leave. It happened once. On that morning he finished putting on his shoes and socks in the bus. Thereafter, he was ready on time.

In another household, piano practice time was a problem. In this case the problem was more complicated than usual because the mother was also the piano teacher. Television seemed to interfere with the practice time, so the mother established the rule that the child could choose to practice a certain amount of time and prepare the lesson adequately, or forgo television privileges the following week.

None of these examples is presented as the best way to handle a problem situation. What works in one household may not work in another. The task of parents is to find a consequence which is logically related to the misbehavior and which works.

Silberman and Wheelan (1980) suggest that parents maintain a few standard penalties that can be used in a variety of situations, in case more logical consequences are not available. Among the most commonly useful are prohibiting watching television, playing or going out with friends and riding a bicycle or using the car. Another means of determining the consequence is to ask the child to come up with a penalty for the misbehavior.

Parents sometimes feel like they've tried everything and nothing works. Kenneth Kaye (1984) suggests that parents who feel helpless make a list of everything they do for their children. The list is to include every cent spent on the children within the last month, every instance the parents helped with anything, every minute devoted to their needs and desires. Then they are to go back and cross out items related to food, clothing, shelter and health care (which parents are obligated to provide).

> *Everything else* that you do for your children is something
> that you can stop doing if they are uncooperative, inconsid-
> erate or abusive. Different parents have to choose for them-
> selves, from their own list, which services they are prepared
> to withdraw and in what order. . . . I am not suggesting that
> you stop doing those particular things. My experience indi-
> cates, however, that once you have made a complete list and
> ranked all the items in terms of your willingness to withhold
> them as consequences, you will no longer feel so helpless.
> *Something* works; you just have to find it! (Kaye, 1984, p.
> 80–81)

The basis for parental power is the child's dependence, not the
parent's coerciveness. The adage, "You can lead a horse to water, but
you can't make it drink," is true. You can't coerce a horse into
drinking. But what you can do is stop leading it to water. Eventually
it will become interested in drinking.

The logical consequences which work best are those which are
neither too light nor too severe. Research suggests that children are
more likely to internalize prohibitions if the deterrent is strong
enough to make the desired behavior preferable to the undesired
behavior, but mild enough to leave them with a sense of choice. In
an experiment, elementary school children were introduced to an
attractive toy, but then told not to play with it. Some were given a
severe threat and others were given a mild threat in regard to the
consequences of disobedience. They were then given opportunity to
play with the toy as a test of obedience. The two levels of threat were
about equally effective in producing obedience.

But several weeks later a striking difference between the two
groups showed up. When the children had another chance to play
with the toy, about three-fourths of those who had been severely
threatened for playing with the toy did so freely. In contrast, only
one-third of the children who had been mildly threatened for playing with the toy did so.

The researcher's explanation for this is that the children who had
been severely threatened had sufficient reason for not playing with
the toy, and this reason was external—they would be severely
punished if they disobeyed and were caught. Later, when the authority was absent they no longer had sufficient reason for not
playing with the attractive toy. In contrast, the group that was mildly
threatened had to struggle a bit with their consciences the first
opportunity they had to play with the forbidden toy. There was less

external reason for resisting temptation, so they had to create internal reasons for resisting. They did this by devaluing the toy, which showed up in their choice of toys weeks later (Freedman, 1965).

So logical consequences work best if they are neither too mild nor too severe. There also needs to be a balance between an absence of rules and too many rules. In some households, children seem to be on their own; their parents impose few if any demands and consequences. In other households, rules are so numerous that enforcing the rules requires almost constant vigilance by the parents. Logical consequences work best if parents target only a few misbehaviors at a time.

A basketball game in which the officiating is too lax is impossible to enjoy. The attention of players and spectators is on the lack of control and they become anxious about unfairness, injury and retaliation. On the other hand, a game which is called too closely is equally hard to enjoy. Intensity on the floor cannot be sustained because of the whistles, and players are taken out of action or play tentatively because of foul trouble. Basketball is most enjoyable when referees exercise a judicious amount of control, finding a balance between letting the game get out of control and making so many calls that the pleasure is taken out of the game.

The same is true of the control which parents exercise in the home. There need to be enough rules and consequences for breaking the rules that the household is run in a fair and orderly manner, but if there are too many rules, attention is on the rulekeeping, and the pleasure of living together as members of the household is diminished.

Facts-Feelings-Demands-Consequences

At this moment it is June, and as I write, the Kansas wheat harvest is getting underway. From my third floor office window, I can see the fields just beyond the campus. I imagine a wheat farmer. There is a smile on his face because he is a friendly farmer. He is driving a combine (see Figure 11.6).

Friendly farmer drives combine. FFDC. This mental picture serves as a device for remembering the four strategies of the Parent's Problem Area covered in this chapter and the previous one: Facts-Feelings-Demands-Consequences.

The four strategies can be applied separately or in any combination. But they are especially effective if applied in the FFDC sequence. Since parental power increases with each step in the FFDC sequence, parents will use the minimal level of power required to take care of misbehavior if they begin with facts and move to the other levels only as needed.

Inside a combine, wheat goes through a process called threshing. Threshing is a combination of hitting, which knocks the grain from the stalks, and rubbing, which removes the chaff from the grain. The process takes place when the wheat passes between a cylinder and a concave grate. The threshing action is determined by the distance between the cylinder and the grate and also by the speed the cylinder turns.

If the threshing action is too weak, the grain is not removed from the chaff. It passes out the back of the combine with the chaff and is lost. If the threshing action is too vigorous, the chaff is removed but the grain is cracked. The grain then loses quality because of the oxidation which occurs, and its value goes down. Neither millers nor livestock like it as well when it is cracked. Threshing action which removes the chaff but leaves the grain intact is best.

Figure 11.6
Friendly Farmer Drives Combine

The same is true of the use of parental power. If used insufficiently, the socialization process is thwarted. But if used too vigorously, the self-respect of the child is damaged and the parent-child relationship suffers a loss.

Consider how the FFDC sequence would have improved the way a school principal dealt with Mike, a middle school student. Mike's shoes had been making black marks on the school floors. Mike either had not noticed them or had decided they were insignificant. The school principal noticed, however, and regarded them as serious. He required Mike to stay after school and scrub the marks off the floor.

Mike came home from school later than usual that day, found his mother working in the laundry room and burst into tears. His mother dropped the clothes she was folding, moved to his side and asked what happened. He sobbed for a few moments and then told her that he had gotten in trouble at school because of his shoes. Mike pointed to his hiking boots, which before this day had been a matter of pride. They were just what he wanted when he had picked them out a month earlier — suede leather, a built-in cushion at the top of the boot, wide red shoestrings and waffle soles.

"If he had told me to stop wearing my boots, I would have. I didn't know he was so mad about it. I had to scrub the floor after school when everybody was in the halls and the kids thought it was funny. I hate these shoes and I hate school!"

If the principal had followed the FFDC sequence, he would have started with *facts* and the conversation might have gone like this:

"Mike, your shoes make black marks on the floor."

"Lots of kids wear shoes like these."

"You're right about that. I have been watching to see if I could figure out which ones are making the marks and it seems to be yours."

This information probably would have taken care of the problem. Mike would have stopped wearing the boots to school.

It's possible, however, that Mike would have considered this information and decided to keep wearing the boots, but walk carefully to avoid making marks. Since doing so is virtually impossible, the principal's concern would have continued. He could have expressed his *feelings* about the situation next:

"Mike, I'm still concerned about the marks your shoes make. It really bothers me to see these marks when the custodian works so hard to keep the floor looking good."

Mike hardly could have ignored this message if he wanted to

maintain the principal's approval. At this point he probably would have taken the principal's feelings about the matter into account and worn other shoes.

Suppose, however, that Mike decided that he liked his shoes so much that he would wear them in spite of the principal's disapproval, or that he decided to challenge the principal's authority over the shoe issue. At this point the principal could have made a *demand* and established logical *consequences:*

"Mike, I want you to stop wearing those shoes because they make marks. You have a choice. Either wear other shoes or stay after school to clean the marks off the floor. You decide." He would state this to Mike in a matter-of-fact tone of voice and he would do it privately to avoid a public confrontation. But he would be firm enough to leave no doubt about the consequences if Mike chose to disregard the demand.

If Mike protested, the principal could have acknowledged Mike's disappointment, agreed that the boots are fine boots and that other students wear boots that are similar. Nevertheless, he would have reiterated that Mike must stop wearing them to school. He would not have expected Mike to be pleased about the request, so he would not have argued, scolded or belittled Mike into approving the plan. He would have moved ahead without Mike's approval.

Had the principal followed the FFDC sequence, he would have used just enough power to put an end to the marks from Mike's shoes, which was what he was after, and he would have done so in a way which upheld self-respect for both Mike and himself.

Mornings at Tony's home provide another example of the use of the FFDC sequence. Tony's parents were bothered by their teenager's procrastination. Each morning he waited until the last minute to get up and get ready for school. His parents and sister Tara would remind him to hurry, but each morning he would not be ready until the last minute. Tony and Tara would bolt out the door, drive as quickly as possible to the high school grounds and rush to their classrooms, sometimes arriving after the bell had sounded. Tony's parents decided to work at the problem in this manner:

"Tony, every morning you and Tara are late or almost late for school because she has to wait for you [fact]. She doesn't like to arrive late. She prefers to arrive a few minutes early. We also don't like the way you speed on your way to school and we don't like the morning hassles we've been going through [feelings]. From now on, we want you to be ready fifteen minutes before the time school starts, because that is when Tara is going to leave [demand]. If you want to ride with her in the car, you will need to be ready. Otherwise you will need to get there some other way [consequence].

A teenager told about an FFDC sequence her father used with her when she was younger:

I used to come to the table with dirty hands. Finally, one day my dad sat me down and told me how much dirty hands at the table irritated him. From then on I had the choice of washing my hands or missing dinner.

Another teenager told how his parents responded after he drove the car one evening when he was home alone, before he had a license:

Dad figured out that I had driven the car; he told me he wasn't too happy about it. Mom was really upset, too, because I could have gotten hurt. They told me I was never to do it again, and if I did, they would postpone the time I was to get my license.

Amelia's carelessness about putting things away provides a final example of the FFDC sequence. She was in the habit of dropping her books, papers and other things on the floor inside the door when she came home from school. Her mother told her:

"Amelia, you have a cupboard to put your things in, but you just leave them on the floor inside the door [fact]. I feel like I am always picking up after you, to keep the house looking neat, and I am tired of it [feelings]. From now on, I want you to put your things away when you come home [demand]. If you choose to leave your things on the floor, I will pick them up, but I will put them in a box in the basement where they will stay for the rest of the week [consequences]. You decide."

Using the FFDC strategies in sequence as needed helps parents retain flexibility and avoid overemphasis on any one strategy. No method, at any level of parental power, is effective if relied on too much to solve the problems of the Parent's Problem Area. Balance is required.

When parents choose consequences for misbehavior, one of the common choices is physical punishment. The next chapter explores some of the issues involved in punishment and offers suggestions about using punishment most effectively, if it is used.

Questions for Thought and Discussion about this Chapter are on page 300.

12. Using Punishment

Punishment ranks above all other parenting topics in controversy and uncertainty. The question of physical punishment inevitably arises whenever a parenting expert is interviewed on television or leads a discussion group. And experts do not speak with one voice on the issue — there is considerable disagreement among them.

Expert opinion also changes across time. Bigner (1979) analyzed several women's magazines from 1950 to 1970 and found that in the early 1950s physical punishment (spanking) was condoned, but by the 1960s it was discouraged. A survey of readers of *Psychology Today* in the mid-'80s found them to be evenly divided — 49 percent thought that children should never be physically punished, and 51 percent thought they should be (Stark, 1985).

It's no wonder there is confusion and disagreement among parents; some are convinced that spanking is an essential part of parenting, and others are equally convinced it has no place in good parenting. Many waver in their position, using physical punishment at times but feeling disappointed in themselves and their children for the need to do so. This was the experience of Lorna and me, as I will explain later in the chapter.

My desire for balance leads me to regard with caution the extreme positions on the punishment issue and to search for the path of reason which I assume lies between the two. Let us first differentiate among the types of punishment. This will provide a vocabulary for thinking through the issues and for determining when (if ever) the different types of punishment are appropriately used.

Four uses of punishment will be reviewed: to render retribution, to make restitution, to inhibit undesirable behavior, and to communicate displeasure. I will argue that the first use, to render retribution, is the most common rationale for punishing but is the least defensible. The other uses are less frequently articulated but are more justifiable.

Punishment Used to Render Retribution

The most common use of punishment grows out of the notion that when people do something bad, something bad needs to happen to them. This is why the Peanuts cartoon character Peppermint Patty said to her teacher, "I stepped on a bug on my way to school. I feel so guilty. Punish me, ma'am . . . Give me an 'F' in something."

The concept of retribution refers to the use of punishment to redress grievances. When someone wrongs another, an equal amount of wrong is done to the culprit to even the score. The law of Moses in the Old Testament book of Leviticus commanded the Hebrew people to use punishment as retribution: "If anyone injures his neighbor, whatever he has done must be done to him: fracture for fracture, eye for eye, tooth for tooth. As he has injured the other, so he is to be injured" (24:19-20, NIV).[1]

In the modern legal system retribution takes the form of prison sentences, since we don't require an eye or a tooth in a literal sense (although a mandatory death sentence for taking someone's life is retributive justice). Following a crime against society, the debt to society is repaid by time in prison.

In the home, punishment as retribution is seen when parents assume that punishment is obligatory following a child's misbehavior. The child does something wrong and punishment automatically follows because that is the order of morality. Punishment as retribution takes place in the home when a parent decides how severe a punishment should be. Just as a judge fits sentence to crime, the parent decides how many swats a child deserves or how long a teenager should be grounded following a misdeed.

[1] Some Old Testament scholars suggest that the original purpose of the "eye for an eye" law of Moses was to prevent the escalation of violence. Retaliation was permissible up to the level of retribution, but was not to exceed it. Later, under Roman influence, retribution was seen to be mandatory, and it is this interpretation of the law which we inherited. Instances in which retribution was not rendered (e.g., King David's affair) are cited as evidence that retribution originally was not mandatory.

While the use of punishment to render retribution may be appropriate in the theological and legal realms, this type of punishment is not necessary in the discipline of a child. According to research by the late cognitive developmental psychologist Jean Piaget (1965), children themselves come to reject the logic of this type of punishment as they mature. Piaget posed situations like the following to study the development of children's ideas about justice:

Once there were two children who were stealing apples in an orchard. Suddenly a policeman comes along and the two children run away. One of them is caught. The other one, going home by a roundabout way, crosses a river on a rotten bridge and falls into the water. Now what do you think? If he had not stolen the apples and had crossed the river on that rotten bridge all the same, would he also have fallen into the water? (p. 252)

Young children perceive the misdeed and the punishment to be inseparably one. Punishment inevitably follows even when carried out by inanimate objects like bridges:

"Why did the boy fall in?"

"Because he had eaten the apples."

"He had his punishment too."

"Because he should not have stolen."

"If he hadn't fallen into the water he would have been caught."
(p. 253–254)

Piaget called this notion of young children *immanent justice.* It is accompanied by the belief that punishment defines an act as having been wrong. Certain things are bad things to do because one gets punished for doing them. At this level of moral development, children do not distinguish between misbehavior which is intentional and that which is accidental. They also favor retribution as the most fair, when asked to select among several punishment options.

In late childhood, however, children begin to recognize that misdeeds can be considered independently of punishment:

"Why did he fall in?"

"Because the plank was worn out."

"The punishment was what he deserved, but it was a coincidence."

"If the bridge was going to give way, it would have given way just the same." (p. 254–255)

In late childhood children recognize that people sometimes do bad things and aren't punished, since it is not the punishment which defines the act as wrong. Wrongness is defined by the intention of the actor and the social consequences of the act. At this level of moral development, children do not regard retributive punishment as a moral necessity. If punishment is to be used, older children recommend a punishment which entails putting things right and which makes the guilty one endure the consequences of the action (Piaget, 1965, p. 201).

A few years ago a faculty colleague took his daughter along when he moved some furniture with a rental truck from his home in Kansas to the home of relatives in Missouri. Midway in their journey she became ill and began vomiting. He took his eye off the road for a moment to care for her. In that moment he allowed the truck to wander onto the shoulder of the highway and then was unable to bring it back onto the highway as it swayed out of control. They ended up in a water-filled ditch with the truck on its side.

They were not injured, fortunately, but there were other consequences to pay. Jill was ill and now badly frightened as well. Jim was concerned for her well-being, remorseful about his lapse of attention to driving and embarrassed about causing the public scene which such an accident creates. Appliances in the truck were dented, fragile items broken and upholstery water-damaged. A tow truck was required to get them upright and out of the ditch, which cost them time and money. Jim was responsible to the rental company for the damages which the truck received. And to top off the events of a bad day, a Kansas Highway Patrol officer issued a ticket to Jim for careless driving and he had to pay a fine.

In Jim's case, the ticket and fine weren't necessary (although the officer evidently felt they were). There were consequences inherent in the situation — emotional duress, damages to the furniture, reparations to the rental company, inconvenience and so on. And the likelihood that Jim would do this again was slight; he was not characteristically a careless driver and following the accident he was sure to be even more careful than usual.

Much of the punitive action of parents is like the action of the officer. I remember well the moment that I realized that this type of punishment doesn't make sense. It happened when our son Jeff was partially toilet trained. I say partially trained, because when he paid attention to his bowels, he could use the toilet successfully. But if he became engrossed in play he would ignore the messages his intestines were sending until it was too late. That's what happened one day as he was playing in the sandbox in the backyard. I was working in the garden nearby when I saw him jump up and run for the house. He stopped just before he got to the back door and I knew he had lost the race.

I was frustrated because he seemed to be regressing; if he could manage to get to the bathroom on time on some occasions, why couldn't he do it all the time? Now I had another mess to take care of because of his procrastination! I scolded him, carried him to the bathroom to clean him up and then spanked him.

Later, after I had calmed down, I asked myself what good the spanking had done. The look on his face when he stopped short of the back door indicated that he was as dismayed as I by what happened. He didn't like the messes any better than I did and he wasn't making them to challenge my authority. Yet I was reacting as if it were a personal battle. Engaging him in battle was not something I felt good about, given that I was a 165-pound, intelligent adult and he was a little boy dependent on me for care.

In this incident spanking was a way for me to express my frustration, but it did little to move him towards the goal of success in toilet training. Following this incident, I spanked our children less and less, convinced that there were better ways to achieve our goals of childrearing than to use punishment as retribution.

In both the truck mishap and the messed pants incident, what happened was accidental and not due to willful disobedience. But that does not alter the point: the use of punishment to render retribution is not a moral necessity. Other kinds of responses to misbehavior are possible and preferable.

Punishment Used to Make Restitution

Restitution means restoring what was lost or taken away. Restitutive punishment requires the culprit to undo what was done to the victim. To play on the words of the Golden Rule, you undo to others as you would have them undo to you. This is in contrast to retributive punishment (which we just considered), which requires that something be done to the culprit because the culprit did something to the victim.

The criminal justice systems of many states in recent years have been altered to include restitution in legal sentences. Formerly, this was not the case. Sentences were to deter crime and to rehabilitate criminals, but had little to do with making restitution. Some years ago in a neighboring state, a young man in a jealous rage threw acid in the face of a young woman. He was arrested, tried, convicted and sentenced. Today he is in prison and the state is spending over $20,000 per year to keep him there. Meanwhile, the family of the young woman has had enormous medical bills and has received no help from the convicted man nor the state to meet the payments.

But this is changing. Kansas, for example, established a crime-victims reparations board several years ago to help determine compensation to victims; judges now commonly order restitution. Other states have instituted similar changes.

If systems as cumbersome and impersonal as courts can incorporate restitutive punishment, surely families which are small and personal can do so. The victim-offender reconciliation programs of church groups have led the way in judicial reform by demonstrating that a different kind of response to antisocial acts is possible; their message of reconciliation applies to the family as well as to the larger society.

When Jeff was about six years of age, we were in the garage one day. I was repairing something at the workbench and he was playing nearby with a small metal bar. After a while he began using the bar as a fly swatter. I told him to be careful and not break anything, but otherwise didn't pay much attention. As you probably are imagining already, the game ended when he swung at a fly that landed on the window of the garage door—and I had another repair job.

If I had chosen to respond to what he did with a retributive form of punishment I would have had to decide how wrong his act was and then punish him accordingly. How wrong is a broken window? Two swats' worth of spanking? Four swats? As wrong as being sent to bed without supper? As wrong as being banished from the garage? About the same as having a muscle pinched, the ear tweaked or the head thumped?

I rejected all of these options in favor of a restitutive form of punishment which asks a different kind of question: What were the consequences of Jeff's act? Did he feel remorse about having caused them? Could he be given some responsibility for undoing them?

So I had no interest in punishing him because he had broken a window, but I was interested in teaching him about repairing broken windows. He was by my side as I removed the shards of glass and helped hold the tools as I scraped and measured the frame. We took a nominal amount of cash from his bank and then went to the lumber yard to get a new pane. He watched intently as I installed the window and helped me to put things away.

I was satisfied by then that he felt badly about what had happened and that his discomfort was put to good use by helping to undo the damages. I also was confident that he would play more carefully around windows in the future. As in many instances of misbehavior in the home, nothing more than restitution was needed.

What happened to Jeff after he broke the window may not seem like punishment, but restitution is a type of punishment. He was required to bear some consequences—mental anguish (fright, shame, guilt) and financial loss (a portion of what he had saved to buy a toy). Since the misbehavior in this case was an isolated incident and not an ongoing pattern of destructiveness, these consequences were sufficient. Had the misbehavior been a recurring problem, consequences may have needed to be more substantial. (The previous chapter, Chapter 11, explains how to use logical consequences.)

Punishment Used to Inhibit Undesirable Behavior

Since the 1940s one branch of psychology has been studying the effects of punishment empirically. These are the learning theorists and social learning theorists, among whom B. F. Skinner has been the most influential. This line of inquiry has been motivated by a desire to understand better the principles of learning and punishment's role in the learning process. Learning researchers pursue such questions as: Under what conditions does punishment effectively suppress behavior? Are there side effects to the use of punishment? Are the effects of punishment long-term as well as short-term?

After several decades of experimentation, there is now no doubt that punishment suppresses behavior. How powerful the suppressive effect is, whether or not undesirable side effects are produced and how long the suppressive effect lasts depend on several factors: the timing, intensity, consistency and frequency of punishment; the use of reasoning with punishment; and the nature of the relationship between the parent who is doing the punishing and the child who is being punished.

The *first* factor to be considered is *timing*. The most effective timing is when the punishment is applied the moment the act is initiated; the longer the delay between the act and the punishment, the less powerful the suppressive effect is. In the home parents rarely intercept a forbidden act the moment it is initiated. Usually they deal with the misbehavior some time after it has taken place. A young person remembered an incident in which he was punished long after the act took place:

We were visiting another family. I was playing with the daughter of the family when we got in a fight. I yelled, "I'm going to kill you!" which sent her crying to her parents. Her parents told my parents, who were really upset because you weren't supposed to say such things in our peace-loving family. Dad led me to the car and without saying a word drove for what seemed like an eternity. He finally found a shed in the country where he gave me the spanking of my life. I still resent the way he handled it. If he wanted to spank me, I don't know why he didn't do it right away in town.

In past years it was common to wait until the father got home for the punishment to be delivered. A college student remembered:

When we were younger, mother would not discipline [punish] us, but say, "Just wait until Dad comes home." I vividly remember waiting and when he did come we would all stand in line and wait our turn for a spanking before we went off to bed.

Research results do not support this practice. Punishment is more effective when it is immediate rather than delayed.

A *second* factor in determining the effectiveness of punishment is *intensity.* Punishment is most effective when it is moderate in intensity. If too mild, it has little effect, and if too strong it produces emotionality, which interferes with the learning process and produces undesirable side effects. For example, fines are used as punishment to inhibit speeding on the highways. If the fines were too small they would have little impact on the behavior of drivers. Speeders would take their chances of being caught, and if caught, be merely inconvenienced. On the other hand, if consequences were substantial (loss of license, impounding of a car, a fine so large as to be difficult to pay or incarceration), speeding would be reduced. But the threat of such heavy penalties would also result in tenseness behind the wheel for fear of doing something wrong, efforts to evade detection or escape apprehension, resentment towards the officers who wielded such heavy clubs and stress related to the disruption of work and family life for those who were punished. The moderate level of punishment which is usually applied for speeding is preferable. It is effective in inhibiting fast driving but does not produce the disruptive side effects.

Punishment which is too intense calls attention to what happens to the culprit. Mild punishment is preferred because it allows the culprit's attention to be focused on the issue involved. As one young adult recalled, "A light spanking made me think about what I'd done more than a hard spanking did. After a hard spanking I just felt humiliated and angry."

A *third* factor which determines the effectiveness of punishment is *consistency*. Punishment which follows violation of rules in a consistent, predictable manner is more effective than punishment which is erratic and unpredictable. Inconsistency occurs when parents respond to a particular behavior one way on some occasions and another way on other occasions. It also occurs when parents communicate different notions from each other about what is punishable, as in the following incident recounted by a young adult:

> My father used to sleep in his favorite chair with his mouth open, snoring. Once when I was six my mother told me to go and pour water into his mouth. I did and he woke up with a snort. It made him angry and he spanked me. He wouldn't let me explain why I did it and my mother kept quiet. Later she came to my room where I had been sent, but I didn't feel like talking. I felt confused and betrayed.

Inconsistent punishment creates confusion and anxiety and is not conducive to learning the desired behavior.

Animal research suggests that punishment which is unpredictable and inescapable leads to despair and an inability to cope (Seligman, 1975). Researchers placed dogs in a harness from which they could not escape and then shocked their feet in an unpredictable manner. Next, the dogs were placed in a box with a metal grid floor through which shocks could be delivered. These shocks were predictable — a signal was given and followed ten seconds later by shock. These shocks also were escapable if the dogs jumped over a barrier from one side of the box to the other. Dogs which had not received the unavoidable shocks could do this; in fact, they quickly learned to cross the barrier within the ten second warning period and avoid the shock altogether. But dogs which earlier had received unavoidable shock failed to learn to escape it when they could — they lay down and absorbed the shock, whimpering quietly.

Seligman suggested that people learn to be helpless and depressed in this manner. Emotionally and physically painful events which are unpredictable and unavoidable create a sense of powerlessness. Inconsistent punishment does not teach children what to do, it teaches them to quit trying to cope with their world.

A *fourth* factor is the *frequency* of punishment. When punishment is used frequently, it becomes less effective as a means of guiding behavior. As one student wrote:

> Spanking was my parents' main form of punishment. It got
> to the point where spanking didn't work. I would do some-
> thing wrong knowing that I would get spanked. I just didn't
> care any more.

Another said, "My mother's answer for every problem was to spank.
It might have made her feel better, but it did nothing to help my
behavior. It just instilled fear."

In contrast to these two persons, a third could recall very few
instances of punishment, but she remembered one especially well:

> When I was about 13 I went through a period of rebellious-
> ness. On this particular occasion I was yelling at Mom about
> something I didn't like. She passed me with her arms full of
> laundry and I said something mouthy as she went by. A few
> seconds later she came out of the laundry room and slapped
> me across the mouth so hard it stung. She told me she hoped
> to never hear me talk so disrespectfully again. I was shocked.
> But it cured my talking back! I never did it again.

I do not recommend slapping, but the incident illustrates the importance of the frequency factor. The slap was effective because it was
rare, so unlike the mother's usual manner.

Frequent slapping would have a much different effect. There is
considerable evidence that the repeated use of physical punishment
is correlated with various forms of anti-social behaviors like delinquency and aggressiveness (e.g., Feshbach & Feshbach, 1971). What
children seem to learn when they are punished often is to respond to
frustration with aggression, battling their way through life as their
parents have done.

A *fifth* factor involved in the effectiveness of punishment is the
amount of *reasoning* (also called cognitive restructuring) that is used
with the punishment. The use of reasoning with punishment is more
effective than punishment by itself. The combination is illustrated
by this account of a teenager who was involved in a vandalism
incident:

> After a day of talking to the police and cleaning up the mess,
> I came home exhausted. I knew that Dad had been notified
> and I had to face him yet, which I dreaded. When he arrived
> he gave me a smile and a hug and said, "Kind of rough, isn't
> it?" Then he had me tell him all about what happened. At the
> end we talked about what my punishment at home was to be
> and why.

Another young person was talking about the time she jumped on her bunk bed after her parents had told her not to:

> After several jumps the slats gave way and the mattress and I fell on top of my little brother, who was below. My parents heard the crash and Ryan's screams and came running to see what had happened. They first made sure that he was all right, then explained to me that that was why they had told me not to do it, and then they spanked me. I was worried about my brother and felt guilty about what I had done. I deserved the spanking I got and have not jumped on a bed since then.

I find that many of the memories of being punished which children retain involve punishment which is undeserved. Another incident about jumping on beds illustrates this type of memory:

> Our family was helping to hang drapes in a new retirement center. We kids were running around the new building checking out the rooms and helping the adults whenever they called us. All of a sudden Dad called us into one of the rooms and wanted to know which one of us had been jumping on the new bed. We all said we hadn't been. Dad had noticed footprints on the mattress, so he measured our shoe sizes with the size of the prints on the bed. Mine were the closest, so I got punished. Dad spanked me, put me in a room and made me sit there until they were ready to go home which was a long time. But I hadn't done it and I didn't know who did. I wish he had been willing to talk about it and listen to me. I've often wondered why he punished me and how he feels about it.

If parents reasoned with their children and were open to reason in turn, misapplied punishment like this would be less likely to happen.

The *sixth* and final factor involved in the effectiveness of punishment is the *relationship* between parent and child. It is so important that its influence overrides the other five factors. After many years of reviewing research and listening to numerous people talk about their childhoods, I have become convinced that the moderate use of physical punishment doesn't make as much difference in how children turn out as people who take extreme positions would have us believe. Spanking in a child's background deserves neither the credit nor the blame it so often gets in determining whether children turn out to be winsome, successful adults or loathsome failures. What does make a difference is the level of affection and how the affection is played out in the many ways by which parents influence their children.

In a home where a child feels accepted and loved, physical punishment is interpreted by the child as evidence of concern, provided that the spankings are moderate in severity, infrequent and just. The following memory illustrates this:

> One time I snotted off to my dad and stomped up the stairs. He ran up after me and I knew by the look on his face that a spanking was coming. He swatted me good. I pleaded, "No, no, I'm sorry," and bawled. I didn't cry because it hurt physically, but because I thought I was being treated unfairly. Later I realized I was being treated fairly—I deserved the spanking.

This girl's parents are intelligent, reasonable, loving people who occasionally lost their patience with her and spanked. Today the daughter is doing very well, on schedule developmentally, pleasant and responsible. But this is not because she was spanked. Her parents did so many things right in the way they raised her that spankings played a minor role. While spankings were not very beneficial to her development, neither were they detrimental. Since the home environment was so positive, she interpreted the spankings in a positive manner.

Contrast the home environment of the case above with one where spankings were unpredictable, frequent and unjust:

> I was a quiet child because I was afraid of my dad. If he raised his voice at me, I would cry. This made him mad, so he'd yell at me to shut up. If I didn't quit crying he would whip me to give me something to cry about, as he put it. If I would hiccup after crying, this made him all the madder, especially if it happened in front of company. I got whipped for talking to company without being spoken to first, for turning my back on my dad when he was speaking to me and also to make me agree that he was right. Sometimes I got whipped just for walking by him when he was in a bad mood.

Such punitiveness obviously is poor parenting. But even in such an extreme case, it is not the physical punishment by itself which is the cause of developmental problems. Growing up in the household of a person like this would leave a child emotionally damaged, regardless of how much she was actually whipped. Punishment is only one part of discipline, and the father's techniques in the other areas were equally poor. The whippings were but one manifestation of a mean spirit.

Research would lead us to predict that this girl is at high risk for developing her own psychopathologies. Fortunately she became involved in a supportive, church youth group in adolescence. Today she attributes the resilience which enabled her to survive the abuse and rejection of her home to a religious conversion. Although emotionally scarred and struggling, she is doing remarkably well as she approaches the end of her teen years.

Punishment Used to Communicate Displeasure

The final use of punishment is as a means of nonverbal communication. Sometimes parents—even those who do not want to spank or approve of spanking—do so out of desperation. Their frustration heats up and finally boils over. Every parent feels the urge to strike at the child in those moments of impatience and anger. Fortunately, most are able to control the impulse. For those who occasionally give in, the use of the following guidelines will protect them from getting carried away. This requires *parental* discipline.

1. When you become so frustrated that you feel like you have to spank, view the spanking not as punishment, but as a message which you are sending to:
   a. obtain the child's immediate attention
   b. remind the child of your authority
   c. quickly terminate a dangerous behavior
   d. convey how upset, angry, frustrated you are
   e. let the child know how strongly you feel about the misbehavior

   Afterwards, regard the spanking as an indication that words failed, that communication broke down. Fix the problem by sending the message more adequately in other ways at other times. A spanking is an exclamation point—not a complete sentence.

2. Be spontaneous. Don't threaten to do it, do it. Do it when it expresses honestly and quickly how you are responding emotionally to the situation. A spanking delivered after you have cooled off is calculated and mechanical; what is really an emotional expression of frustration is then disguised as a rational act, and that is confusing. This is why Mark Twain thought his advice "Never strike a child except in anger" was an

improvement on the old adage, "Never strike a child in anger." It *is* better to wait until you have cooled off, of course, but the reason it is better to wait is because a spanking isn't needed then. When you wait you have time to figure out how to deal with your frustration in a more rational way.

3. Use your hand, never an object, and only on the child's bottom, which is a naturally padded area. Some experts, including James Dobson, recommend using an object because the hand "should be seen by the child as an object of love rather than an instrument of punishment" (Dobson, 1982, p. 159). But a spanking is an intimate act, as intimate as a hug. It expresses deep concern about what is going on between the two of you, and you need to express the concern in a personal way, not in an impersonal, objectified manner.

   Even more important, using your hand rather than an object safeguards against your crossing the line from punishment to abuse, which is a fine line easily violated in the heat of the moment. Your hand is softer and will not leave the welts and bruises which switches and paddles leave. Your hand also is enervated, able to send feedback to your brain about the sting of the blow, which a paddle cannot do.

4. Use one or two quick swats only. Remember, your goal is to get the child's attention, not to inflict pain. Fitzhugh Dodson recommends a "pow-wow" type of spanking: your "pow" followed by the child's "Wow!" (Dodson, 1970, p. 227). A teenager stated, "I was horrified by my father's spankings, but all they amounted to was one pat on the rear. The effect was entirely psychological and I always learned my lesson well."

5. Since the purpose of a spanking is to communicate displeasure, it is not a good time to deliver other messages about how you are doing this for the child's good, how it hurts you more than him or her or how upset God is by the child's disobedience. It is your displeasure which is being expressed in the spanking. Use words which fit the nonverbal message:

   > "Don't do that again!"
   > "Stop it!"
   > "I will not let you do that!"
   > "Not in this house!"
   > "Enough! I can't take any more of that!"
   > "I am really upset about this!"
   > "Listen to me!"

"Pay attention!"

"I'm serious!"

6. After a spanking, don't force children to apologize, make up or ask for forgiveness. While an apology might be due, it can't be produced upon demand. As stated in the Old Testament book of the Psalms, apologies come from "a broken and contrite heart" (51:17, NIV), not from a sore bottom. Before reconciliation is possible, grievances and feelings need to be acknowledged. Often this takes time. Parental suggestions about gestures of good will can pave the way for reconciliation if timed well, but forcing apology too quickly suppresses feelings and adds insult to injury:

> When we brothers and sisters did something to hurt each other, we were told to kiss and make up. Sometimes our parents would stand back and laugh while we did this, not a mean laugh, but a joking laugh. Anger would boil in me, but I'd go ahead and do it because I didn't want another spanking. It was humiliating.

In regard to your relationship with the child, after the two of you have recovered sufficiently from the spanking and you feel like making up, then reaffirm your love and care for each other. If you regret that you lost your temper and reacted as you did, apologize. Welcome whatever signs of contrition the child shows—but don't demand remorse. And if you are inclined to pray, do so about *your* need for patience and wisdom, and *your* desire to live in loving relationship with your child. If your child expresses similar yearnings, be grateful— but don't demand them.

7. Don't dwell on what happened. View the child's misbehavior as a mistake and get on with life. Steph remembered the period following a spanking this way:

> Mom told me to stay in my room alone until I was ready to come out and be happy. I wasn't about to come out quickly, because I felt so sorry for myself. I fell asleep, woke up a couple of hours later and decided to join the others. I tried my hardest to be mad at everyone and make them feel sorry for me, but they refused to do so. Instead they said things like, "Oh, was that a smile?" which made me laugh. Actually I was glad they didn't drag the punishment out. I wanted to forget it too.

Since the purpose of spanking in this manner is to communicate displeasure, it represents a failure of other means of influence. Therefore, parents minimize spankings when they teach what is to be learned in other ways, at other times—by demonstrating on a daily basis how to treat people, by sharing stories and concerns during No Problem moments, and by clarifying expectations and providing feedback about the child's behavior earlier, before disapproval builds to the point that its release is explosive. Parents can feel successful in this if they never spank twice for the same reason, or at least work towards the elimination of the need to spank.

Our Experience with Spanking

Lorna and I spanked our first child, Jeff. We spanked him because we didn't know what else to do. He was a very intense child, becoming engrossed in whatever activity caught his fancy, which meant that sometimes he forgot about, or was oblivious to, our instructions. We thought it was proper and necessary to spank to direct his attention. However, when Julie came along two years later, I discovered it wasn't necessary with her. I could induce tears and compliance very quickly with just a stern look, because she was so sensitive to my approval and disapproval. With Nathan, three years younger than Julie, we had no need to spank. He was such an easy child to manage that the thought of spanking him (or Jeff and Julie, by this time) was distasteful. By this time we were experienced parents, less anxious about misbehavior and more competent with other skills of the Parent's Problem Area.

The pattern of our experience seems to be fairly common. Most parents spank, at least occasionally. Studies of parents in England and the United States reported that 84% to 97% used physical punishment at some period in their children's lives (Steinmetz & Straus, 1973; Steinmetz & Straus, 1974). Although these data are old, I doubt that the situation has changed much. I consistently find among college students that being spanked in childhood follows the design of a bell-shaped curve—a few report never being spanked, a few report being spanked very often and the large majority remember being spanked occasionally.

Our family's experience is common also in that children born earlier in the birth order tend to be spanked more than those born later. Those born later are reared by parents whose expectations have been modified by experience and who have developed a

Figure 12.1
Uses of Punishment

Use of Punishment	Illustrative Phrase	Goal	Recommendation
To render retribution	"Eye for eye, tooth for tooth."	To equalize wrongs	Don't use. Not a moral or practical necessity.
To make restitution	"Undo to others as you would have them undo to you."	To right the wrong	Use. Calls attention to consequences to others, rather than self.
To inhibit undesirable behavior	"Does it work?"	To suppress misbehavior without producing unwanted side effects.	Depends on several factors. Effective in short-term if timed well, not too intense, consistent, infrequent, and especially effective if accompanied by reasoning. Long-term effect depends on quality of parent-child relationship.
To communicate displeasure	"Stop it!"	To get child's attention	Other means of communication preferable. But normal and appropriate if kept within guidelines.

variety of ways to influence their children, compared with the novices who raise firstborns.

Since spanking is such a common technique among parents, I am not surprised when young parents assume that they need to spank, nor do I tell them that they should never do so. My wish for them is that they gain confidence in their resourcefulness as parents, so that spanking comes to play a small part and not a lead role in the drama of their parent-child interactions.

Parents who used to spank and now regret it, like Lorna and I, needn't be hard on themselves. In the long-term it isn't going to make much difference. More important than whether or not they spanked is the quality of their relationships with their children. How they live with their children in the present is far more important than anything that happened in the past.

A Word to Religious Parents

Thus far in this chapter I have not made reference to the biblical wisdom in the book of Proverbs, "He who spares the rod hates his son, but he who loves him is diligent to discipline him" (13:24, RSV). I must do so, however, since it has been given a position of prominence in parenting advice. Some parents seem to base their entire thoughts about discipline on this one verse and questions about sparing the rod are inevitably raised whenever punishment is discussed.

Old Testament scholars suggest that the term rod had several different meanings. One meaning no doubt referred to an instrument which was used to punish, just as people today refer to a paddle or switch. Several other references from the book of Proverbs seem to use the term in this way; for example, ". . . a rod is for the back of him who is void of understanding" (10:13b, KJV).

In the Old Testament book of Exodus, rod also was used to denote authority, equated with the king's scepter which was carried as a badge of command. (". . . and in his hand Moses took the rod of God" (4:20b, RSV.) A third meaning is its reference to a stick used by shepherds to guide and protect sheep (for example, "your rod and your staff, they comfort me," in the 23rd Psalm).

When modern readers attend only to the punishment reference of the term, they do not fully understand what the proverbs about the rod meant to the original readers. Even when rod refers to an instrument of punishment, as it probably does in the "spare the rod" proverb, the term would have evoked more than the single image in the mind of the ancient Hebrew.

The fact that modern readers interpret the "spare the rod" proverb too narrowly is seen in that its first half, which focuses on physical punishment, is well known. However, its second half, which speaks of discipline, is virtually ignored; "He who spares the rod hates his son, but he who loves him is careful to discipline him." The construction of the sentence does not imply that the opposite of sparing the rod is using the rod. The opposite of sparing the rod is disciplining the child. To the Hebrew this involved more than physical punishment; it had to do with incorporating the child into the community of faith which took place in the process of living together, as noted in the Old Testament book of Deuteronomy:

> These commandments that I give you today are to be upon your hearts. Impress them on your children. Talk about them when you sit at home and when you walk along the road, when you lie down and when you get up. (6:6-7, NIV)

Punishment is but one part of discipline and cannot be its basis.

Determining what a passage of scripture meant to the original reader is only half the job of scriptural interpretation. The other half is to apply the essence of what it meant originally to the life of the modern reader who is in a different historical and cultural setting.

The books of the Bible were written for different purposes, with their content derived from a variety of sources and directed to different audiences. The book of Proverbs is part of the "wisdom literature" of the Old Testament and consists of a collection of the court wisdom and folk sayings of that time. Since using the rod was the wisdom of that time, it was included in the collection of admonishments which the people of God treasured. But times change, and so does advice.

Proverbs also says, "Drink water from your own cistern, flowing water from your own well" (5:15, RSV). Does this mean that we shouldn't use water from the city water supply? Of course not; the wisdom of Proverbs was oriented to the conveniences of that time. There undoubtedly were good reasons for following that advice then, but today we have a steady supply of safe water.

So too with child-rearing. Advice changes. The essence of much of the advice from Proverbs is that we are to take seriously our task as parents to pass on our faith and values to our children: "Train up a child in the way he should go, and when he is old he will not depart from it" (22:6, RSV).

According to Proverbs, whatever we do, including parenting, is to be moderated by patience and kindness. "A man of quick temper acts foolishly, but a man of discretion is patient" (14:17, RSV). Even our animals we are to treat kindly: "A righteous man has regard for the life of his beast, but the mercy of the wicked is cruel" (12:10, RSV).

I think Proverbs calls for us to continually pursue wisdom and understanding, the wisdom and understanding which will see us through times of social change, so that we will neither resist change nor be buffeted about by it. Wisdom is needed today as much as ever. Perhaps even more. In one of his poems, T. S. Eliot asks, "Where is the wisdom we have lost in knowledge, where is the knowledge we have lost in information?"

The stabilizing and adaptive wisdom which is good for all times comes from God, as stated in the Old Testament book of Proverbs:

For the Lord gives wisdom;
from his mouth come knowledge and understanding;
he stores up sound wisdom for the upright;
he is a shield to those who walk in integrity,
guarding the paths of justice
and preserving the way of the saints. (2:6-8, RSV)

May each of us be granted the wisdom we need to develop many resources for rearing our children, so that we use the old method of physical punishment by the rod less and less.

Questions for Thought and Discussion about this Chapter are on page 301.

13. Applying Behavior Modification

Psychologists working with rats and pigeons in research laboratories in the 1930s, '40s and '50s observed how animals acquire, maintain and get rid of habits of behavior. They observed that habits are acquired when behavior is rewarded; when the behavior is not rewarded, habits tend to disappear. This concept is simple, but its potential for application was demonstrated by training animals to do unusual things; for example, pigeons to play ping-pong or rats to play the piano. More serious projects included training whales to recover objects from the ocean floor and pigeons to guide missiles and to search for people lost at sea.

The key to these achievements is that the trainer starts with something the animal does and gradually changes the exact response that is reinforced. The behavior is "shaped" in small steps, closer and closer to the final desired response.

Since the 1960s, psychologists have been teaching parents and teachers to manage behavior of children by using techniques based on the same principles of reinforcement used in the animal projects. In clinics, schools and homes, the techniques have been employed to control the wild behavior of the aggressive child and the bizarre behavior of the autistic child; to teach speech and self-care skills to retarded children; and to curb such habits as tantrums, bed-wetting, thumb-sucking, overeating, whining and procrastination. Programs which use reinforcement principles to alter behavior are known generally as behavior modification programs.

Behavior modification emerged in the 1960s at the crest of the wave of behaviorism.[1] As behaviorism declined in influence, behavior modification became less visible in the American psychology scene. Nevertheless, it remains an important tool for parents, teachers and counselors, and deserves to be studied. Whether or not parents apply behavior modification in a systematic way, the study of behavior modification will help them to understand how they and their children influence each other's behavior in daily life.

One goal of this chapter is to teach the step-by-step application of behavior modification to problems of the Parent's Problem Area. Another goal is to teach the proper use of the vocabulary of behavioral psychology, which must be learned before behavior modification can be applied effectively (or criticized fairly). The concepts underlying behavior modification are easy to grasp if terms are used precisely.

These concepts will be explained as each step of the procedure is covered. Use of the procedures will be illustrated at the end of the chapter with several applications to problems of the Parent's Problem Area.

Step I: Specify the Behavior to Be Changed

In behavior modification, a specific behavior which is bothersome to the parents is targeted for improvement. Parents might be critical of a child's messiness, for example. But messiness is too broad for specific focus. Does it include sloppy handwriting? Disgusting table manners? Dirty or wrinkled clothing? Cluttered bedroom? Items dropped on floor of family room? Unkempt hair? Worn-out or untied shoes?

Behavior modification requires parents to pick a specific behavior

---

[1] Behavior modification is based primarily on B. F. Skinner's (e.g., 1953) work in learning and the experimental analysis of behavior, and the social learning theory of Albert Bandura (e.g., Bandura & Walters, 1963). Skinner concentrated on the role of reinforcement in learning, and Bandura studied learning which occurs vicariously through the observation of models. Parent education programs built on this foundation emphasize the use of instruction, role play, modeling, rehearsal and cuing (coaching) to change the behavior of parents.

Among the best parent education materials, in my opinion, are Wesley Becker's *Parents Are Teachers: A Child Management Program* (Becker, 1971), Roger McIntire's *For Love of Children: Behavioral Psychology for Parents* (McIntire, 1970), and Gerald Patterson's *Living With Children: New Methods for Parents and Teachers* (Patterson, 1976). Numerous newer pamphlets, tapes and films are available today for training parents in behavior management techniques. The best source is Research Press.

to modify, rather than tackle the general trait "messy." As a rule of thumb, the behavior should be defined so specifically that someone else could observe it and carry out the reinforcement program.

Following are several general concerns of parents which are too broad for behavior modification. Each is followed by a specific, behavioral definition of the problem:

- Child is "slow." Child wears pajamas for a long time in the morning before getting dressed.
- Child doesn't take care of teeth. Child doesn't brush after meals or before going to bed.
- Child is "shy." Child doesn't greet guests.
- Teenager is "irresponsible." Teenager uses car without replacing gasoline.
- Teenager stays out "late." Teenager does not return by 10:00 on week nights and 12:00 on weekend nights.

Behavior modification is not concerned with the child's "personality" because the concept of personality is too general. But since a child's personality consists of characteristic ways of behaving, the child's personality can be altered to the extent that the specific patterns of behavior can be altered.

Behavior modification *is* concerned with clearly defined behaviors, and the concern is limited to a small number of such behaviors at any one time.

Step II: Obtain a Baseline Count

A baseline count is obtained by counting how often the specified behavior occurs over several days. This is to make the procedure more objective, since parents can become so reactive to the problem behavior that they exaggerate its frequency and are poor judges of improvement.[2]

For the problem behaviors mentioned above, baselines like these could be obtained:

- At about the same time each evening, count how many items are dropped on the family room floor.

---

[2] Behavior modification's emphasis on objectivity is due to its origins in behaviorism. The radical behaviorists who developed the methods of the "scientific analysis of behavior" insisted that behavior which could be observed and measured was the only behavior worthy of study. This emphasis on objectivity resulted in a foundation of research findings upon which behavior modification rests. Behavior modification's claims about what works and what doesn't work tend to have more empirical support than the claims of other parent education programs.

- Keep track of the number of minutes the child spends in pajamas before being dressed for the day.
- Fill in a chart showing whether or not teeth are brushed after meals and before bed.
- Note the instances of household guests and the child's response upon their arrival.
- Use a chart to record the times the car was used and whether or not gas was replaced.
- Write on the calendar the time the teenager returns home at night.

In psychological research, the baseline count probably would be made without the child's knowledge. But in the home situation, it can be done with the child's knowledge. Explaining in an unemotional way that a record of a particular behavior will be kept, and placing the chart where the child can see it, are likely to have a positive impact on the problem. In fact, sometimes the baseline count eliminates the problem and the parent doesn't need to go beyond this step in the procedure.

Step III: Terminate Reinforcement for the Undesirable Behavior

Most behavior, including misbehavior, is assumed to be learned. If misbehavior is learned, it can be unlearned. The process of unlearning a behavior is called extinction. Each of these concepts will be explained in this section.

Misbehavior is Learned

From the behaviorist point of view, people do most of what they do because they have learned to do so. Their style of dress, the type of music they listen to, their choice of friends, their work habits, their vocabulary and speech accent are all behaviors that are learned.

The word "learn" in the language of behaviorists has a more technical meaning than the word has in ordinary use. In the language of behaviorists, learning refers to changes in behavior which are a result of experience. The principle governing changes in behaviors like those mentioned above, is that behavior which is rewarded tends to be repeated; behavior which is not rewarded tends to disappear. When behaviorists use the word "learning," they are referring to the "acquisition," "maintenance" and "extinction" of behaviors. The connection between a particular behavior and its reinforcer is called a "contingency." The study of the learning process, in the behaviorist tradition, is the study of behavior-reinforcement contingencies.

Behaviorists argue convincingly that parents are constantly teaching their children how to behave by the ways they reinforce them. Sometimes parents teach children desirable behaviors and sometimes they teach children undesirable behaviors. This happens whether or not parents are aware of it. For example, if a child cries and screams at the grocery store and finally gets the gum he wants, he has been reinforced for crying and screaming and is more likely to do it again. If a baby smears food on her face and the family laughs, she is learning to smear food on her face.

Children teach parents how to behave, also. If parents nag and nag until finally the child complies with a request, the parents have been reinforced for nagging and are likely to continue the practice. If parents allow a child to stay up later than usual and the child is unusually cooperative, the rewarding behavior of the child increases the likelihood that the parents will postpone bedtime again in the future.

From this point of view, understanding the way reinforcement works is the key to understanding the behavior of children. For example, if children are honest, this view assumes that they have been reinforced for being honest in the past. On the other hand, if children cheat, it's because cheating has paid off for them in the past more than honesty has. Similarly, children learn to be courteous and they learn to be rude. They learn to complete their chores and they learn to shirk their duties.

Understanding how reinforcement works is also the key to correcting misbehavior. The principles of reinforcement can be used to extinguish inappropriate behavior and to shape appropriate behavior to take its place.

Extinction

Extinction is the process of reducing the frequency of a behavior by ending its reinforcement. Behavior modification assumes that the misbehavior occurs because it has paid off in the past. Children get what they want by whining, tattling, procrastinating, hitting and so on. Sometimes the attention of the parent is the pay-off.

On the surface, it doesn't seem like parental nagging, scolding or even punishment could be reinforcing to children, but attention is a powerful social reward, even when it comes in negative forms. At any rate, something is reinforcing the misbehavior or it wouldn't exist. Behavior modification helps parents to figure out what reinforcers maintain the misbehavior and to establish more desirable contingencies.

To break the cycle of misbehavior and negative control which parent and child have gotten into, Step III calls for the parent to stop responding to the misbehavior and ignore it, unless there are reasons why it cannot be ignored (reasons of safety, for example).

When reinforcement is terminated, the behavior will not disappear immediately. In fact, the initial effect may be that the behavior will *increase* in frequency and intensity. The parent has changed the rules of the interaction to which parent and child had become accustomed, so when the parent stops responding, the child will probably try harder than ever to get a response, using the method which worked in the past. If the parent stops responding to temper tantrums, for example, the child probably will throw bigger tantrums than ever for awhile.

But if the parent steadfastly remains unemotional and withdraws attention when the misbehavior occurs, it will begin to decrease in frequency. This means not criticizing, not looking angry and not threatening to punish physically. Instead of using these negative control methods, the parent concentrates on terminating the payoffs, whatever they were, and using attention withdrawal as a consequence. Since attention is a powerful social reinforcer, its withdrawal is a powerful punisher. This is especially effective with such misbehaviors as clownishness, excessive dependence, tattling and whining.

Reprimands

If the misbehavior is the type that can't be ignored, parents can respond to it with brief but firm reprimands. Reprimands are most effective if they specify exactly what the child is to stop doing:

"Franny, stop teasing your sister!"

"Michelle, you may not drop your food on the floor!"

"Stop right there, Ellie! Take those muddy shoes off and put them on the porch."

In order to keep reprimands from becoming out of balance, Van Houten (1980) suggests parents do something each time they reprimand, to remind themselves to deliver praise before they reprimand again. For example, a wrist watch can be used as a reminder. After a reprimand is given, the watch is turned over so that the face is not showing. Before another reprimand can be given and the watch turned back, a praise must be given.

Time Out

Time Out is a procedure which helps parents to stop reacting to misbehavior in ways which are inadvertently reinforcing; it also helps them withdraw their attention in a systematic way. Time Out means time out from positive reinforcement.

Time Out requires a place where misbehaving children can be placed for a few minutes without social interaction. Patterson (1976) recommends the bathroom for this purpose. Crary (1979) suggests a hallway or a small area screened by a piece of furniture. The ideal location is far enough away from the social activity that children will be unable to provoke attention, but near enough to social activity that they will know what they are missing.

Suppose the parent is attempting to reduce the teasing behavior of a child. When teasing occurs, the parent says, "That was a tease. Go to Time Out. You can come back when you are ready to play nicely." This places emphasis on the desired behavior (playing nicely), rather than on punishment of the misbehavior (teasing). It also gives the child responsibility for making the decision to cooperate with others or to remain isolated.

If this doesn't work, parents can use a timer to determine the end of Time Out. "I'll set the timer by the door for two minutes. When it goes off, you can come out."

The parent stays calm when placing a child in Time Out, even though the child is likely to fuss about it the first few times. If the child kicks the door or screams, the parent can say, "OK, that's another minute." If the protest continues, the parent can tell the child that the time begins after he or she becomes quiet.

If the child makes a mess in the Time Out area, the parent instructs the child to clean it up. If the mess isn't cleaned up, the parent does it, but removes some privilege (watching television for a given period, for example).

Time Out periods are brief, only two, three or four minutes. Several short Time Outs are better than one long one, because the parents have more opportunity to teach the lesson, and children have more opportunities to learn from the Time Out experience. Longer periods tend to be punitive ("Now I've had it! Go to Time Out for 100 minutes!"), and that kind of punitiveness is what behavior modification is designed to avoid. Time Outs should be viewed as a calming device for both parent and child, rather than a form of punishment. Neither should Time Outs be used as threats

("You do that one more time, and you get a Time Out!").

Since the Time Out technique is not recommended for the very young child, Elizabeth Crary (1979) suggests an adaptation called the Tiny Time Out for toddlers. It serves the same purpose, but does not isolate the young child as much. The parent interrupts an unacceptable behavior by lifting the toddler out of the situation and setting him or her down a short distance away. As the toddler is moved, the parent explains briefly and assertively why (for example, "No hitting people!"). The parent then takes care of the first situation if attention there is needed. After a few moments the parent returns to the offending toddler to engage the child in social interaction, once again repeating the rule.

For children from about two to about 11, Time Out (or the Tiny Time Out) is an effective tool, if used in a consistent and firm manner. Time Out is not recommended for adolescents. There are other kinds of reinforcers which can be applied to the older child.

Step IV: Reinforce the Desirable Behavior

Step III calls for parents to stop reinforcing the misbehavior, but this by itself does not necessarily take care of the problem. At the same time that the misbehavior is extinguished through nonreinforcement, the behavior which is to take its place needs to be made more likely to occur through positive reinforcement.

The Competing Behavior

For every misbehavior, there is an opposite or competing behavior to take its place. This is what is reinforced in Step IV. The opposite of dropping things on the floor is putting them away. The opposite of staying in pajamas is getting dressed. Not brushing teeth is replaced by brushing teeth. Not greeting guests is replaced by greeting guests. Not buying gasoline is the misbehavior; buying gasoline is the desired behavior. Coming in late is the misbehavior which cannot occur simultaneously with coming in on time.

Modifying the Environment

The parent can make the desired behavior more likely to occur by modifying the environment. For example, putting things away is more likely to occur if there are adequate storage shelves, boxes and hangers. A child is more likely to get dressed if favorite clothes are laid out conveniently. Teeth are more likely to be brushed if the sink, mirror, toothbrush and toothpaste are conveniently located and attractive to the child.

Catching the Child Being Good

In order to reinforce the desired behavior, parents need to catch children being good. Sometimes this means that they plan ahead to be ready for the competing behavior when it appears. Suppose a parent is bothered about the fighting and yelling which take place in the back seat when she drives the children to school. She considers having some treats on hand to use to get them to quiet down, but decides that that would be rewarding the boisterous behavior which she wants to extinguish. Instead, she keeps the treats beside her and the first chance she has to reinforce a period of cooperative play in the back seat she passes out the treats.

Shaping

Some behaviors would never be reinforced if parents waited until they appeared to reinforce them. Instead of waiting, therefore, parents can break down the desired behavior into small steps of improvement. Then with each small advance in the preferred direction, reinforcement is used. The parent gradually requires the child to show more and more improvement to earn rewards. This process is called shaping, because the parent shapes the behavior in closer and closer approximations to the goal, just like a sculptor shapes an object out of clay.

To shape better behavior in the car, for example, the mother could announce as they leave home that she has some rewards for them if they remain quiet. Then after a brief period of quiet, she rewards them. On the next trip, she makes the reward contingent on a slightly longer period of quiet. She might decide then to work on pleasant conversation. She starts by rewarding a single incident of pleasantness. On subsequent trips she requires more and more of the behavior she wants. Pleasant, cooperative behaviors eventually replace the fighting and yelling behaviors.

Positive Reinforcement, Negative Reinforcement and Punishment

Four different types of consequences follow behavior (not counting a neutral response as a consequence): (1) something pleasant can be added, (2) something unpleasant can be added, (3) something pleasant can be taken away and (4) something unpleasant can be taken away (see Figure 13.1). (1) and (4) are reinforcing, and (2) and (3) are punishing. For example:

(1) A child visits amiably at the table and at the end of the meal is kissed by a parent. The amiable behavior resulted in the addition of

something pleasant (assuming that the kiss is pleasant to the child). When something pleasant happens after a behavior is performed, the behavior is positively reinforced and is more likely to occur in the future. Kissing was a positive reinforcer for visiting.

(2) A child exaggerates an event during the table conversation, and the others ridicule her. Her stretching the truth resulted in the addition of something unpleasant. When something unpleasant happens after a behavior is performed, the behavior is punished and is less likely to occur in the future. Stretching the truth was punished by ridicule.

(3) A child quarrels with the others at the table, and at the end of the meal is told by her parents she will get no dessert. Her quarrelsome behavior resulted in the removal of something pleasant. Taking away something pleasant punishes the behavior which preceded it, and the behavior is less likely to occur again. Taking away dessert was a punishment for quarrelsomeness.

Figure 13.1
*Four Ways of Changing a Behavior through
its Consequences*

| | | **Condition** | |
		Pleasant	*Unpleasant*
Added		*Positive Reinforcement* *(strengthens behavior)*	*Punishment* *(weakens behavior)*
Action			
Removed		*Punishment* *(weakens behavior)*	*Negative Reinforcement* *(strengthens behavior)*

(4) Because a child, who usually is quite quarrelsome, goes through an entire meal without fighting with the others, her parents excuse her from having to do the dishes. The removal of something unpleasant (doing the dishes) negatively reinforces the behavior which preceded it (being fun to be around) and *increases* the likelihood that that behavior will occur again. Not having to do the dishes negatively reinforced good behavior at the table.

Note that both positive reinforcement and negative reinforcement increase the occurrence of the preceding behavior. Negative reinforcement, in spite of the way its name sounds, is not one of the two types of punishment (shown in Figure 13.1). To remember what negative reinforcement is, think of it as *relief,* which would have been a more apt term for this type of consequence.

In behavior modification, positive reinforcement of desired behavior is emphasized, and punishment of undesired behavior is downplayed. Without training in behavior modification, parents often do just the opposite; they take good behavior for granted, rather than reinforce it, and rely on punishment to suppress misbehavior. When I ask children and adults to talk about ways problems were handled, they rarely tell stories which illustrate the use of positive reinforcement to increase good behavior, but they have many punishment stories to tell.

Types of Positive Reinforcement

Positive reinforcers can be divided into three categories: material, activity and social (see Figure 13.2). Material reinforcers are concrete objects: food, candy, toys, games, books, marking pens, clothes and so on.

Activity reinforcers include the many things individuals enjoy doing. Examples include watching television, doing a special project, going out to see a movie or to eat, entertaining guests, sleeping late and so on. Any activity which is more preferred can be used to reinforce a less preferred activity. This is known formally as the Premack Principle (named after the psychologist who described it); informally, it's called Grandma's Rule (because parents have long known that this is an effective means of behavior control).[3]

Social reinforcers include attention, approval and affection in the many ways these are expressed, both verbally and nonverbally:

---

[3] The Premack Principle stated more technically is that a behavior which occurs more frequently (given the opportunity to do various behaviors) will serve as a reinforcer for a behavior which occurs less frequently.

Figure 13.2
Potential Positive Reinforcers

Age	Material	Activity	Social	Tokens

Preschool	Balloons
	Toys
	Books
	Puzzles
	Favorite snacks
	Stuffed animals
		Play with
		  friends
		Read to child
		Tell stories
		Go to park, for
		  walk to
		  favorite store
		Play with child
		  in yard
		Extended
		  bedtime
		Skip nap
		Watch TV
		Help in kitchen,
		  garage or
		  yard
		Choose menu
			Specific praise
			Hugs, kisses,
			  squeezes
			Toss in air
			Piggyback rides
			Praise child to
			  someone else
			Take picture of
			  child doing
			  well
				Stars on chart
				Pennies, coins
				Stickers
				Happy faces

Elementary
School
	Stickers
	Books, games
	Puzzles
	Favorite food
	Tape player,
	  radio
	Allowance
		Play with
		  friends
		Overnight with
		  relative or
		  friend
		Help in kitchen,
		  yard, garage
		Eat out
		Watch TV
		Freedom from
		  chores
		Extended
		  bedtime
		Time with
		  parent alone
			Specific praise
			Hugs, kisses,
			  smiles
			"Ok" gesture
			Ruffle hair
			Pat on back
			Praise child to
			  someone else
			"Give me five"
				Marks on chart
				Points
				Poker chips
				Happy faces
				Stars
				Special badges

Middle School	Music tapes
	Favorite foods
	Clothes
	Books,
	  magazines
	Items for
	  make-up,
	  hair styling,
	  shaving
	Allowance
		Free time
		Watch movie
		Decorate room
		Freedom from
		  chores
		Extended
		  curfew
		Overnight with
		  friends
		Transportation
		  (with
		  friends) to
		  shopping
		  mall,
		  restaurant,
		  movie
		Sleep late
		Time with
		  parent
			Specific praise
			Hugs
			Smiles
			Joking around
			Words of
			  friendliness,
			  praise,
			  appreciation
			Thumbs up
			"Ok" gesture
				Points
				Coupons
				Contingency
				  contracts

High School	Books
	Tapes
	Sports
	  equipment
	Tools
	TV
	Computer
	Telephone
	Clothes
	Favorite food
	Car keys
	Money
		Decorate room
		Watch TV,
		  movies
		Talk on phone
		Free time
		Shopping
		School activities
			Specific praise
			Eye contact
			Physical
			  contact (if
			  comfortable)
			Thumbs up
			"Ok" gesture
			Words of praise,
			  appreciation,
			  support
				Coupons
				Contingency
				  contracts

listening, smiles, praise, hugs, pats on the back, stars or checks on a chart, public esteem, acceptance into groups and so on.

Token Economies

Points, coupons or "tokens" (for example, plastic chips) are used sometimes in behavior modification. After a certain number of points or tokens have been earned, they are exchanged for material objects or activity privileges in the same way that adults work for two weeks to earn paychecks which are used to purchase consumer goods and services.

One of the advantages of tokens is that the child is able to select the reward from an array of possible rewards, which makes the contingency more likely to be successful.

Contingency Contracts

A contingency contract is an agreement between parent and child that each will deliver something the other values. For example, a parent might want the child to hang up items of clothing instead of drop them on the floor. The child would like a new jacket. So they make a contract which specifies that the child is to hang up clothes for a certain period of time after which the parent is to take the child shopping for a new jacket.

Step V: Obtain Another Count and Compare With the Baseline

In Step V the parent counts the misbehavior, using the same procedures to measure it that were used in Step II, to see if there has been any change. (In many programs, the parents keep continuous records, so that the Step V comparison with the baseline can be done at any time.) If the misbehavior has been satisfactorily reduced, the behavior management plan has been effective, and the parent goes on to Step VI.

If the frequency of the misbehavior has not improved satisfactorily, the parent goes back to Step IV and tries again with different reinforcers[4] or with smaller steps. Not every attempt will be successful. A reinforcer which works for one child may not work for another. Some children, for example, respond to charts. Other children resent that kind of record keeping but will work for special privileges. For some, money is an incentive, and for others it is not.

---

[4] A "reinforcer" technically is not a reinforcer unless it affects the behavior. The consequence of a behavior can be called a reinforcer (or punisher) if it changes the frequency of the behavior, but not just because it sems to be a desirable or undesirable condition.

Most children value gestures of affection but some resist such displays. The parent needs to find what works.

Another reason programs fail is because too much change is expected too quickly. If this is the case, parents can go back to Step IV and try again by reinforcing smaller improvements, shaping the behavior more gradually.

Step VI: Shift from a Continuous Reinforcement Schedule to an Intermittent Schedule; from Material Reinforcements to Social Reinforcements

When the desired behavior is established, parents can "thin" the reinforcement by shifting to an intermittent schedule. They also can diminish the use of material reinforcers while maintaining the frequency of the desired behavior with social reinforcers.

Intermittent Reinforcement

In Step IV parents select a reinforcer to use when the desired behavior begins to appear. At first, reinforcement is given each time improvement occurs. This is called a continuous reinforcement schedule. Later, after improvement has become established, reinforcement is delivered occasionally rather than continuously. This is called an intermittent schedule of reinforcement.

One reason for doing this is that most reinforcers, if used too often, lose their reinforcing value. This is obviously true of things like toys and food; children become satiated with them fairly quickly. But it's equally true of money, privileges and even praise and affection. All lose their effectiveness as reinforcers after the level of satiation is reached.

Another reason for shifting to an intermittent reinforcement schedule is that it frees the parent from the constant supervision which continuous schedules require. Fortunately, occasional reinforcement is effective. Children (and adults) will work hard for an occasional pay-off. For example, persons who don't golf well may still play frequently. They hit the ball well occasionally, and this is so satisfying that they keep playing, hoping for another good stroke each time they swing. Children will greet guests in a friendly manner if they are complimented on their friendliness occasionally.

Behavior which is maintained with occasional and unpredictable reinforcement is highly resistant to extinction. Suppose there are two children who have the habit of throwing temper tantrums. The parent of one gives in each time a tantrum occurs (continuous reinforcement). The parent of the other usually doesn't give in, but occasionally does (intermittent reinforcement). Now suppose that both parents decide that never again will they give in to a tantrum. Which child will persist longer with the tantrums? The second one will, because the change in contingencies is less noticeable. Behavior which is reinforced after a long period of nonreinforcement is difficult to extinguish.

This partial reinforcement effect applies to the maintenance of desirable behavior, just as it applies to the unintended maintenance of misbehavior. Once a child has learned to put things away, rather than drop them on the floor, an occasional word of appreciation will maintain the neat behavior. The child that has been trained to get out of pajamas and into daytime clothes more quickly doesn't need to be complimented each time this occurs.

Maintenance With Social Reinforcers

Social reinforcers almost always are used in behavior modification, if not by themselves, then coupled with material or activity reinforcers. The material and activity reinforcements are gradually withdrawn so that the desired behavior eventually is under the control of social rewards only.

In one preschool classroom, for example, teachers wore carpenter aprons filled with M&Ms at the beginning of the year. Whenever an M&M was awarded, teachers also smiled, touched or complimented. By Thanksgiving, M&Ms had been replaced by tokens which were exchanged for marking pens, scissors, pads of paper, coloring books and so on. Social reinforcers continued to be used. By early spring, classroom privileges, rather than objects, were used in the token exchange. By late spring, the social reinforcers alone were used to reward good behavior of the children.

Summary of Basic Concepts Underlying Behavior Modification

Misbehavior is assumed to be learned. If it is learned, it can be unlearned, and appropriate behavior can be learned to take its place. To achieve this goal, the parent rewards the desired behavior more and the undesired behavior less. To reward the desired behavior more, three categories of positive reinforcers are used: material, activity and social. Of these three types, social reinforcers are emphasized for long-term control of the behavior. Intermittent reinforcement is used to maintain the desired behavior after it has been acquired in order to free the parent from continuous monitoring of the behavior, to avoid satiating the child on the reinforcer and to make the desired behavior more resistant to extinction.

Several applications of behavior modification procedures follow. In some the six steps (see Figure 13.3) were followed thoroughly, and in others the procedures were less thorough and more informal. Each used positive reinforcement, however, to achieve the desired change in behavior.

Figure 13.3
Behavior Modification Procedures

I. **Identify Behavior to be Changed**
   Write down exact behavior to be changed. Be specific.

II. **Obtain a Baseline Count**
   Record how often the misbehavior occurs over several hours or days.

III. **Terminate Reinforcement of Undesirable Behavior**
   Ignore undesirable behavior and do not criticize. (Undesirable behavior may increase for awhile.) Use Time Out if necessary.

IV. **Reinforce Desirable Behavior**
   When improvement in desirable behavior occurs, reinforce it with combination of material reward or behavioral privileges and social rewards. Modify environment, if possible, so that desirable behavior is more likely to occur.

V. **Obtain Another Count and Compare it With the Baseline**
   If there has been improvement, go on to Step VI. If there has not been improvement, go back to Step IV and try a different reinforcement or smaller steps.

VI. **Shift from a Continuous Reinforcement Schedule to an Intermittent Schedule; from Material Reinforcements to Social Reinforcements**
   When the desired behavior is improving, begin to reinforce less often. Keep using social reinforcers and diminish material reinforcers, if social reinforcers are sufficient to maintain the desired frequency.

Example of a Program to Deal with Child's Noncompliance

Step I: The parents of five-year-old Greg regularly ask him to do something five or six times before he begins to do it. They define the misbehavior as an instance in which a request goes unheeded by Greg.

Step II: Greg's parents count the number of "noncomplies" over a three-day period. The first request was not counted, but each reminder was counted as a noncomply. The average was 18 noncomplies per day.

Step III: Greg's parents became more aware that his noncompliance paid off. It led to arguments about the request, and while he ignored their request, he controlled their attention. Sometimes he got away with noncompliance because they forgot about the request, did it themselves or gave up. At the least, his noncompliance bought him time.

Greg's parents decided that they would make a request once, minimize their reminders and that they would not argue with him about requests.

Step IV: Greg's parents told him, "There are a lot of things you do which we really appreciate. But there is one thing you do which bothers us. When we ask you to do something, many times you don't do it. So we are going to use this chart to help you obey us better. Each time you obey you can put a star in the box on the chart. When you have earned five stars, you will get a special reward. When you don't obey, we will put a mark on the chart down here."

Each time Greg did what he was asked to do, he was given a star, touched affectionately and told how pleased they were: "That's great! You did it right away. Would you like to put the star on?"

His parents bought a variety of small, inexpensive items which are appealing to young children. They put them in a grab bag for use as rewards. As promised, they let him draw out a special reward after each set of five stars.

Step V: Greg's parents marked noncomplies on the bottom of the chart so they had a continuous count. After several days, noncomplies had dropped to an average of about three per day.

Step VI: After a few days, the number of stars required for a special gift was increased to six, then seven, and so on, until finally they gave him a treat once in awhile. They continued to compliment him for his minding right away, but no longer complimented him every time.

Example of Program for Carelessness at the Table

Step I: The Diller children frequently spilled their glasses at the table.

Steps II, III, IV: The usual parental responses to the accidents were that the mother complained about having to clean up the spills, and the father was critical of those who spilled and sent them from the table. Although the parents didn't understand how this could be maintaining the high rate of accidents, they decided it was time to try something else. They announced on Sunday that the family would go to their favorite ice cream place Friday night if they made it through the week without spilling their glasses.[5]

Step V, VI: The first week was successful; there were no spills and the family went out for ice cream. They did it again the following week and once again were successful. At that point, the program was discontinued. The children had learned that they were capable of not spilling, and the parents had learned that they didn't need to scold. The children spilled their glasses occasionally, but not as frequently as before. Once in awhile, after an enjoyable meal the family went to the ice cream store for dessert.

Example of Program for Putting Clothes in Hamper

The father of a three-year-old decided to teach her to put her dirty clothes in the hamper in her room by reinforcing the desired behavior with praise, as he was helping her get ready for bed. Since she was in the habit of using the hamper only about once a week, he waited until the next time she did so and immediately said, "Ruthie, I'm really pleased that you put your dirty clothes in the hamper." The next night she did it again and he said, "Hey, that's great! You remembered to put your clothes in the hamper!"

By the end of the second week the father decided to change the reinforcement schedule. The next time the daughter threw her clothes into the hamper he pretended to be involved in something else. She appeared to be disappointed that he didn't notice what she did and praise her for it, but he said nothing.

---

[5] The parents' choice of contingency turned out to be successful, but it probably would have been better to break down the desired behavior into smaller steps, rather than to seek such substantial improvement immediately. If too much improvement is expected, the desired behavior is too difficult for the children to attain, and the parents never get an opportunity to reinforce it. They could have started by reinforcing a single meal without accidents, then a single day, then two or three days and finally a week.

The following evening she put her clothes in the hamper again. This time, he paid attention to what she was doing and said, "Ruthie, you're really doing well! You remember to put your clothes in the hamper even when I'm too busy to watch." From then on she continued to use the hamper regularly, and he complimented her occasionally.

Example of Program for Helping Around the House

A parent was bothered that his son, Doug, wasn't helping as much as he should have been with household tasks. It seemed to the father that Doug resisted doing what he was told; the dad had come to think of Doug as lazy and irresponsible, and criticized Doug often. After reading about behavior modification, he decided to give it a try.

The father began by looking for things which Doug did which could be praised. In the next couple of days Doug mowed the lawn and took out the trash without being reminded to do so. However, when Doug was asked to go to the neighborhood store on an errand, he protested, and he left his dishes on the table after meals, in spite of the rule that all family members were to help clear the table.

Nevertheless, the father commented on how nice the lawn looked and how much he appreciated the help with the trash. Doug smiled at the recognition he had received but said nothing.

The next day Doug washed the car without being asked to do so and helped fold a load of clothes. That evening his dad told him, "Doug, you're really getting to be a help around the house. And I sure appreciate having a clean car!" He then asked Doug if he wanted to go to the football stadium parking lot to practice driving. Doug responded enthusiastically. They went to the stadium and both enjoyed the activity.

During the following weeks Doug helped more willingly with household tasks. Even though there were times when he was slow to respond to a job that needed to be done, his behavior was improved. His dad was pleased about the additional help the family was getting from Doug, and also pleased with the improvement in his relationship with his son.

Criticisms of Behavior Modification

Behavior modification has received more criticism than any other type of parent education program. I will present several criticisms and respond briefly as proponents of behavior modification would respond. I do not intend to be an apologist for behavior modification, but its defense deserves to be heard.

One of the criticisms is that behavior modification is superficial, since there is a lack of attention to emotional causes of misbehavior. Modifying the behavior is like treating symptoms and not the disease, critics claim. Proponents reply that symptoms are what people suffer from, so treating symptoms is worthwhile. Furthermore, emotional problems can be improved or alleviated if patterns of troublesome behavior are altered. The relationship between emotional problems and behavior problems is bi-directional. Each affects the other. For example, children who are overweight or who are aggressive suffer emotionally. Rather than focusing on the emotional needs, however, it might be more important to teach them better eating habits or better social skills.

Another criticism is that the strict behavior modification model treats the pigeon, rat and child alike — as if the child's mind doesn't exist. The reply of the strict behaviorist is that paying attention to the mind isn't necessary. Control over behavior is possible by modifying behavior-reinforcement contingencies.[6]

Another criticism is that the procedures (observing, recording and rewarding) are so demanding of parents that the procedures are impractical. Time, energy, concentration, use of such recording devices as counters and charts, and a supply of rewards are required. Proponents reply that the procedures help parents to be more objective and systematic about their attempts to control their children's behavior. The empirical base of behavior modification is what makes the case for giving up ineffective control methods and adopting more effective methods.

Those who find such forthright control of others distasteful are critical of behavior modification because it seems too manipulative or contrived. Proponents argue that parents are already attempting to influence their children, and the attempts are not always sucessful. They might as well do it in an informed and effective manner. Using *positive* reinforcement to bring about *positive* changes in behavior is not unethical. In fact, in situations where the child and family would best be served by behavior modification, it might be unethical *not* to use it.

---

[6] In practice, few psychologists today follow the strict behaviorist line. Behavioral researchers now pay more attention to the role of the mind in the learning process. For example, mental rehearsal of the behavior and knowledge of the behavior-reinforcement contingencies have been shown to speed learning. The phrase "cognitive behavior modification" is heard frequently in the clinical setting today.

A related criticism is that behavior modification techniques involve bribery. Proponents argue that this is not the case, if the techniques are used correctly. Bribery is a pay-off for an antisocial behavior. Behavior modification is designed to help parents *not* do this. Catching children being good in order to reward them is not bribery.

A final criticism, and the most important one, in my opinion, is that using external reinforcers (for example, material objects) works against the development of internal control of behavior. Critics have evidence that this can happen. In one study, for example, children who received a reward for drawing were less likely to draw at a later opportunity when rewards were not given, compared with children who had not been previously rewarded for drawing (Lepper, Greene & Nisbett, 1978). Psychologists concluded from this study and others similar to it, that children sometimes come to regard the reinforced behavior as work, and it loses intrinsic interest. This is most likely to happen when the reward is inappropriately large or inappropriate in type.

Proponents acknowledge that this can happen and recommend, therefore, that over-rewarding be avoided. Silberman and Wheelan (1980) suggest that external rewards are most appropriate if the desired behavior is very difficult, anxiety provoking or unappealing. There are enough instances like this that behavior modification is a useful tool to get the child's behavior moving in the right direction. External rewards can be withdrawn as soon as possible. Such internal rewards as self-determination, self-esteem, achievement, problem solving and creativity can also be supported by parents. Parents don't have to choose between external rewards and internal rewards for their children.

Contributions of Behavior Modification to Balanced Parenting

Behavior modification is not a complete approach to parenting. It fills only one small part of the circle of the Balanced Parenting Model. For example, behavior modification tends to disregard the emotional concerns of children. But balanced parents have another set of skills for the Child's Problem Area, and need not rely on behavior modification to do something for which it is not well suited (see Chapter 8, "Listening," and Chapter 9, "Encouraging Autonomy").

The use of behavior modification in the No Problem Area is inappropriate for parents who are able to enrich the parent-child relationship without couching what they do in behavioral language. For them, behavior modification in the No Problem Area is unnecessary and unnatural; they already possess relationship building skills.

However, behavior modification has potential for use in the No Problem Area by families with poor parent-child relationships. Love for one another is *felt* when loving behaviors are *performed*. The activities of the No Problem Area (playing in the yard together or doing favors for each other, for example) can be thought of as *relationship behaviors* which are reinforced through mutually satisfying affiliation with one another. Behavior modification can help parents establish more mutually rewarding contingencies.

Behavior modification is most appropriately used in the Parent's Problem Area, but even there it is but one tool. Other means of handling problems are possible, and for many parents and children, preferable, due primarily to the cumbersomeness of behavior modification. Keeping track of misbehaviors and desired behaviors, dispensing rewards and contriving reinforcement schedules all require effort. If parents can take care of problems with simpler, more natural methods, there is no need to bother with behavior modification procedures.

Behavior modification is best viewed, in my opinion, as remedial discipline. With children who lack the mental capacity or the social development to respond to other methods, behavior modification may be the best strategy. In general, the more abnormal the situation is, the more useful behavior modification is. An example of a family which could benefit by behavior modification is one in which a child is very aggressive and out of control. Behavior modification can help the parents to regain control of the home.

For parents, one of the most useful applications of behavior modification is in regard to their own behavior. The principles of contingency management can be used in self-modification programs for such things as weight control, social skills (letter writing, for example), exercise or other personal goals. Teaching children to use self-modification techniques by modeling them is a worthy parenting activity.

One of behavior modification's contributions comes through the study of the principles involved. Behavior modification enables parents to understand better how they and their children influence each other's behavior. When parents understand this, they can be more intentional in the way they use their influence. They control many of the reinforcers which operate in children's lives. Most parents can use the reinforcers more effectively on an informal basis, if not in a highly structured behavior modification program.

Behavior modification will always be limited in its usefulness, however, because its assumptions about human interaction are inadequate. When interactions of the home are reduced to behavior-reinforcement contingencies, too much is left out. Parents and children are subjectively reactive to each other, which makes their interactions more complicated (and more interesting) than that described in behavior modification.

Questions for Thought and Discussion about this Chapter are on page 301.

Part V
The Mutual Problem Area

The Mutual Problem Area is formed by the overlap of the Child's Problem Area and the Parent's Problem Area. Mutual problems are bothersome to both parent and child, and threaten the relationship. Mutual problems commonly involve school work; dress and hair styles; cleaning up messes and doing household chores; money; the use of the car, telephone or television; going to bed, sleeping in, practicing music and other uses of time; and parties, drinking and other activities with friends.

Many of the strategies for the Mutual Problem Area are the same parenting strategies used in the Child's Problem and the Parent's Problem Areas, since it is formed by the overlap of the two. Chapter 14 explains how they are combined for the Mutual Problem Area. In addition, the ability to compromise judiciously is important in the Mutual Problem Area. Chapter 14 illustrates the process of solving shared problems in a mutually satisfying manner.

Chapter 14 also suggests that sometimes the best strategy for parents is to give up the problem, since attempts to solve it often make the problem worse. The reason for this is explained in Chapter 15, which looks at problems in the context of family relationships. This view sometimes reveals parents to be participants in the problems of children. Chapter 15 suggests ways for preventing or managing problems by altering the parent's activity in the family system.

Both the ability to compromise and the ability to stand firm are needed in the Mutual Problem Area. The balanced parent can do both, according to the occasion. If parents compromise too much, children take advantage of them and the household is chaotic. If parents are too rigid, on the other hand, the parent-child relationship is damaged and the child's normal development is disrupted.

Even though control is eventually turned over to the child, parents must never relinquish control completely as long as the child is living in the parents' household. It is the *parents'* household; parents are in charge. However, parents don't need to work as hard at retaining control as so many do. Parental control will be present naturally if they develop skills in each of the four areas. The best way to manage problems is by preventing them — by storing up good will and mutual respect which can be drawn on in times of conflict, by practicing the art of listening and by assertively clarifying expectations.

Questions for Thought and Discussion about this Chapter are on page 303.

14. Managing Conflict

Young adults tend to think that people who love each other and who communicate will be able to reduce conflict or perhaps even eliminate it from their relationships. A relationship troubled by conflict, they assume, is one in which the parties "don't communicate" or have experienced a "communication breakdown" or a "communication gap."

But as young adults grow older and gain experience in relationships, they discover that communication doesn't necessarily prevent conflict from occurring. In fact, communication is as likely to *reveal* conflict as to *reduce* it. The more any two people share with one another, the more opportunity they have to disagree about some things. The fact that they love each other doesn't change this.

A parent-child relationship troubled by conflict isn't necessarily one lacking in communication or love. The problem may be that they have communicated enough to reach disagreement and don't know what to do about it. They lack the skills of conflict management.

In the Balanced Parenting Model, the Mutual Problem Area is formed by the overlap of problems which are bothersome to both parent and child. The parenting skills which apply to the Mutual Problem Area, therefore, are a combination of the skills for the Child's Problem Area (listening for the child's feelings and interests) and the Parent's Problem Area (clarifying one's own feelings and interests). Additional parenting skills specifically for the Mutual

Problem Area include defining and sticking to the issue, compromising assertively and giving up the problem (see Figure 14.1).

Figure 14.1
Parenting Skills for the Mutual Problem Area

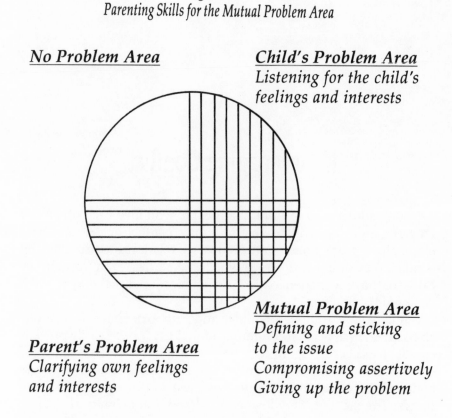

No Problem Area

Child's Problem Area
Listening for the child's feelings and interests

Mutual Problem Area
Defining and sticking to the issue
Compromising assertively
Giving up the problem

Parent's Problem Area
Clarifying own feelings and interests

Listening for the Child's Feelings and Interests

One of the key ingredients to successful conflict management is seeing the situation from the other person's point of view. This is as true of conflicts in the parent-child relationship as it is of conflicts in other relationships. To do this, parents use the listening skills of the Child's Problem Area. The listening skills include *being available to talk, using door openers, observing nonverbal messages, paraphrasing content, listening actively for feelings* and *granting wishes in fantasy* (see Chapter 8).

To see the situation from the child's point of view doesn't mean that the parent agrees with the child or accedes to the child's demands. It means that the parent perceives the child's feelings and interests accurately, and treats the child's point of view respectfully.

Another reason listening is important in conflict management is that the ability to listen actively enables parents to acknowledge the feelings which are generated in the course of the conflict itself. Most people, including children, take disagreements personally. They attempt to save face, attack the other when threatened, and feel unloved, unappreciated, misunderstood, depressed, angry or sorry for themselves. For example, a teenager remembered an incident this way:

> One time I was helping Mom clean house and all she did was gripe about how much work there was. She went on and on about what I needed to do. I made a smart-aleck remark under my breath which she happened to hear, and boy, did the sparks fly! Then I dropped a bottle of Lemon Oil, and she accused me of throwing it down. I was really upset and we ended up in a big fight over one little phrase. It was not such a bad thing that I said, but it sure hit her wrong. I really felt misunderstood.

Teenagers are especially likely to end a conflict nursing personal injury. At this age their social status is moving up, but is still below that of the parent. Because of their sense of vulnerability and because of the self-centeredness at this age, they become offended by comments which older adults overlook. My daughter Julie once wrote me a note in which she expressed regret that she and I had been experiencing so much conflict. I was surprised because I didn't feel that we had experienced so much conflict. But her perception of our relationship was important information and helped me to be more sensitive to her feelings when we disagreed.

In a relationship between two people with different levels of social status, the person of lesser status tends to remember the *feelings* of the last interaction. The person of greater social status tends to remember the *outcome* of the last interaction. It's important, therefore, that parents soften disagreements with assurances of appreciation and respect. If they can't do this in the moment, then it's important that they find an opportunity to do so soon afterwards, saying something like, "I'm glad we can disagree about this and still love each other. You're far more important to me than this argument."

Clarifying Own Feelings and Interests

Since a problem in the Mutual Problem Area bothers the parent, too, all of the techniques of the Parent's Problem Area are appropriate to use. These techniques include *using facts and reasons, sending I-messages, making assertive demands, taking a position, avoiding arguments by fogging, persisting like a broken record* and *setting up logical consequences for misbehavior* (see Chapters 10 and 11). Each of these techniques serves to get the child to listen to the parent's complaint and to take the parent seriously, just as the listening skills enable the parent to take the child seriously.

As parents listen for the child's feelings and interests, and clarify their own, they *differentiate* themselves from their children. This, too, is an important ingredient in successful conflict management. Emphasizing differentiation of selves helps both parent and child to solve the problem without reacting so strongly to each other.

Parents can restrict a child's independence and nurture the child's sense of self at the same time. Independence and differentiation of self are not the same thing. To illustrate, a quadriplegic is dependent on other persons for care but can still possess a strong sense of self. Differentiation has to do with getting one's feelings, wishes, beliefs, desires and preferences untangled from those of other people. It has to do with the ability to take a position which is at odds with the emotional climate and, conversely, the ability to hold a position without imposing it on others.

The process of differentiation begins at birth as parents respond to infants as individuals who are separate from themselves and different from all other children. Conflicts offer opportunity for parent-child differentiation to be accented, with such statements as:

"I realize that you feel that way about it. I feel differently."

"Life would be boring if everybody agreed all of the time, wouldn't it?"

"I'm glad you didn't turn out exactly like me. You make life interesting!"

"I know you're upset about what happened at school today. You've got a right to feel grumpy, but the rest of us don't have to be grumpy just because you're feeling grumpy."

"That's a choice you're making. There are other things you could do about it."

These statements might sound unnatural for use in conflict situations. But when parents bear in mind the importance of differentiation, they can learn to respond to conflict in ways like this.

A sense of humor helps ease conflict. When members of the family laugh as soon as possible about their peculiarities which emerge in conflicts, differentiation is enhanced and anxiety is lowered.

In our family, this means that every member gets a share of good-natured kidding. We still laugh about the time Julie and Jeff were preschoolers fighting over a toy. Through her tears, Julie began to sing "Share with one another. . . . This is the happy way, to share with one another." Her singing made Jeff laugh, and he gave her the toy she wanted.

Another favorite family story is about Nathan. I had been nagging him to brush his teeth and get to bed. He ignored me for a long time and finally I yelled, "Nathan, get in there and brush your teeth and go to bed!" That got him moving towards the bathroom, but he grumbled all the way, "Nathan, do this! Nathan, do that! That's all I ever hear around here!" He slammed the door, and then there was silence. A couple of minutes later he stuck his head out the door and called, "Hey, Dad! What was I supposed to do in here?"

The more parents differentiate themselves as persons, the more likely they are to keep their sense of humor and manage conflict comfortably.

Defining and Sticking to the Issue

Another of the ingredients to successful conflict management is the ability to stick to the issue. Not being able to focus the complaint or bringing in other complaints often results in an escalation of attack and counterattack, which makes solving the problem at hand more difficult. Sticking to the issue is especially important in conflicts with teenagers, because, as psychologist Roger McIntire explains:

> Scapegoating is a common teen activity and a parent should
> be on guard against accepting all blame and guilt:
> "Mom, where are my sandals? I'm late!"
> "I don't know."
> "Well GOSH, Mom!" (McIntire, 1985, p. 221–222)

Children, especially teenagers, place blame more irrationally than adults do. It's difficult to not take their insensitivity and brashness personally and respond angrily, but overt expression of anger usually is not productive in conflict management. Sticking to the issue helps to keep the anxiety of both parties lowered and helps to avoid an escalation of You-messages (see Chapter 10) which blame each other.

The ability to stick to the issue without being drawn into attack and counterattack requires parental assertiveness (see Figure 14.2; also refer to Chapter 11). To manage conflict assertively parents refrain from blaming and arguing, and don't become highly anxious about the conflict.

Figure 14.2
Managing Conflict Unassertively, Assertively and Aggressively

Unassertive Style	Assertive Style	Aggressive Style
Gives in quickly	Sometimes compromises, sometimes doesn't	Seldom compromises; escalates threats and consequences
Becomes uncertain, confused, flustered	Listens to child's point of view (active listening); acknowledges child's point (fogging)	Discredits child's point
Gets silent	Clarifies the issue	Explodes
Pleads	Sticks to the issue (broken record)	Argues
Afraid of upsetting child	Remains nonanxious Differentiates self from child	Uses anger to control child
Blames self for conflict	Doesn't blame Accepts conflict	Blames child for conflict
Allows self to be treated disrespectfully	Retains self respect and respects child	Treats child disrespectfully

Compromising Assertively

Compromise is a necessary part of family life. Individuals cannot live together without making concessions in the everyday give-and-take of family interactions. Mutual problems very often are resolved in ways which parents and children do not find completely satisfying, but not completely unsatisfying either.

Silberman and Wheelan (1980) point out that parents have a number of options for compromising with children:

(1) Parents can give a choice about how or when or where compliance is to take place, or a choice about the consequences if compliance does not take place. In regard to cleaning a room, for example, parents can negotiate how "clean" is clean, the deadline by which it is to be clean or the circumstances under which it is to be clean; they can also negotiate what happens if it is not cleaned.

(2) Parents can say "no" to a request, but provide alternatives:

"I cannot take you and your friends to the mall tonight. How about Saturday?"

"I'm not willing to pay this much for basketball shoes. Let's see if we can find them in the discount catalog."

(3) Parents can make an exchange or some other offer too good to turn down. The art of negotiation consists of finding a way to get what you want by offering something the other party wants. In parent-child conflicts, parents want something, too. They have the option of getting it by making the child's compliance worthwhile to the child. With young children who resist bathtime, for example, parents can entice them into the tub by adding food coloring to the water or by placing plastic containers for water play in the water. With older children, parents can offer to do a routine chore for the child in exchange for help with an unusual project.

(4) Parents can compromise by meeting children halfway. Parents and children can negotiate to get part of what they want by giving up part of it. This is commonly done in conflicts about the family schedule, household chores, allowances, hours and use of the telephone or car. If the conflict has to do with a difficult or unappealing task, parents can offer to do it with them.

(5) Parents can ask children to suggest solutions. Parents don't have to make the first offer: they can invite offers. For example, in a parent-child conflict about late night movie-watching, parents can ask for ideas about limits. Children sometimes make surprising offers. An advantage of this option is that children have more

invested in solutions they suggest and are more likely to abide by the terms of the agreement.

(6) Parents and children can seek a solution jointly. This option is what Thomas Gordon in *Parent Effectiveness Training* calls the "No-Lose" Method for resolving conflicts (Gordon, 1970, p. 194). It's called no-lose because both parent and child get their needs met by finding a solution which satisfies both. This is in contrast to parental power methods by which parents "win" in conflict situations, but children "lose." It is also in contrast to parental permissiveness which makes children conflict winners and parents conflict losers.

The problem-solving steps Gordon recommends consist of defining the problem, generating possible solutions to the problem, evaluating the solutions, deciding on a mutually acceptable solution, implementing the decision and reviewing the level of satisfaction with the decision.

The "raincoat" story, which was used in the introduction to Chapter 3 of this book, illustrates the No-Lose method of P.E.T. In this incident, Gordon's daughter did not want to wear her raincoat which was different from what other kids were wearing. But he was not willing for her to go without a raincoat. She suggested that she wear her mother's coat with the sleeves rolled up, which was a mutually acceptable solution.

Giving Up the Problem

The long-term goal of parenting is to turn over control to the child. This is why Roger McIntire (1985) entitled his book about parenting teenagers, *Losing Control of Your Teenager.* Both parent and child are doing what they should be doing when they negotiate the gradual transfer of responsibility from one to the other. It is rarely achieved without conflict, but it is an inevitable and ultimately rewarding process.

Tom Mullen, Quaker educator and writer, tells the story about a conflict between his wife, Nancy, and daughter Sarah. When Sarah was about nine years old, she put on socks which didn't match the rest of her outfit one morning as she got ready for school. Her mother saw her and asked her to change her socks. Sarah ignored her. Her mother asked her again, but Sarah protested, saying she liked the socks. Finally her mother told her that she couldn't go to school looking like that, she had to change her socks. Sarah went to her bedroom to change, and returned with a different *outfit* on, one which matched the socks.

This kind of conflict occurs because of normal developmental challenges; the conflicts are common, predictable and temporary. This does not mean that developmental problems are easy to manage at the time they occur; it's hard to maintain a balance between too much control and too little control, while the child's need for control is changing.

Furthermore, children sometimes demand more autonomy than they are ready for. Sometimes children want parents to set their boundaries so that they don't have to take a position on their own within the peer group. Sometimes parents underestimate the capabilities of their children. Sometimes parents worry too much about risks their children face and permit too little opportunity for their children to learn from experience. Sometimes parents hold children back because of their own emotional needs, and sometimes they sabotage the efforts of their children to be more autonomous.

There are many reasons why a normal developmental conflict between parent and child can evolve into something more serious. Whether or not the problem fades as the child matures depends on how the parents respond to the child. If parents respond with common sense, patience and a sense of humor, the conflict eventually fades. But if parents react intensely to the problem, the problem will not disappear like it normally would.

Monica got sick one day at school and vomited, but for some reason was not permitted to go home. Following this incident, she became worried that if she were sick again, she wouldn't be permitted to go home. To avoid the risk of throwing up again, she stopped eating at school. Her parents became concerned about her not eating and tried various methods to get her to eat. Her mother packed a lunch for her and included special items. Monica was encouraged to eat breakfast before the rest of the family, so they wouldn't upset each other about the food issue. Her parents spanked her for not eating. Nothing worked. Finally Monica's mother told her that she was going to stop worrying about it. If Monica didn't want to eat, that was fine with her. Within days, Monica was eating at school again.

When parents are too reactive to a child, the child's normal development is disrupted and the parent-child relationship itself becomes problematic. Little issues (like what to wear to school or eating habits) take on significance beyond what they should, because the fears and needs of parents have become more important than the needs of the child for reasonable guidance.

According to family systems theory, emotional entanglement of one person with another is revealed by their reactivity to each other. Imagine a father and a daughter at home alone. They are busy with their activities, visiting occasionally and comfortable with each other. The son arrives, and within a few minutes the brother and sister are upset with each other and the father is feeling irritable. Even though there has been no "conflict," tension is in the air.

This "twitchiness" in each other's presence is what is meant by reactivity. It's somewhat like the old Johnny Mathis song, "Chances are . . . that my composure sort of slips the moment you come into view." The song is about being in love, but reactivity takes negative forms as well as positive. When two people fall in love and are positively reactive to each other, they overlook problems which others would be aware of. When they are negatively reactive to each other, they focus on problems others wouldn't see or wouldn't be anxious about. Their reactivity creates and sustains problems.

The same is true of parent-child relationships. If the parent feels anxious about a mutual problem, and the problem becomes a long-term pattern, it's likely that the parent has become part of the problem. Instead of trying harder to solve the problem in the same manner, the parent needs to "give up" the problem and be less anxious about it. This will cause the child to respond differently to the problem, too, and both will strike a new balance in the child's independence and dependence struggles.

One of the parenting goals for the Mutual Problem Area is to provide stability and guidance in the child's life, but to do it in a flexible and nonanxious way. If parents are able to manage conflict without being highly reactive, most parent-child disagreements will diminish in time. (Chapter 15, Changing the Family System, suggests a number of ways parents can reduce their reactivity to their children.)

The parent-child relationship is permanent, which makes it far more important than any independence issue under negotiation. (The subtitle of McIntire's book referred to above is *Ten Rules for Raising an Adult while Keeping a Friend*.) When conflict becomes too intense, parents need to find ways to lower their anxiety about it—by keeping their sense of humor, being patient, seeing the relative long-term importance (or unimportance) of the problem or by giving it up.

Conflict Management Case: The Family Telephone

Mother: Sandy, we need to talk about the telephone [expressing desire to talk about mutual problem]. You've been on the telephone so much in the evenings that the rest of us have trouble using it [fact].

Sandy: But I have to talk with my friends. Do you expect me not to talk with my friends?

Mother: I realize that you like to talk with your friends, and I'm glad you have friends [active listening and I-message]. But the phone has been tied up too much [broken record].

Sandy: Well, it seems to me like you don't want me to have any friends, or else you don't like them.

Mother: This has nothing to do with whether or not I like your friends. It has to do with the phone being available for the rest of the family [sticking to the issue].

Sandy: It's not my fault if I have more friends than everybody else.

Mother: The number of friends isn't the issue. The issue is being able to use the phone [sticking to the issue].

Sandy: Well, I need to use it, too. Until I'm old enough to drive, that's the only way I can talk to my friends.

Mother: The phone is really handy, and I'm glad we have one [fogging]. But sometimes I need to make calls in the evening because I work all day, and I feel resentful if I don't have a chance to do so [I-message].

Sandy: I'm not always on the phone.

Mother: That's true [fogging]. But the phone is not available enough to make or receive calls [broken record].

Sandy: You just want the phone to be *available*. I want to *use* it. That's what phones are for.

Mother: You're right. The phone is to use [fogging]. But it's for the whole family to use. It has to be shared, like the TV [sticking to the issue].

Sandy: If someone tries to call you and I'm talking, they can call back later. That's what a busy signal is for.

Mother: That's true [fogging], but one of my friends recently told me she had been trying to call me for several days [fact].

Sandy: Last night I was off the phone a long time and nobody called.

Mother: That could be [fogging]. But the phone needs to be available more than it has been [broken record].

Sandy's mother decided to impose a 10-minute time limit on Sandy's calls. Within a few days it became clear that Sandy wasn't paying attention to the passage of time, so her mother instructed her to use a timer. This didn't work well either. Sandy would fail to set the timer right away, or would reset it, or would have a long goodbye after it went off. Sandy's mother began setting the timer herself, reminding her when the time was about up and finally telling her when time had run out. The following conversation took place after two or three weeks.

Mother: Sandy, I'm still not happy with the telephone situation [expressing desire to talk about the problem]. You're not keeping to the rule [fact]. I don't want to keep going through what we've been going through [I-message].

Sandy: I can't just hang up when 10 minutes are up! That's rude!

Mother: You have 10 minutes. That's the rule [sticking to the issue].

Sandy: Some calls are less than 10 minutes, so why can't others be more?

Mother: You have 10 minutes [broken record].

Sandy: I have to spend 5 minutes of my time explaining the situation to my friends and 5 minutes apologizing for my parents.

Mother: You have 10 minutes to do whatever you want to do [differentiating].

Sandy: My friends are going to stop calling me (said in a blaming tone of voice).

Mother: [doesn't respond to guilt induction tactic of daughter]

Sandy: They all think you're too strict, and if Dad answers the phone, my friends hang up because he sounds so mean.

Mother: That could be [fogging]. I know that sometimes he gets tired of being your answering service [fact].

Sandy: None of their parents have 10-minute limits.

Mother: I probably am different from them in some things [differentiating].

Sandy: Does everyone else in our family have a 10-minute limit? What about you and Dad?

Mother: For now, a limit isn't needed for anybody else [differentiating].

Sandy: That's not fair!

Mother: I'm not concerned with being fair. I'm concerned with making the phone more available [sticking to the issue].

Sandy: The problem is that there isn't enough time for everybody to talk on the phone. As far as I'm concerned, the 10-minute rule just makes things worse.

Mother: I know you get angry when I make you get off the phone, but that's the way the rest of us feel when we can't get on [active listening and I-message]. I'm still not happy about the situation, either [I-message]. Maybe there is some other way we could solve the problem [expressing desire to keep talking about mutual problem].

At this point, Sandy and her parents decided to figure out a better way to handle the telephone problem. Her parents remained assertive about their own interests which were at stake, but were flexible enough to consider a compromise. They also insisted that Sandy share more of the responsibility for solving the problem. They considered withdrawing her telephone services completely [logical consequences] until she became more willing to help solve the problem, but didn't need to do so.

They generated these possible solutions:

Sandy could use the phone without interference between 9:00 p.m. and 10:00 p.m., but she had to stay off the phone before 9:00 and could not disturb the family with her calls after 10:00.

If another member of the family wanted to use the phone, other than between 9:00 and 10:00, Sandy could hang up and call back later.

The family could get the kind of service which has an incoming call signal.

They could get a second phone number, for her. They could split the cost of monthly service and she could pay for all toll calls.

Sandy's parents offered to split the cost of a second phone and obtained information about the cost. Sandy considered this and decided that it cost more than she was willing to spend. They finally settled on the 9:00–10:00 solution. It worked fairly well. There were occasions when Sandy needed to be reminded of the agreement, but she was more cooperative after the conflict management process than she had been before, and the rest of the family felt better about their access to the telephone.

Conflict Management Case: The Homecoming Plans

When Julie was a high school senior, she was one of the candidates for Homecoming queen. Lorna and I were proud of her, as parents typically would be, but we were not enthusiastic about the plans the members of the Homecoming court were making as the event approached. Their plans were to do what previous courts of this high school had done — leave the Homecoming activities early, get a room at a motel or hotel and spend the rest of the night celebrating the special occasion together—swimming, snacking, watching TV, visiting and so on.

The parents of the candidates decided to meet to share concerns, suggestions and, if possible, to present a united front to the teenagers. In the meeting, we learned that two or three of the eight families involved approved of the plans the teenagers were making, two or three disapproved, and two or three were reluctant to give their consent, but would probably do so. It was also clear that all of us resented the pressure we felt to keep alive a tradition we did not wholly support. So we decided to negotiate a compromise with our teenagers, with the hope that they could settle on a plan which all of the families approved, and that future Homecoming groups would be able to plan more creatively if this group broke the tradition.

In the parents meeting, a number of suggestions were made for approving the teenagers' plans, provided that certain conditions were met. One suggestion was that parents choose the hotel, because of parental worries about late night activity in certain locations. Another preference was that the location be a hotel complex (with a dome, for example), rather than a traditional motel. One parent suggested that the plan be approved if the teenagers would agree to stay inside the hotel complex after arriving and not go onto the street. Yet another suggestion was that the plan be approved on the condition that a "sponsor" be there. The sponsor could be a person or couple nominated by the teenagers. The sponsor would not need to be with the teenagers all of the time, but would serve as an adult presence, available in case of need.

The parents decided that they would not oppose the plans the teens had made, if the teens were willing to meet these conditions. However, they also decided that even with the conditions, they were not wholly supportive of going to a hotel. Their first choice was that other plans be made. So they suggested to the teenagers that they find a location other than a hotel to spend the time together. The parents also offered to host the group in a home and provide a late night meal or breakfast.

Several other ideas were generated by the parents about activities which could be exchanged for canceling the original plans: renting a limousine to take the teenagers to a late dinner, chartering a plane or booking them on a commercial flight for a meal in some other location, arranging for them to go to a nice restaurant the following evening or sending them by train to another location for recreation.

Attitudes of both teenagers and parents moved closer together as a result of the parent-child discussions which took place. The parents told the teenagers that they didn't want to spoil their fun and, in fact, wanted just the opposite — to help them create a good memory of an event which happens only once in a lifetime. But they also had some anxieties which they couldn't overlook. Their initial reaction was negative, they admitted, because getting a room in a hotel just didn't sound good to them. They were anxious about drunkenness and sexual activity of the group, the possibility of others crashing the party and the risk of late night incidents in general.

The teenagers replied that it was time to stop being so anxious and controlling, since they were 17 or 18 years of age, just a few months from being on their own in college.

In regard to sexual activity, the teens pointed out that there were no dating couples among the members of this Homecoming court. In regard to drinking, they reminded their parents that they all were members of a varsity team or cheerleading squad and faced suspension if drinking was reported. Finally, in regard to others crashing the party, they told the parents that this activity was a special event for the members of the court, and they wanted to do it together. Nobody else would be there and, conversely, it was important that all of them be allowed to go.

The result of the discussions was that parents became less resistive and more supportive, and teenagers became less resentful and more reassuring.

At this point, the parents asked the teenagers for their suggestions. They met and came up with none. Unfortunately, by this time they were so curious about what we were going to suggest, that some of their initiative was lost.

The Homecoming court and parents met to evaluate the various suggestions. The teenagers judged some of the suggestions to be unappealing and rejected them outright. Additional information proved some of the suggestions to be impractical and others to be prohibitively expensive. The teenagers were intrigued by the train idea, however, because of its novelty. The train schedule also appealed to them in that a train passed through the depot nearby about the time they wanted to leave the high school.

The teenagers decided this suggestion was worth further study. A couple of days later they presented to their parents details about what they wanted to do (see Figure 14.3). All of the parents endorsed the plan and offered to help in various ways with the preparations.

Figure 14.3
Conflict Management Case: The Homecoming Plans

Candidates' Trip

Schedule

1:30am	Leave Homecoming
2:00am	Leave Newton by train
6:00am	Arrive in Kansas City
	Taxi to Crown Center*
6:30am	Check in, relax, clean up, etc.
9:00am	Breakfast in Crown Center
10:00am	Get van from parents
10:30am	Shop, sightsee, lunch, movie, etc.
4:30pm	Back to hotel to swim, rest
5:30pm	Go to nice restaurant to eat
7:00pm	Leave for home (no problem with falling asleep — 3 drivers)

Reasons for room: change clothes, use facilities, swim

Cost Per Person	Train (one-way Newton-KC)		$42
	Hotel suite ($80 divided by 8)		10
	Meals		
	breakfast	$4	
	lunch, snacks	5	
	dinner	13	
	total		22
	Van, taxi ($40 divided by 8)		5
	Total (appx.)		$79 per person

Maintaining Balance in the Mutual Problem Area

All parents experience conflict with their children from time to time. But how much conflict parents experience varies greatly. Some parent-child relationships are characterized by constant tension. Their homes are the scene of daily skirmishes about rules, dress, school and peer activities. These parents talk as if this were inevitable, especially in the teenage years. They are fond of saying to parents of younger children, "You think parenting is tough now? Just wait! You haven't seen anything yet!"

In homes where conflict is extensive, conflict is being managed in a way which generates more of it and in a manner which damages the parent-child relationship. Conflict to this extent is not inevitable or desirable.

At the other extreme are those who think the ideal parent-child relationship is characterized by an absence of conflict. They work to eliminate conflict or at least to appear as if there were no conflict. But no two people respond to events in exactly the same way, since their personal interests, needs, values and perceptions are never identical. Inevitably, there will be times when parents and children disagree.

Homes where parents and children appear to be in constant agreement manage conflict in a way which works against the differentiation of individuals. Since differentiation is a prerequisite to intimacy, these families sacrifice intimacy for the sake of agreement.

Too much conflict and too little conflict *both* indicate problems in the parent-child relationship. The goal for the Mutual Problem Area is to manage conflicts in such a way that the process does not generate additional conflicts nor suppress differences (see Figure 14.4).

Figure 14.4
The Goal of the Mutual Problem Area is to Manage Conflict in a Manner That Does Not Generate More Conflict Nor Suppress Conflict

Suppression of Conflict
Tactics to deny disagreement result in
- *too much agreement and a*
- *manipulative relationship.*

Generation of Conflict
Tactics to force agreement result in
- *too much disagreement and a*
- *broken relationship.*

Acceptance of Conflict
Tactics to manage conflicts result in
- *differentiation and an*
- *intimate relationship.*

Mutual problems are not easy to manage, and I don't want to give that impression. Few parents are comfortable with conflict; most manage it badly. Parents who are best skilled in the Mutual Problem Area possess common sense and patience, and have the ability to keep their anxiety in check. The suggestions of this chapter may help in managing conflict more comfortably, but no magic formulas exist.

Questions for Thought and Discussion about this Chapter are on page 304.

15. Changing the Family System

Since the 1970s, a revolution has been taking place in counseling psychology. The movement is called "family systems theory." Problems of individuals, in this theory, are traced to the emotional limitations of members of the individual's family and their patterns of interaction with one another.[1]

In family systems theory, such problems as academic failure,

[1] Compared with other schools of thought within psychology, systems theory is still in its early stages of development. Most of the early work took place in the 1950s, but the movement did not have wide impact until the 1980s. Early pioneers included Gregory Bateson, Jay Haley and Virginia Satir, founders of the "communications school" of family therapy on the West Coast. The communications school of thought emphasizes opening up lines of communication and speaking in a nonaccusatory manner.

Another pioneer was Salvador Minuchin, who developed the "structural school" of thought at the Philadelphia Child Guidance Clinic. The structural school focuses on the patterns of communication, primarily triangles, boundaries, coalitions and hierarchies.

The most influential theorist in recent years has been Murray Bowen. Bowen, who began his work at the Menninger Foundation in Kansas, and then moved it to Washington, D.C., is founder of the "differentiation" or "family systems" school of thought. He emphasizes the way family members handle their anxiety, and especially the patterns for doing so which are passed from generation to generation. Bowen family systems therapy includes the construction of a family diagram (sometimes called "genogram") for gathering data to reveal the generational transmission of patterns.

This chapter is based primarily on Bowen's (Kerr and Bowen, 1988) description of family processes but does not cover all of family systems theory. The emphases on generational patterns and the work with family diagrams, for example, do not appear here.

Peoplemaking by Virginia Satir (1972), *The Family Crucible* by August Napier and Carl Whitaker (1978), *Intimate Partners* by Maggie Scarf (1987), and, especially, *The Dance of Anger* by Harriet Goldhor Lerner (1985) are some of the best introductions to family systems ideas.

obesity, cancer, heart disease, schizophrenia, teenage pregnancy, delinquency, alcoholism, depression and phobias are regarded as symptoms of problems in the patterns of relationships in the family. The theory suggests that parents, without being aware of it, help to perpetuate these kinds of problems.

In one sense, this observation is not surprising. It's easy to see that parents rarely form ideal relationships with their children. All parents have unfulfilled needs, insecurities and fears which affect their relationships. Children tend to react to their parents in the same way that friends, work colleagues and others outside the home react to the parents. Parents do not change their characteristic anxieties and interaction styles at the door when they leave or enter the home. This is why the kinds of interpersonal problems parents experience out of the home tend to show up also in the home.

What is surprising about family systems theory is that it suggests that parents often prolong the problems of children by their efforts to end the problems. While this analysis seems to cast parents in a negative light, it also offers hope—hope that by viewing problems in a different way, parents will be able to avoid the downward spiral they and their children so often are pulled into by mutual problems.

This chapter covers a series of suggestions for applying family systems concepts to parent-child relationships. The emphasis of the chapter is on a way of thinking about emotional maturity and its impact on relationships, rather than on specific skills for relating. The vocabulary of family systems theory is important; accurate use of the terms and comprehension of the concepts go together.

Viewing Problems in the Context of Family Relationships

Bonnie, a college freshman, came to see me one day. She had just received her mid-term grades, and they were very low. "What grades were you expecting?" I asked.

"Well, to be honest, I thought they would be low. There were several papers I didn't turn in, and my attendance hasn't been very good."

"I see."

"In fact, last week when I talked with my folks on the phone, I told them my grades weren't going to be very good."

"What did they say?"

"They were pretty upset. Mom cried, and Dad reminded me that they are putting out a lot of money for me to be here. We agreed on the phone that I would at least finish the term."

"What do you think the problem is?" I had seen her college entrance test scores, and knew she was capable of better work.

"I don't seem to have any motivation. Lately I've been feeling kind of depressed, and I just don't care about my grades. This is what I wanted to talk about."

Bonnie and her parents faced a serious mutual problem. She was failing her first semester of college, didn't seem to care and was depressed. Her parents were worried about her emotional state and concerned about how much money was being invested in her college education for so little return.

The traditional view of problems like this is that something causes the problem: A causes B (see Figure 15.1). This linear model of human behavior is sometimes called the "billiard ball" model. One person (or an event or condition) does something to another person which causes a reaction, just as one billiard ball strikes another and causes the second one to move. In this model such concepts as cause-effect, stimulus-response and action-reaction are employed to explain behavior.

Figure 15.1
Relationships as Linear Action

A "problem" is seen as what one person does to another. The problem is caused by individual action.

Terms for Explaining Behavior
cause-effect
action-reaction
stimulus-response
culprit-victim

Perhaps Bonnie's problem was caused by lack of motivation. Perhaps it was caused by lack of good study habits. Perhaps the cause was a lack of direction for her life. Or perhaps she was so worried about something that she was unable to concentrate on her studies.

In the linear view, there are solutions as well as causes. The solutions have to do with changing the events or conditions which cause the problem (for example, by getting the person who caused the problem to apologize). In Bonnie's case, the solution could have taken the form of helping her to develop better study habits. Or perhaps her problem would have been overcome through career counseling and goal setting. (Her parents called to suggest this solution.) Perhaps she could have been helped by talking about her depression. (This is why she came to see me.)

Since the 1970s, counselors have been viewing problems like this in another way. In this model of human behavior, A influences B, but B also influences A—the influence goes in both directions. Furthermore, both A and B are reactive to C and D, which affects the way they influence each other. In other words, human behavior occurs in a system of relationships. Each member of the system affects all other members and, in turn, is affected by all other members.

This view of human behavior rejects the billiard ball model because humans do not react to one another according to the laws of physics as wooden balls do. Humans are *subjectively* reactive to each other. When A does something to B, how far B moves and the direction B moves are determined by B's reactivity to A. In some instances, B might not move at all. In other instances B moves if A is merely present.

The linear view of behavior uses forms of the verb "to be" to explain behavior of individuals: "Ricky is shy"; "Ricky's mother is overprotective." The systems view uses language which connects behavior to its social context: "Ricky behaves shyly in the presence of his mother, who behaves overprotectively in the presence of Ricky." If Ricky's mother were to conceptualize her systemic interaction with Ricky, she could say, "With me the way I am with him, he is shy."

Virginia Satir (1972) proposed that a hanging mobile be used as a model for human relationships (see Figure 15.2) in place of the billiard ball model. The parts of a mobile maintain a balance among themselves; whenever one part moves or the distance between two

Figure 15.2
Relationships in Context of System

A "problem" is seen as a symptom of anxiety in the family and is sustained by the system.

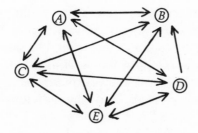

Terms for Explaining Behavior

interactions	*adaptation*
patterns	*reactivity*
cycles	*closeness-distance*
balance	*stress*
stability	

parts changes, the balance of the entire mobile is affected. The balance of the family mobile is affected by such changes as children leaving home, the addition of in-laws, new alliances within the family, distancing caused by conflicts, tugs from factors external to the family (for example, a change in the farm economy) or illness and death. In family systems theory, such concepts as interactions, patterns, cycles, balance, stability, adaptation, reactivity and closeness-distance are used to explain the dynamic ways people relate to one another.

In a case like Bonnie's, a family systems counselor would not attempt to figure out what happened to her that caused the problem nor search for a solution to "fix" her. This would be the linear model. Instead, a family systems counselor would look for family interaction patterns which sustain the problem. Perhaps Bonnie's failure in college was serving the family by distracting them from a larger problem. If so, attempts to "fix" her problem were not likely to be successful. Her grades would be more likely to improve if there were an adjustment in the family interaction patterns which gave her permission to leave home and succeed in college.

Because my approach to counseling has been influenced by family systems theory, I asked Bonnie questions about relationships in her family and about changes they were adjusting to. Within a few minutes I learned that her parents argued often and had talked about separating. Although Bonnie was worried about a divorce, she sympathized with her dad's desire to get out of the relationship. Her view of the marriage relationship was that her mother was driving her dad away because she was so critical of him.

Family systems theory suggests that a family "gets" something from the problems of an individual member. Sometimes it gets a distraction, so that something worse is avoided. Anxiety about a more basic relationship issue may be redirected to the individual's problem, and a crisis averted. Thus, the individual's problem helps to stabilize the system and, in turn, the system sustains the problem. Even though this pattern is dysfunctional, the problem will be incorporated into the family's way of functioning because of the benefit which is derived from it. As long as the individual's problem is the focus of anxiety, the family system will keep the problem.

In Bonnie's family, there was stress in the marriage relationship. Somehow Bonnie invited the family to spill the anxiety about the marriage relationship onto her. The diverted anxiety was focused especially on the issue of leaving home, since family members expected a crisis to occur at the point that the parents didn't need to stay together "for the sake of the children."

I suspected that the family system needed Bonnie to stay young and immature, and to fail at college so that she could be cared for at home and not have to leave. My hunch about this was confirmed, I think, by additional information. I learned that when Bonnie was a junior in high school, her dad told her confidentially that he and Bonnie's mother very likely would separate after the two children (Bonnie and a younger brother) left home. Bonnie's depression began the day of her eighteenth birthday. (This is unusual. Normally the eighteenth birthday is experienced as a happy occasion.) I learned also that Bonnie had never earned money of her own and, even now, indicated no desire to do so. In high school she worked for her parents, who gave her money as she needed it. Her mother picked out and purchased her clothes.

Bonnie was not aware of how her failure at college stabilized the family system. She was as anxious about the low grades as her parents were and thought something was wrong with her. As I talked with her, I helped her to see that, indeed, there was nothing she could do about her parents' relationship. That was up to them. What she could do was increase her tolerance for their anxiety and withdraw from their conflicts. She could also be more responsive to her own needs for growing up.

In the months after our first conversation, she made some progress. She began to shop for herself, for example. However, her independence continued to be the focus of family anxiety, as she argued with her parents about a dating relationship and choice of college.

Seven-year-old Todd tends to be a picky eater. He often refuses to eat what is prepared for meals and then demands to be fed between meals. His mother, Virginia, is bothered by the problem and alternates between scolding him and indulging him.

A linear view of this problem is that Todd needs to develop better eating habits, and that Virginia needs to develop better child management techniques so that she can train him more effectively. Viewed in the context of family relationships, however, Todd's eating problem is seen as a symptom of another problem in the family system.

The other problem is in the marriage relationship. Todd's father, Gary, is obese. His weight is such an emotionally charged issue that Gary and Virginia never speak of it. Many nonverbal messages leave no doubt that she is repulsed by his obesity, and that he is aware of this. He tends to tell himself, "If she loved me, she would accept me the way I am." She tends to tell herself, "If he loved me, he would take better care of himself." Both of them are frightened that their relationship would not survive if the obesity issue were addressed openly. Todd's eating problem showed up as a symptom of the level of anxiety in the home.

In a family systems analysis, a problem is no one member's fault. No one is to blame; there is no culprit or victim. Todd does not misbehave with food to upset his mother or to get his dad off the hook. Virginia does not intentionally use Todd as a scapegoat. Gary does not overeat to spite his wife. They don't intend to do these things to each other, but they do, as if they had an unspoken agreement. They all contribute to the pattern, which is why the problem is no one's fault.

They all benefit by it as well. Todd's eating difficulty serves as a distraction from a problem about which the family is even more anxious, the marriage relationship. What would happen if Gary were honest about his desire to eat, his loss of control and his body image? What would happen if Virginia were honest about her feelings about Gary's size and about appearing with him in public? What would they be left with if Gary lost weight? Would they find their intimacy to be blocked by other issues and their relationship still problematic?

Questions like these raise the possibility of frightening answers. The family prefers to struggle with the conflict surrounding Todd's eating habits than to learn the answers to the questions. Todd's problem helps the family avoid a crisis by stabilizing the marriage relationship as it is.

The fact that the family's anxiety is focused on Todd's eating is somewhat coincidental. Food obviously is an emotionally charged issue in the family, but the anxiety could have spilled just as easily onto the older daughter, Lynn, and her activities with her friends, for example. What is predictable is that as long as the level of anxiety remains as high as it is, problems will be present as symptoms of the anxiety.

The examples of Bonnie's and Todd's families both emphasize anxiety about the marriage relationship. Families are anxious about many other issues, of course. But problems of children are related to stress in the marriage relationship so frequently that Virginia Satir stated, "If the child feels the pain, the pinch is in the marriage." The health of the marriage relationship is revealed by the presence or absence of symptoms in members of the family.

The following questions can be used by parents as frames for viewing problems in their context:

1. How does this problem help to avoid a crisis elsewhere in the family system?
2. How does this problem benefit me? What would I be left with if the problem went away?
3. What am I afraid of? What would happen if my worst fears about the problem came true? Could I adjust?
4. What would happen if I stopped trying to prevent the problem from getting worse? Am I willing to take some risks to find out?
5. What am I willing to give up to enable the child to give up the problem?

Balancing Togetherness and Separateness

The difficulty of balancing the needs for togetherness and separateness became clearer to me when our children reached college age. They decided to attend the college where I teach, which raised many questions regarding my level of involvement with them. How involved was I in their decision about where to go to college? (How much choice did they really have, given the web of family connections with the institution?) Should I make recommendations about courses? If they enrolled in courses I teach, could I comfortably relate to them as both student and son or daughter? When I was with faculty colleagues, would I feel compelled to ask questions or make suggestions regarding my son's or daughter's affiliation with them? How much did Lorna and I need to know about their dormitory life and other social activities? How often did I expect them to stop by my office or to come home to visit?

Figure 15.3
Fused, Distant and Differentiated, But Close
Relationships

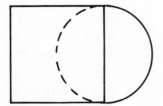

Fused Relationship

Obscure boundaries
Excess communication
Over-involvement
Reactivity
Mechanisms of control

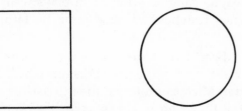

Distant Relationship

Rigid boundaries
Communication blocked
Detachment
Reactivity
Escape

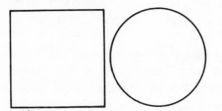

Differentiated but Close Relationship

Permeable boundaries
Flow of communication
Mutual support
Nonanxious presence
Intimacy without control

The balancing of togetherness and separateness desires did not emerge for the first time as an issue for our family when our children entered college. These circumstances merely magnified an issue which had been present since their births. Neither was the issue unique to our family. Togetherness and separateness desires are present in every parent-child relationship, and every parent seeks a balance of the two.

How successfully parents achieve a balance is determined by what family systems theorists call personal boundaries. In a relationship which is out of balance because of too much closeness, personal boundaries are so vague that individual identities are lost. In such a fused relationship (see Figure 15.3), individual responsibility for successes and failures, feelings, preferences and fears is lost. The individuals give up personal responsibility for the sake of togetherness. In a desire to be close, they develop mechanisms for controlling the other's feelings in order to react as one. This creates emotional entanglements and inappropriate interventions in each other's lives.

Following are several examples of fused, over-close parent-child relationships:

> The parents of the Nolan children become so upset when one of their children doesn't make the team or get the desired role in a musical program, that they call the principal to complain.

> Whenever Sandy Raber's daughter, Jill, comes in from a date, Sandy pumps her for information.

> After a Little League game in which Tim plays well, his father is elated. When Tom has had a bad game, his father is in a bad mood.

> The parents of Michael, a toddler, have rarely gone out together since he was born. On the few occasions when they left him with a sitter, Michael protested their departure and they were so anxious they were unable to enjoy the evening.

> A 30-year-old wife and mother calls her mother, who lives in another state, at least once a week. They react in tandem to whatever their husbands have done.

At the other end of the separateness-togetherness continuum, parents and children are cut off from each other. At this extreme, personal boundaries are rigid and communication is minimal. In verbal and nonverbal ways, they say to each other, "Leave me alone.

I don't want to be involved in your life or you to be in mine." They escape from each other into work, peer relationships, television, silence or geographical separation.

A relationship which is distant can be as fused as one which is over-close. In fact, a cut-off often follows overcloseness. One member creates distance as a means of recovering the self which was sacrificed:

> My father was really strict. As a teenager, I wanted more freedom than he thought I should have. Finally, at the supper table one evening when I was 17, I told him I was going to do something which he didn't want me to do. He told me that if I was at his table and living under his roof I would do as he says or find another place to live. The next morning at 4:00 I left home and have never returned since.

Distancers reduce contact, but as long as they remain reactive (rebellious, resentful, unforgiving, unaccepting or judgmental), they remain fused.

A female in her late teens described her distant relationship with her parents this way:

> I left home at age 17 because I felt there was nothing for me there. Two months later I moved back home and my parents didn't talk about my leaving home very much. Then I was in an accident and was forced to stay put. But as soon as I could walk again, I was on my own again. My parents refused to talk to me. At this point we really don't know what to say to each other.

Figure 15.4
Balancing Togetherness and Separateness Desires

Separateness		*Togetherness*
Fused	*Differentiated but close*	*Fused*
Reactive	*Nonanxious presence*	*Reactive*
Uninvolved	*Involvement without interference*	*Over-involved*
Cut-off	*Mutually supportive*	*Manipulative*
Parent avoids	*Parent is comfortable*	*Parent uses*
child because	*with self and with child.*	*child to meet*
of fears.		*emotional needs.*

Parents who are cut off from their children avoid the anxiety they feel when they are close, but aren't involved enough in their children's lives. Because they are absorbed in their own worlds, they find out little about their children's needs and offer little support.

The ideal parent-child relationship is close but not emotionally entangled. Their personal boundaries are permeable enough to permit a flow of communication, but not so obscure that personal identities are diffused between the two. Since their personal identities are differentiated, their boundaries do not overlap.

Increasing differentiation is the goal of family systems therapy. Persons who are less differentiated make choices based on the flow of emotion in the people around them. Relationships among persons who are less differentiated are characterized by attempts to bind or escape one another. They blame, induce guilt, obligate the other, persuade, intimidate, feel victimized and helpless, run away, become silent and complain. Because of these mechanisms of control, unfettered intimacy is unlikely to be experienced by persons who are less differentiated.

Individuals who are more differentiated are able to make choices based on reason rather than emotion. They are comfortable with themselves and tolerant of disagreement with others. Since they can be close without needing to use the mechanisms of control, they are more likely to experience intimacy with each other.

The degree of differentiation of parent and child is indicated by their reactivity to each other; the more reactive they are, the more fused and less differentiated they are. Reactivity takes negative forms (embarrassment about a child, ridicule or sarcasm, nagging about a behavior pattern, frequent arguments or hurt feelings). Reactivity also takes positive forms, equally undesirable — pride in a child's accomplishments, such close ties that the child's relationships with others are hampered or so much concern about a child's problem that the problem becomes the focus of family anxiety.

Parents are not absolutely fused with their children or absolutely differentiated from them. Differentiation is a matter of degree, a matter of balance (see Figure 15.4). The majority of parents tend to have fused, over-involved relationships with their children. Some are fused and cut off. Some are simply distant and indifferent. Many go back and forth in their attempt to seek a balance, depending on the child, the age of the child, the issue at stake and the amount of anxiety present in the family system.

Since my tendency is to be over-involved with our children, the position of "mild interest" serves as a useful corrective device for me. I say this cautiously for fear of being misunderstood, but I believe that my relationships with my children are healthier when I am mildly interested in their affairs, rather than highly interested. I remind myself of this when they are on the campus where I teach, and the experience so far has turned out to be a mutually supportive, enjoyable one.

The following questions are gauges for measuring the parental balance of the togetherness and separateness desires. "Yes" answers indicate fusion (either over-close or cut-off) and suggest that parents need to move towards the position of "mild interest," which will tone down their reactivity to their child and increase differentiation.

1. Are you uncomfortable being with your child? Is it hard for you to be "nonanxiously present"?
2. Do you become embarrassed by your child's behavior?
3. Do you show off your child's successes?
4. Do you praise your child often?
5. Are you generally dissatisfied about how your child is doing? Are you frequently after your child to change a pattern of behavior?
6. Do your children easily "get a rise" out of you? Are you easily "hooked" by things they say or do?

Fostering Individuality of Family Members

If fusion is a problem in parent-child relationships, differentiation is the solution. Fusion represents loss of self for the sake of the relationship. When fused persons make a move to support their sense of self, they use mechanisms of control to get other persons to move with them, since they are emotionally yoked.

But a sense of self is not gained through blaming, inducing guilt, feeling sorry for oneself, complaining, running away or becoming silent. Self comes from self. As individuals become more comfortable with their own individual differences, they become less reactive to others, less anxious about relationships in general and have less need to use the mechanisms of control.

Therefore, one of the most important gifts parents can give children is permission to be separate individuals. In regard to children growing up and separating from their parents Maggie Scarf wrote:

> What healthy separation involves is not necessarily geography, but the *transformation* of the original love attachments into something less highly charged, less self-defining, less

urgent. Being truly separate from one's parents means having the ability to be *different* from them and not experiencing
that differentness as a loss or a betrayal of what has been. An
individual may be a separate and differentiated being yet live
very near to his original family; he may, on the other hand,
live a continent away and—in the internal, psychological
sense—never have parted from them at all. (Scarf, 1987,
p. 325)

From a family systems point of view, the goal of parenting is to
create an emotionally healthy family—a group of unique individuals who relate well together and enjoy each other's company, but
do not think and react as one. Members are freed to be different from
one another and are comfortable with the differences.

Following are several suggestions for fostering the individuality of
children.

1. Assume your children are capable of a wide range of behavior. They are neither all good nor all bad. If you think so, you
   surely are too reactive to them.
2. Look for the things which make them unique—but don't be
   surprised by their ordinariness.
3. Avoid labeling children ("He's my little helper." "She is just
   like her Aunt Kate." "He's the smart one in the family." "She
   is always the last one to get ready.") Labels indicate fusion,
   since parental selection of traits grows out of parental reactivity to the traits. If you do label, focus on positive traits, but
   remember that even positive labels are binding. Keep labels
   few, flexible and open to revision, not rigid and permanent.
4. Don't succumb to the demands of children to be treated
   "equally" or "fairly." This is impossible, and attempting to do
   so leaves parents in a weak position. Children are different,
   situations are different and parents are different. Expect each
   child to be able to defer gracefully to the others without
   keeping score.
5. Work towards the goal of making each child feel special, but
   do it without alliances and secrets.
6. Be supportive of children's interests which are different from
   your own. Conversely, don't push your own interests. There
   is no need to, since your children usually will share your
   appreciation of those activities which you genuinely enjoy.
   However, if your children feel bound to your interests, they
   may need to escape them.

7. When you make demands of your children, keep clear the distinction between demanding behavior and demanding feelings or thoughts. Demand appropriate behavior. Don't demand agreement in feelings or thoughts.
8. Permit emotional reactivity in your children. Respond to it in nonanxious ways.
9. Express your own feelings in nonbinding ways (avoid blaming, inducing guilt, feeling sorry for yourself).
10. Don't use "invasive" language, which tells children what they are feeling or thinking, or what they should be feeling or thinking: "You're bored. Find something to do." "I'm cold. Put your sweater on." "We love Grandpa, don't we."
11. Most importantly, remember that your children ultimately gain their sense of self from themselves. You can't do it for them. What you can do is differentiate yourself from your children, so that they will more easily differentiate themselves from you.

Avoiding Rigid Roles for Parenting

In a fused relationship, the two individuals often develop complementary mechanisms for coping with each other: one pursues, the other distances; one becomes over-responsible, the other becomes under-responsible; one becomes over-emotional, the other becomes unemotional. Each one attempts to counteract the other by doing more of what the other reacts to.

Complementary mechanisms characterize many marriage relationships. Maggie Scarf (1987) refers to them as "collusive bonds." Collusive bonds occur because individuals sometimes deal with their anxiety by forming relationships which allow the partners to repress their fears and wishes, and project the fears and wishes onto each other.

For example, Donna has trouble making assertive demands. Her husband, Mark, is uncomfortable offering comfort. They form a collusive bond in which he becomes the expert in making demands, and she becomes the expert in offering comfort. With their children, she plays the nurturing, understanding parent role. He plays the role of enforcer of family rules.

Unfortunately this does not resolve the original issues, which are Donna's anxiety about asserting herself and Mark's anxiety about nurturing another person. What they have done is externalize onto the other what is intolerable within themselves. This is only a short-range solution to their problems, because it simply sustains their individual anxieties. She sets him up to be the "disciplinarian" in their parenting styles and then criticizes him for being so hard on the children. He sets her up to do the nurturing work with the children and then criticizes her for being so easy on them. Her perception of him as strict causes her to become more solicitous; he, in turn, counteracts her softness by becoming harder. Over time, they become more and more polarized in their parenting styles.

Another common pattern in polarized parenting styles is an over-involved parent (usually the mother), who is counter-balanced by a detached parent (usually the father). There are many kinds of anxieties which initiate this pattern. Perhaps the mother needs to nurture to fill an emotional void in her life. Perhaps she is uncertain and anxious about what else she could do besides parent. Perhaps the father is anxious about his career and puts his energies there with little left over for the family. Perhaps he feels incompetent as a parent. Whatever the personal anxieties are, the couple makes a collusive bond. One becomes an over-involved parent, and the other bows out or is pushed out.

Once the pattern is established, it perpetuates itself. She nags him for his lack of involvement with the children. But when he does become more involved with them, she criticizes him because he isn't as good at it as she is. She may even sabotage his efforts or set the children up to reject him out of loyalty to her. This causes him to feel more inadequate and he withdraws from parenting even more.

To counteract his lack of involvement, she becomes over-involved. He then criticizes her for being too smothering, not letting the children go, not developing outside interests, being too tied down, not doing something with just him and so on. This causes her to become even more involved in her parenting, since she believes it's all up to her. They both react to the specialized role of the other by doing what they do with greater intensity. When they become polarized in their parenting styles, it is hard for them to be anything in between.

What the parents in these examples have done is move the site of the struggles with their personal anxieties from *within themselves,* to their *relationships.* This is common, which is why those traits which attract partners to each other sometimes turn out later to be the irritants in the relationship. They divide up their personality potential in order to specialize, intending to form a complementary partnership: "You take spontaneity, I'll take caution." "You take logic,

I'll take emotionality." "You take friendliness, I'll take restraint." "You take softness, I'll take hardness." "You take competence in the home. I'll take competence in the world." But in so doing, they trade off part of their selves and are unable to relate to each other (or their children) as whole persons. And they end up fighting in each other the traits they disown in themselves.

Once again, differentiation is the key for unlocking a dysfunctional pattern. Roles are less specialized and rigid when parents are able to relate to each other as separate, whole persons. Their wholeness comes from within themselves—not from trading off parts of self and each other. When they own their personal inadequacies and fears, and are honest about their struggles, they fight their battles within themselves rather than in the relationship. When they stop trying to gain advantage or correct their partners, working instead to correct what they can in themselves, their anxiety in each other's presence goes down. Then they can be the mutually supportive partners in parenting that they would like to be.

There is nothing wrong with taking roles in the parenting partnership, as long as parents aren't locked into the roles. Rigid roles limit personal growth of parents and block healthy interaction of family members. The goal is to keep roles flexible and adaptive to changing circumstances so that children's needs are met, and so that both parents reap the personal rewards of parenthood.

Following are several suggestions for avoiding rigid role specializations:

1. Share the nurturer and enforcer roles, so that neither one of you is rigidly cast in one role.
2. Don't vie for position as favored parent. To the extent that you do, you are meeting your own emotional needs, not those of the children or the family.
3. Develop your own relationship with each child. Don't relate to children primarily through your spouse. Take the initiative for making each relationship what you want it to be.
4. Give your blessing (mentally) to your spouse to develop better relationships with each child. You are partners for meeting the needs of your children, not competitors for their affection.
5. Give your blessing (mentally) to your children to develop relationships with your spouse. Improvement in parent-child relationships should not be a matter of loyalty or betrayal; the children need both of you.
6. Admit that your parenting abilities are a mixture of good and

bad, and that you have ambivalent feelings about your parenting style. Recognize the same in your spouse. No parent is all good or all bad.

7. Expect your spouse's parenting style to be different from yours. Don't sabotage it so that it fails. On the other hand, don't rush in to correct or to rescue your spouse's parenting problems. Get out of the way so that the other style has a chance to work — or to fail — on its own.

8. Be the parent that you are. Don't think that you have to be exactly like your spouse, or that your style is necessarily inferior. Don't sell yourself short. Your children need both of you.

Staying Out of Triangles

A two-person relationship (dyad) is the most basic human relationship. In the dyad, persons experience the greatest support and intimacy (see Figure 15.5). The dyad also has the greatest potential for hurt and fear. Because the emotionality of the individuals is concentrated on such a small system, the dyad is very sensitive to anxiety and becomes unstable very easily (see Figure 15.6).

Figure 15.5
The Dyad

A ——————— B   *A and B are in a relationship.*

Figure 15.6
The Dyad Under Stress

A B   *The relationship between A & B is stressed.*

The inevitable tendency, when the dyad is unstable, is for one of the members of the dyad to bring in a third person for support. This causes a shift in the tension. At least one of the two persons in the original dyadic relationship experiences some tension relief because the third person now carries some of the anxiety. However, nothing in the original relationship has changed (see Figure 15.7). This is illustrated by the following teenager's account of a family problem:

> My father was transferred to California about three months ago. The rest of us will join him as soon as we sell our house here. After he left I got a boyfriend, Kevin, who is 19 years old. (I am 15.) When my father came home and found out about it, he had a major cow fit. He wouldn't even let the guy call the house at first. So my mom started sneaking me around so that I could see Kevin. After a couple of weeks, Kevin began calling the house anyway, and my father turned on the silent treatment. He gloated in the fact that we will be moving to California soon and Kevin and I will be separated. But last week Kevin decided to transfer to a college in California near where we will live. Now my father and I are fighting, and I've been crying all week. I still see Kevin because my mom is sneaking me around.

In this case, the daughter-father relationship was stressed, so the daughter triangled in her mother. The daughter now felt a little better because she had an ally, but the relationship with her father remained unchanged. The mother wound up with some of the anxiety from the father-daughter relationship by allowing herself to be triangulated, and this anxiety will stress her relationship with her husband.

Figure 15.7
The Triangle

Person A triangles in Person C for support. Now A and C are allies. The B and C relationship takes on some of the A-B stress. A's anxiety is lowered but nothing has changed in the A-B relationship.

The triangulation process operates automatically and unconsciously in every family system. Triangles are not problematic as long as they are transient and flexible and not rigid and intense. If triangles are transient, they occur in moments of heightened anxiety. However, family members are able to manage the issues about which they are anxious well enough that their anxiety doesn't remain diverted. Communication is maintained among all family members, in spite of occasional conflicts among them.

If triangles are flexible, family members don't get locked into the same position. No one is consistently the outsider when tensions are high. No one member is consistently picked on, taunted, interrupted or the butt of jokes. No one member is locked into the role of counselor or peacemaker. Neither parent consistently sides with the children against the other parent.

Figure 15.8
The Triangle Under Stress

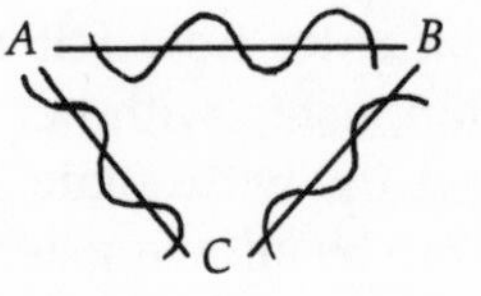

If C allies with A, the B-C relationship is stressed.

If C defends B, the A-C relationship is stressed.

If C attempts to improve the B-C relationship, A feels betrayed.

If C attempts to mediate to solve the problem for both A and B, both are likely to reject C's solutions; the A-C and B-C relationships are stressed and C carries more of the anxiety.

If relationships in a triangle are intense, they all tend to deteriorate, perceptions become distorted and reactivity goes up. Other persons are triangled in to form complicated sub-systems of triangles.

If triangles are intense and rigid, all of the relationships involved tend to deteriorate (see Figure 15.8). Perceptions become distorted, reactivity to one another escalates, alliances are formed and the family's capacity for problem-solving is diminished. This is illustrated in the account above about the boyfriend situation.

The growth of individuals and relationships is stymied by triangles because emotional energy is diverted from the conflicts which would yield the greatest satisfaction if resolved. The potential for intimacy in the marriage relationship, for example, is reduced by an affair. The marriage relationship is cheated of the undivided attention it needs to thrive and is plagued by heightened anxiety from fear of detection or reaction to betrayal.

Intimacy is reduced in the same way if a child is triangled into the marriage relationship. For example, the relationship between Norma and her husband Greg is strained. In order to relieve herself of some of the anxiety she feels about her husband, Norma triangles in their four-year-old son Paul. When Norma and Greg talk, she allows Paul to distract them by interrupting, tugging at her or climbing into her lap. When Greg plans to take Paul someplace, Norma sets Paul up to protest being taken (and then complains to others that Paul doesn't like his daddy very much). At night she frequently allows Paul to sleep with them, or she spends excess time in his room because of his fears and discomforts. Thus she avoids sexual contact with her husband and the focus on their relationship which sex requires. (This describes Norma's part of the triangle. Neither Greg nor Paul is a victim of Norma, of course, because all three participate in the triangle, and all three benefit by it.)

All three relationships will deteriorate if the triangle remains as it is. The marriage relationship will get worse, because Norma uses the care of her son as an excuse for not communicating directly with Greg, and Greg withdraws. Greg and Paul will become more and more detached from each other. The mother-son relationship will be fused and emotionally destructive.

Triangles result in individual dysfunction, as well as relationship deterioration. Triangles channel anxiety away from certain issues and individuals towards others. If the triangles are rigid, the anxiety pools onto certain members. These are the members who develop problems as symptoms of the anxiety in the family. Paul is likely to become sick, be in an accident or be socially immature in order to maintain the over-involvement of Norma and keep the family's anxiety off the marriage relationship. Or Greg could become more and more dysfunctional in the family by becoming workaholic, alcoholic, depressed or by having an affair.

Following are several suggestions for staying out of triangles:

1. Be aware of your tendency to triangle in another person when you are upset with a family member. Minimize the tendency by not gossiping or complaining to others. Increase your tolerance so that you are less reactive to the situation, or else put your energies into dealing directly with the person with whom you are upset. For example, if you disagree with your spouse about the handling of the children, either withdraw from the conflict and tone down your anxiety about it, or else, with your spouse, search for a mutually acceptable solution.

2. Be alert to family triangles which become rigid. Is one child often picked on? Interrupted? Blamed? You might be able to alter the pattern by pointing it out to the others or by responding to the child yourself in the opposite manner for awhile. (A change in one side of a triangle causes the other two sides of the triangle to adjust; a change in one triangle causes adjustments in all other intersecting triangles.) Your attempt to change the pattern must be done in a nonanxious manner, however, or you'll create more anxiety for the system to handle. This would make the problem worse or create other problems.

3. Resist being triangled in as the third party when your children tattle on each other, criticize their teachers or complain about their friends; when your spouse objects to conditions at work[2]; or when your parents list the faults of each other. Listen sympathetically, but remain neutral and resist the temptation to offer advice.

   If you find yourself becoming anxious about the other person's grievance, you are being triangled in. This doesn't happen against your will, of course, since triangulation requires the collusion of all three persons.

4. To step out of a triangle, you must respond to the other

---

[2] Note that the three members of a triangle aren't always persons. "Members" can be institutions, agencies, teams, companies, events or beliefs.

Note also that you don't have to be personally involved with both parties to be the third party. Triangulation occurs as an emotional/mental process and has nothing to do with physical proximity. The concept of triangulation, like other concepts in family systems theory, is a way of thinking about relationships. Deal with the triangle in your mind, not necessarily in person, in the same way that "family" systems therapy can be used with one member of the family.

person's complaint nonanxiously. Show mild disinterest. Use humor to lighten the situation. Change the subject as soon as you can do so tactfully. Say that you have nothing to offer in the way of advice. If necessary, disclose that you prefer not talking about another person or that the other person is also important to you.

5. Keep your anxiety lowered by maintaining confidence in your children's (or your spouse's or your parents') abilities to take care of their problems. Sometimes intervention is needed, but this is less often than most parents think (see Chapter 9, Encouraging Autonomy). Many times the best way to be supportive is to leave the responsibility for the solution where it belongs, with such replies as:

"I'm sure you will figure something out."

"That's between you and her. Talk to her about it if it's bothering you."

"Try to work it out the best you can."

Replies like this need to be stated in a genuine manner. If stated in a sarcastic, cold or belittling manner, they are not nonanxious responses.

6. Getting out of a triangle doesn't mean that you need to relate any less closely to the two individuals involved. Harriet Goldhor Lerner recommends that persons "stay calm, stay out and stay emotionally connected" (1985, p. 205) to get out of a triangle. By staying connected, she means staying in touch with *both* persons involved, not cutting yourself off from either one. A cut-off is not a nonanxious response.

Your relationship with one of the others might need to be de-intensified, at least about this particular issue, and your relationship with the other might need to be opened up. But this is in regard to *your* relationship with each, not in regard to assuming a mediator role to fix *their* relationship.

7. Speak for yourself ("in your own voice") and not for someone else, when you have a feeling or thought to express.

Don't say: "Jenny sure appreciated her present, Grandma."

Do say: "Thanks for remembering Jenny's birthday, Mom. I appreciate it."

Don't say: "Terry sure is upset with you."

Do say: "I don't like what happened tonight."

Don't say: "You're in trouble at school. You've got to get there on time."

Do say: "I found out that Mrs. Roth is concerned about your tardies. I'd suggest that you talk with her about it."

Speaking for someone else is a movement towards triangulation.

Speaking for yourself is a step out of a triangle.

Preserving Generational Boundaries

One of the most important themes in family systems theory is that fusion in a parent-child relationship prevents problems in the family system from being solved and creates other problems. Most of the examples of this chapter, in fact, have been about fused, over-close parent-child relationships.

John Drescher wrote of the importance of the marriage relationship to parenting:

> If I were starting my family again, I would love the mother of my children more. That is, I would be freer to let my children know that I love their mother. . . . I'm persuaded that probably nothing gives a child so great an inner bubbling of joy and peace as when he feels and sees parents' love for each other, while the child who lives in conflict or in the suspicion that parents do not love, develops ulcers and bellyaches. (1979, p. 13, 16)

Charlie Shedd made the same point in *Promises to Peter*, a book about his relationship with his son Peter: "[I learned that] the greatest thing I could do for my boy was to love his mother well" (1970, p. 64).

Parent-child fusion is less likely to occur if the marriage relationship is kept primary and generational boundaries are preserved. A few suggestions for preserving generational boundaries are offered here:

1. A child should not be a confidante or marriage counselor to a parent. Although this might relieve anxiety in the moment, it eventually creates all of the problems of triangulation and over-involvement if it occurs on a regular basis. In the work setting, a supervisor and subordinate can never be peers. The peers of supervisors are other supervisors, and the peers of subordinates are other subordinates. The same is true of families. The natural peers are those of the same generation.

2. Avoid secrets, especially those which cross the generational boundaries. Mother to son: "Don't tell your dad about your speeding ticket; he has enough on his mind without this."

Father to son: "Don't tell your sister that Mom was pregnant when we got married. I don't want her to tell everybody or to go out and do the same thing."

Secrets raise the level of anxiety in the family system. Friedman (1985) points out as evidence of this, that after an initial period of being more upset, family members usually experience relief when a secret is finally revealed. Secrets "create unnecessary estrangements as well as false companionship" (1985, p. 52). This is illustrated by the following story of a college student:

My dad was always the one to spank us, and I knew he hated it. I could usually get him to end the spanking quickly by crying quickly. One day he came home from work and my mom told him to spank me. He took me into his room, like he usually did, but this time told me he was too tired to spank. So he said that every time he struck the bed, I was supposed to scream and act like I was getting spanked. The plan worked. He "spanked" me like that from then on, and my mother never found out about our secret until my nineteenth birthday.

Options with secrets are limited: keep them, reveal them or not get into them in the first place. Some secrets surely are better kept than revealed, once privy to them, especially those which emerge out of a person's vulnerability and trust. However, long-term family secrets often are the issues around which family patterns for handling anxiety are passed on. Unless the younger generation knows the secrets, the patterns are unlikely to be broken and replaced by healthier patterns. Long-term family secrets, for the younger generation, are like receiving a wrapped package which is not to be opened; one simply does not know what to do with it.

In the course in which I teach family systems analysis, I require students to gather information about their families of origin. In so doing, they often discover such secrets as alcoholism, affairs, desertions, illegitimacies, elopements, business swindles or conflicts with the church. I am impressed again and again by the calming and differentiating impact discoveries like these have in the lives of the young adults, as illustrated by the following note I received:

Something really great is happening for me right now within my family. I made contact with my grandfather

(Dad's dad) who lives in Michigan, and he invited me to spend Thanksgiving with him and his wife. This is special for me because I have never met him. He and Dad got into a fight 20 years ago and haven't spoken since that time. I had not even seen a picture of him until two weeks ago when he mailed me one right after I called. He cried when we talked on the phone. I'm glad I initiated the contact, because if I hadn't, I never would have known that he wanted to get to know me, and he is old and in bad health.

Of course, this caused some friction with my dad, but he knows that I will be going to see his dad with or without his approval. I let him know what was going on immediately, so that he wouldn't find out from gossipy relatives.

Long-term family secrets need to be revealed at the appropriate time.

Secrets within one generation are less problematic. Expect your children to share information with each other which they withhold from you. Don't probe or use your influence to get them to break confidences.

One way to avoid emotionally tangled cross-generational secrets is to tell your children (or your parents), whenever the matter of a secret comes up, that you and your spouse do not keep secrets from each other. In this way you permit the flow of communication without compromising the relationship with your spouse.

3. Don't deny your children's privacy by entering closed rooms without knocking, snooping in drawers and closets, opening mail, reading diaries or eavesdropping on phone conversations. Gaining information in this way is like robbing them of parts of themselves and works against parent-child differentiation; it also raises the level of your anxiety.

4. Protect your own privacy as parents. Establish ways to talk without being overhead or interrupted. Deflect children's queries about your conversations without embarrassment; state matter-of-factly that it is between you and the child's mother (or father). Find ways to make love without disruption or excessive inhibition. (Lock the bedroom door, for example.)

5. Make occasional displays of the primacy of the relationship with your spouse. Once in a while, physically move a child who is between you out of the way. Protect moments of

solitude for each other. Do favors for each other. Resolve a conflict by deferring to your spouse and show pleasure in pleasing the other. When your spouse is experiencing conflict with the children, occasionally come to his or her defense, not to rescue, but to demonstrate where your allegiance will be if alliances are formed.

The Contribution of Family Systems Theory to Parent Education

Because the impact of family systems theory on psychology is so recent, no family systems parent education programs have been developed yet, as far as I know. However, the intellectual excitement about family systems and its potential for improving relationships undoubtedly will be channeled soon into parent education applications. This is revealed already in such books as *How to Discipline Without Feeling Guilty* by Melvin Silberman and Susan Wheelan (1980) and *Taming Monsters, Slaying Dragons,* by Joel Feiner and Graham Yost (1988).

My study of family systems in recent years has influenced my own family relationships and my teaching. Its influence appears throughout this book. Although the Balanced Parenting Model for parent education did not grow out of my study of family systems, I found the two to be intellectually compatible. Maintaining balance is an important theme for both, as is nurturing the individuality and problem solving ability of children.

I also found a compatibility between my faith, with its roots in the adult-believers tradition (see Chapter 4), and family systems, regarding the concept of differentiation. The adult-believers position suggests that spiritual differentiation of parent and child is as important to spiritual maturity as emotional differentiation is to emotional maturity. In fact, they are part of the same process of separating from parents.

Both the adult-believers tradition and family systems seek a balance of individual freedom and responsibility. In the adult-believers tradition, the individual is treated with dignity, yet held accountable to the community of faith. In family systems theory, individuals are free to act, yet always affect and are affected by the systems of which they are a part.

A criticism of family systems is that it seems (initially, at least) to be too complicated for many people to understand. I think this is because it represents a new way of thinking which requires some time to be accommodated, and because much of the family systems information is written in an abstract manner by professionals for other professionals. This needn't be the case. Harriet Goldhor Lerner's book *The Dance of Anger* demonstrated that family systems concepts are within intellectual grasp of the nonprofessional; the success of the book demonstrated that the concepts are appealing.

Another criticism of family systems is that it represents a way of *thinking*, not necessarily a way of *doing*. Parents learn that they are part of a problem but don't necessarily learn what to do about it. Family systems therapists reply that the way of thinking shows a way of doing; however, the doing has to be determined by the individual. Increased differentiation is not attained by being told what to do.

Another limitation of family systems is that it is a description of emotional processes, and emotions do not necessarily submit to the will. What are parents to do when told they need to reduce their reactivity? How do they de-intensify a relationship or an issue? How do they increase their tolerance for another person's anxiety? How do they become nonanxiously present with another person?

Family systems therapists reply to this criticism as to the former one. Granted, differentiation is not increased simply by being told to be less anxious. But when individuals begin to see the connection between their anxiety and the behavior of a child, they are able to think about the child's behavior and the choices they as parents have to respond in a manner which reduces anxiety.

Perhaps the major obstacle to the application of family systems concepts to parent education is the emotional limitations of parents themselves. To what extent can parents change their levels of emotional maturity (i.e., become more differentiated)? Bowen contends that people do not change much. Family systems therapists point out, however, that a small change can have a profound effect on the individual's functioning and on the family system. At whatever level of differentiation, change is a worthwhile goal, even a small amount.

It's too soon to predict the eventual impact of family systems theory on parent education. The influence of the family systems school of thought clearly is increasing. However, family systems theory encounters resistance within psychology, due, in part, to its tendencies to reject all traditional (billiard ball, linear) thinking, and to regard all problems (theoretically, all physical illnesses, mood disorders and social problems) as symptoms of systemic patterns. Those who work with a different frame of reference perceive family systems theory to be grandiose in scope, and wait for family systems to find its place as another way of thinking. Perhaps in time, family systems therapy and the cognitive-behavior therapies and the mood therapies will work together to develop new techniques for the home, clinic and classroom.

There is no doubt that family systems theory makes an important contribution to parent education. It offers a new way of thinking about problems in the home, and it helps to clarify the balance that is needed in parenting skills. It is but one approach, however, and does not replace the others. Parents still need to listen, to provide feedback, to make assertive demands and to manage conflict, in order to change their participation in the family system.

Questions for Thought and Discussion about this Chapter are on page 305.

In Summary

This is an age of much advice. It flows freely for parents-from daily newspapers, monthly magazines, TV talk shows, mothers' and fathers' support groups and concerned grandparents. New books appear regularly promoting the latest techniques and promising success for parents.

The intent of this book is to help parents gain perspective on the requirements of parenting, an outlook which will enable them to make wise choices from the profusion of advice before them.

The Balanced Parenting Model, the conceptual framework explored here, gives shape to the complex task a mother and father undertake. It divides the parent-child relationship into four areas, each of which has distinct objectives and a separate set of parenting skills for reaching those goals.

The No Problem Area

In the No Problem Area the child is not in a struggle with the parent nor worried about other matters, and the parent is not bothered by the child's behavior. These are the moments when parent and child work side by side, play together, attend each other's performances, go shopping or eat out together, converse at the dining table and at bedtime, vacation together and support each other in times of crisis. Although "discipline" is not commonly thought to occur at such times, it does indeed. On these occasions children develop their identity and form patterns for establishing and nurturing relationships which will be followed throughout their lives.

Of the four areas in a parent's relationship with a child, the No Problem Area may be the most important. Those moments, when parent and child are together and neither one is upset, create a sense of family whose members enjoy and care about each other.

If this sense of family is developed, problems will be manageable when they arise, even if the parent's techniques are not the best. On the other hand, if this sense of caring for each other is not created, no technique or method will work well in dealing with a problem.

The Child's Problem Area

The Child's Problem Area contains those situations in which the child is bothered about something and feels frustrated, deprived, hurt, puzzled, defeated, discouraged or inadequate. Here the parent needs to exercise listening and encouraging skills, in order to help the child deal with the troubling situation, but also to refrain from interfering too much in the child's problem. Allowing the child to struggle with such problems as disappointment in an environment of sensitive support and encouragement moves the child towards the long-term goal of being a resourceful and self-accepting person.

As in the other areas, the skills of the Child's Problem Area can be used too much or too little. They are over-used when parents become too involved in their children's problems. Then the child's development is impeded and the parent becomes so responsive to the child's moods that the child becomes manipulative. The well-meaning but overly-concerned mother who tries to make life painless for her children, and the father who regularly bails his children out of trouble are classic examples of excessive use of the Child's Problem Area skills.

Parents also err by using the skills of the Child's Problem Area too little. This happens when parents are indifferent or insensitive to their children's feelings. A child is a person with feelings which need to be acknowledged and a sense of self which needs to be respected and encouraged to become strong. Without the ability to listen and encourage, the package of parental skills is incomplete.

The Parent's Problem Area

The Parent's Problem Area contains the situations in which the child's behavior is bothersome to the parent. This is the area people usually have in mind when they talk about "discipline." (In the Balanced Parenting Model, however, "discipline" is used to mean what happens in all four areas, the sum of things parents do to influence their children to become the kinds of persons they hope their children become.)

Parental skills of the Parent's Problem Area include reasoning, providing feedback in a nonthreatening manner, making demands and turning down requests assertively, and establishing consequences for noncompliance with parental requests.

Parents commonly rely on punishment to correct the child's bothersome behavior, although punishing the child because the child did something wrong is neither a moral nor a practical necessity. If punishment is used, the kind of punishment which requires the child to make restitution to the victim of the misbehavior is recommended.

In certain situations, especially those in which children are lagging in intellectual or social development, the procedures of behavior modification are useful tools for the Parent's Problem Area.

Here again, the skills of the Parent's Problem Area can be emphasized too much or too little. The balance among all four areas is what makes the skills effective. Classic examples of Parent's Problem Area skills carried to an extreme include the father who is so intimidating that his children are afraid of him, and avoid contact with him, and the mother who controls her children so much that their internal control has little chance to develop.

Just as some parents over-emphasize the skills of the Parent's Problem Area, other parents are too weak in the Parent's Problem Area. There are those parents who completely sacrifice their personal lives by catering to their children's whims, and parents who allow their children to be destructive, obnoxious or rude. They look the other way or dismiss the misbehavior as a "stage" which the children are going through, rather than develop the personal competence they need to regain control of the home.

The Mutual Problem Area

The Mutual Problem Area is formed by the overlap of the Child's Problem Area and the Parent's Problem Area. Mutual problems are bothersome to both parent and child and threaten the relationship. Here are struggles involving school work, dress and hair styles, cleaning up messes and doing household chores, money, the use of the car, telephone or television, going to bed, sleeping in, practicing music and other uses of time, and parties, drinking and other activities with friends.

Since the Mutual Problem Area is formed by the overlap of problems which are bothersome to both parent and child, the parenting skills which apply to the Mutual Problem Area are a combination of the skills for the Child's Problem Area (listening for the child's feelings and interests) and the Parent's Problem Area (clarifying one's own feelings and interests). Additional parenting skills specifically for the Mutual Problem Area include defining and sticking to the issue and compromising assertively.

From the perspective of family systems theory, the best parental strategy for the Mutual Problem Area very often is to give up the problem, that is, to be less anxious about it. When a parent is highly concerned about a problem, the parental anxiety itself is a part of the problem. The feelings and preferences of parents and children become entangled and parental attempts to solve problems are emotionally manipulative and unsuccessful. On the other hand, parents who differentiate themselves from their children and who permit their children to differentiate themselves as persons, approach mutual problems with less anxiety, more patience and humor, a respect for individual differences and a willingness to tolerate conflict.

The short-term goal of the Mutual Problem Area is to manage problems so well that growth in the parent-child relationship occurs as a result. If conflict is managed well, parent and child are more likely to regard each other sensitively and respectfully, and are less likely to be callous or to take each other for granted. This will make the No Problem Area moments more enjoyable and problems in each of the other areas more easily solved. Conflict management contributes to a healthy balance among the four problem areas.

The long-term goal of the Mutual Problem Area is to teach conflict management skills to children. The way that parent-child conflicts are handled creates a pattern for the child's ability to deal with conflicts in other areas of life. If whining, badgering, becoming depressed or helpless, bullying or other tactics are modeled, these are the strategies that the child will know best and be most likely to use. On the other hand, if parents respond to conflicts with reasonableness, good will and respect, and insist on the same from their children, children will learn to employ those practices with others.

Evaluating Other Parent Education Programs

The Balanced Parenting Model and its four areas can be used to assess the strengths and weaknesses of parent education programs (e.g., Parent Effectiveness Training, Systematic Training for Effective Parenting, behavior modification) and the advice of parenting experts (e.g., James Dobson). This is done throughout the book, always with a view toward maintaining balance among the four areas as the key to parental success. Overemphasis of any technique or method or any one school of thought will lead parents astray. There is no method which is adequate by itself.

Becoming Emotionally Differentiated

The other theme of **Parenting for the '90s** is the importance of emotional differentiation of parent and child. Parents can feel too responsible for their children and become too involved in their children's struggles, just as they can feel too indifferent and be too uninvolved. Successful parents strive for a balance between these two competing and dynamic tendencies in their relationships with their children.

Parents who are less differentiated tend to be coercive, punitive or emotionally manipulative in their attempts to influence their children, or they withdraw from their children in fear and defeat. This happens because they are unable to separate their preferences and choices from those of their children. Parents who are more differentiated tend to influence their children without being coercive, punitive or manipulative, because they are clearer about their own preferences and choices and respect the preferences and choices of their children. Their firmness as parents comes from inside themselves, from their firm sense of self.

This perspective acknowledges that parents have no guarantee that there will not be problems. Parents do not have control over the disposition the child is born with nor all of the choices the child makes. Respecting the individuality of the child is accompanied always by apprehension and sometimes by disappointment.

From this point of view, parents need not take all the blame (nor all the credit) for how their children turn out. Children are ultimately responsible for their choices. This relieves parents of some of the responsibility they likely feel for their children, but it doesn't let them off the hook entirely. The kinds of persons parents are does affect the kinds of persons children become, and parents *are* responsible for *their* own choices.

This emphasis on the respect for the individuality of the child (developed in religious terms in Chapter 4 and found throughout the book in the terms of family systems theory) presents a view on parenting which is different from the understanding of conservative Christians who emphasize evil, willfulness, obedience and punishment. It is my position that success as a parent does not come through an emphasis on breaking, bending or shaping the will of the child; instead, succeeding is linked to the view of the child as a separate individual, temporarily entrusted to the parent for nurturing to adulthood.

Misbehavior needs to be corrected, of course, and there are many ways of doing so. The task of parents today is to select those techniques which work best for them, which are consistent with what they desire for human relationships, and which form a well-balanced set of skills.

My hope is that the perspective of this book will challenge them to consider in a fresh way what it means to live with children by their side.

Questions for Thought and Discussion

Part I., Gaining Perspective on Parenting Advice, page 9

1. How did your parents become informed about parenting? Through advice from their parents and older relatives? Through observation? Through trial and error? Through reading? (Ask them sometime.)
2. What have been your favorite sources of information about parenting?
3. With what aspects of parenting do you feel informed and confident? With what aspects do you feel inadequately informed and uncertain?

Chapter 1, Balanced Parenting, page 13

1. Identify the owners of the following problems:
   a. Virgil forgets to take out the trash.
   b. Diane doesn't like the color of her coat.
   c. Tim's dad wants him to call Grandma to thank her for the gift, but Tim doesn't want to talk on the phone.
   d. Ann goes with her dad to the grocery store.

    e. Lynn's high test scores earn her a scholarship.

    f. Virgil can't decide whom to invite to Homecoming.

    g. Diane helps her dad with the wheat harvest by driving the grain truck.

    h. Tim dawdles in the bathtub past his bedtime.

    i. Ann breaks her eyeglasses, which she needs to see properly and which were very expensive.

    j. Lynn comes in much later than her parents expected her to come home.

2. Think of things which have happened in your own life which illustrate each of the four areas of the Balanced Parenting Model.

3. What questions are emerging in your mind about problem ownership and the Balanced Parenting Model?

(Answers to Problem Ownership exercise: a. PP, b. CP, c. MP, d. NP, e. NP, f. CP, g. NP, h. PP, i. MP, j. PP.)

Chapter 2, Balance Among the Four Areas, page 23

1. Define discipline in one or two sentences.

2. Evaluate the strengths and weaknesses of your parents from the perspective of the Balanced Parenting Model.

3. In what ways do you sense that the kind of person you are is a result of your parents' strengths and weaknesses?

4. Describe persons you have known who could serve as role models for the different areas.

5. Evaluate your own strengths and weaknesses from the perspective of the Balanced Parenting Model.

6. What reactions do you have to the patterns of imbalance in the roles of the traditional father and traditional mother as they are portrayed in this chapter?

Chapter 3, Three Philosophies of Parenting, page 30

1. Which of the philosophies do the following quotations illustrate?

    a. If we are properly identifying rebellion we will not be content to simply have discovered it, but we will want to do something about it. The something about it is punishment. Rebellion must be met with discipline if we are to establish in the child's mind a healthy respect for authority and his need for submission to it. Sometimes the story is told . . . of the boy who was made to sit in a chair. He did. But he made this comment, "I am sitting down on the outside, but on the inside I am still standing." I'll tell you, those parents had work to do yet. — D. E. Newswanger (1977, p. 60)

b. Most of what we see other people doing represents something they have learned. Talking, dressing, playing, and working at tasks are all things that are learned. It is also true that whining, fighting, or temper tantrums are learned. — Gerald Patterson (1976, p. 3)

c. When a child tells of, or asks about, an event, it is frequently best to respond, not to the event, but to the relationship implied.

Flora, age six, complained that "lately" she had been receiving fewer presents than her brother. Mother did not deny the complaint. Neither did she explain that brother was older and so deserved more. Nor did she promise to right the wrong. She knew that children are more concerned about the depth of their relationships with parents than about the size and number of gifts. Mother said, "You, too, want more presents?" Without adding another sentence, mother embraced her daughter, who responded with a smile of surprise and pleasure. This was the end of a conversation that could have become an endless argument. —Haim Ginott (1965, p. 30–31)

d. In my opinion, the therapeutic value of this kind of psychotherapy is based upon the child's experiencing himself as a capable, responsible person in a relationship that tries to communicate to him two basic truths: that no one ever really knows as much about any human being's inner world as does the individual himself; and that responsible freedom grows and develops from inside the person. The child must first learn self-respect and a sense of dignity that grows out of his increasing self-understanding before he can learn to respect the personalities and rights and differences of others. — Virginia Axline (1964, p. 67)

e. [I] had a holy respect for Dad's razor strap that hung on a big nail on the way downstairs to the coal bin. Dad conducted all his "counseling sessions" in that coal bin. He would never spank me when he was angry, but he waited until I thought he had forgotten all about my disobedience. Then, with a soft voice, "All right, David, let's go downstairs and learn another lesson on obedience." He would turn me over his knee and before he laid a single stripe on me, I'd wiggle like a snake, scream like I was being murdered, and cry like I was about to die. My crying never seemed to frighten or impress him. I got it—hard! Then I had to kneel and ask God to forgive my stubbornness, and after making it right with heaven, I had to put my arms around him and tell him how much I loved him. That is why that stubborn, foolish, disobedient little child grew up to be a minister of the gospel instead of a gang leader! I believe it's time for a woodshed revival!—Larry Christenson (1974, p. 107)

f. If your child finishes everything on his or her plate, *praise* the child and mark the "yes" column on the CLEAN PLATE CLUB form. When you praise your child, do it in a matter-of-fact manner and do *not* refer to times he or she has been unsuccessful. For instance, do *not* say, "I'm glad you ate everything, seeing that you did so badly at lunch." Stress only the positive behavior the child has accomplished at the current meal. —Howard Sloane, Jr. (1976, p. 12)

2. To what extent were your parents influenced by these philosophies?
3. What exposure have you had to these philosophies? What books about parenting have you read? Which of the three philosophies do they fit best?
4. Which aspects of the philosophies appeal to you and which aspects do not? To what extent would you adopt one as your own philosophy?
5. Do some parents not have a philosophy? Do some have one without being aware of it, or without being able to articulate it? Does it make any difference?
6. To the extent that you have one and can articulate it, what is your philosophy of parenting?

Answer to #1 a. Dobson; b. Behaviorism; c. P.E.T., parent as communicator; d. P.E.T., parent as communicator; e. Dobson; f. Behaviorism

Chapter 4, An Alternative Perspective on Parenting, page 46

1. Does the point of view of this chapter appeal to you? Why or why not?
2. To what extent did your parents follow an adult-believers pattern in raising you?
3. How were your parents' religious faiths revealed in the ways they lived? What were their deeply held beliefs? What were their inconsistencies? How were you affected by the ways they lived?
4. If your faith is claimed by your child, what kind of faith will it be? What would you do differently to become a steadier launching pad for your child?

Part II., The No Problem Area, page 58

1. How do you react to the notion that the No Problem Area is a part of the discipline process?
2. Define discipline in a way which includes the No Problem Area.
3. As you were growing up, how full was the relationship account which you shared with your parents? How full is it now with your children (or parents)? Explain.
4. Share reactions to the paradoxes addressed in points 1 through 7 at the end of Part II. Illustrate the paradoxical nature of No Problem moments with personal memories.

Chapter 5, Activities in the No Problem Area, page 65

1. Think of happy memories from your life involving your parents or your children and you. Share them with others.
   a. Family trips, holidays and other celebrations
   b. Shared leisure activities and spontaneous fun.
   c. Working together.
   d. Meal- and bedtime routines.
   e. Mutual support in times of crisis.
2. Do you have other happy memories which don't fit these categories?
3. Grade your family of origin on the size of its No Problem Area. Explain why you chose the grade you chose (A, B, C, D, F).
4. What prevents you from taking advantage of No Problem

moments to a greater extent?

5. What would you like to do to enlarge the No Problem Area? Plan something specific.

Chapter 6, Fighting the Television Battle, page 80

1. How much time do you spend watching TV? (Be honest.) When in your daily and weekly routines do you usually watch?
2. Why do you watch television? How important are the following reasons?
   a. Information (news, weather, sports scores, documentaries, etc.).
   b. Entertainment (to relax, laugh).
   c. To get away from problems or people.
   d. To be with people.
   e. Conversation topics (to be able to talk with others about what is on).
   f. To pass time.
   g. Other reasons?
3. Which programs do you think are the best? The worst?
4. How do you react to the information this chapter presents concerning violence, sex and marriage, parenthood and sex role stereotypes?
5. Are you concerned about the impact of television on your family life? What are your concerns?
6. Do you have other suggestions for fighting the TV battle?

Chapter 7, Keeping Sports in the No Problem Area, page 93

1. How important are play and physical exercise in your life? To what extent do they take place with parent and child together?
2. What memories (both good and bad) do you have of sports activities?
3. What memories do you have of your other kinds of achievements that were commended (or went unnoticed?)
4. Do you have other suggestions for keeping sports in the No Problem Area?

Part III., The Child's Problem Area, page 99

1. People sometimes say, "It's not my problem," indicating indif-

ference to the situation or unwillingness to take any responsibility for the situation. But in the Balanced Parenting Model, to speak of a problem as the child's does not mean that the parent does nothing. When is the child the owner of a problem?

2. What are the parenting goals of the Child's Problem Area? (Review Chapters 1 and 2.)

Chapter 8, Listening, page 101

1. What has been your experience with the skills of this chapter? Is this review of old information or new information for you? Is it easy or difficult for you to apply? Are you convinced or skeptical of the importance of these skills?

2. Reflect back on times when you needed someone to listen to you. What happened? How did you feel about the way the other person responded to you and your problem?

3. With a partner, take turns describing highlights of your lives (honors, accomplishments, times of intimacy with loved ones, moments of insight and understanding, extraordinary aesthetic experiences, times of closeness with nature or God). The one who is listening does nothing but listen, enjoying the pleasurable memories with the other and coming to understand the other person better. At the end the listener says, "Thank you for sharing that with me."

4. Now take turns describing some of the low points of your lives (times you were embarrassed, misunderstood, rejected, defeated, etc.) Again, the one who is listening does nothing but listen, empathizing with the painfulness of the memories and coming to understand the other person better, At the end the listener again says, "Thank you for sharing that with me."

5. Tell about times you listened to children. What were the situations and how did you respond? What were the effects of your responses?

6. Make up a response for each of the quotations below which acknowledges the feeling which the child likely is experiencing. Use a tentative statement for the response, not a question. The list of unpleasant emotions might help in giving the feeling a name.

afraid	angry	annoyed
ashamed	bored	confused
crushed	dazed	defeated
depressed	different	disappointed

discouraged	disgusted	disoriented
dominated	embarrassed	envious
exhausted	exploited	famished
hopeless	horrified	humiliated
hungry	hurt	ill
impatient	indecisive	insecure
lazy	left out	mad
miserable	oppressed	overwhelmed
put down	rejected	resentful
sad	shocked	shy
sluggish	stunned	suffocated
thirsty	tormented	trapped
uncertain	uncomfortable	undesirable
unimportant	unloved	unlucky
weary	weird	worried

a. "Jimmy bosses me around like I'm his servant."
b. "I'll never get this book read in time to do the report."
c. "I hurt Ruth Ann with the point of my pencil today."
d. "Is supper about ready?"
e. "Do you think I should go out for tennis?"
f. "Why can't I go? Everybody else gets to go."
g. "I think I'll go to bed early tonight."
h. "I can't think of anything to do."
i. "Do you like my hair this way?"
j. "I hate these shoes!"
k. "Do you dream bad dreams?"
l. "I wish I were big."
m. "I'd like to drop piano lessons."
n. "I can't sleep."
o. "Praying is no good. I've prayed and prayed and it didn't make any difference."
p. "What a rotten day!"
q. "Kevin still hasn't asked me to the prom."

7. How could the following situations have been handled better by the parents? Role play the situations using poor listening techniques first, then do it again using the techniques of this chapter.

a. If I don't play very well in a volleyball game I'm really discouraged afterwards. I go home and I try to talk about the game with Mom and Dad, but Dad will say something like, "There's no excuse for not getting a serve in." [lecturing] This makes me so upset! I think, "Does he think everything he does in sports is right? He doesn't even know what it's like to play volleyball." It makes me defensive and more discouraged. I wish he could tell me things that are more uplifting.

b. My nose was a big problem all through elementary school and junior high. I was often asked if it was broken. It got to the point where I would hold my hand in front of my face to hide my nose when I talked to people. One day I told Mom and Daddy that I wanted to have plastic surgery on my nose to get it fixed. Daddy came back with, "You do that young lady and I'll disown you. [threatening] You were given that nose and you're not going to have any such thing done to it. [ordering] Think of it this way—it gives you character." [moralizing] Like this was supposed to make me feel better!

c. I dressed for the varsity team all year, and at sectional time I was cut from the tournament squad. I was surprised and upset about it. I didn't think it was fair because I had worked hard all year, even if I didn't play a lot. The coach's reason was that he wanted to give the younger players more experience. When I got home and told my folks Mom said, "Well, the coach is getting paid to coach and you're not. He must know what he's doing." [disagreeing] I felt so humiliated by the situation that I didn't even want to go to watch the game, but Mom and Dad made me go.

Chapter 9, Encouraging Autonomy, page 125

1. Share with others experiences you have had in regard to discouragement or encouragement.
2. Think of encouraging people you have known. What do they do that gives a lift to those around them?
3. How do parents know when to intervene and when to stay out of a child's problem? If they decide not to intervene, how do they remain supportive? If they decide to intervene, how do they do so in a supportive manner? Discuss these questions using the following situation:

    When I was in junior high school, a group of older girls decided they didn't like me and made it their duty to pick on me. They got carried away and would push me around, chase me down the hall and threaten me. My parents realized what was going on and wanted to talk to the principal about it, but I wouldn't let them. I was afraid I would get picked on twice as bad if the principal talked to the girls. It got to be so bad, however, that I was too scared to enjoy school. My parents decided to talk to the principal and to my surprise, things calmed down. The girls still made me feel inferior, but they didn't torment me as openly or as physically as before.

4. Describe cases of the over-responsible/under-responsible pattern which you have observed.

5. Analyze the over-responsible/under-responsible pattern revealed by the following parent-child (college-age) interaction:

Last weekend I had a chance to go to Kansas City with some classmates to visit some friends from back home. We were going to leave on Thursday evening and I could have handled a day of absences from my classes. I was looking forward to the weekend. So I called home to have Mom call my friends in Kansas City to tell them I was coming. Thirty minutes later she called back to tell me that I couldn't go. This was really frustrating to me and made me feel like a child. Her reason for not letting me go was that I have to learn to take responsibility.

6. Role play the following situations. First play the parent's role in a manner which is discouraging, and then go through it again with the parent responding in a manner which encourages the child's autonomy.

   a. One day after going to the grocery store, I decided to make a game out of giving my two older sisters their candy bars. I made notes with clues about where to look for them. At the last minute I changed the hiding place but in the excitement of the game I forgot to change the last clue. My one sister couldn't find hers and she got upset. So I had to tell Mom and she said, "How on earth could you lose a candy bar? You'd better find it!" I retraced my steps and finally figured out where I had put it. I victoriously showed Mom, but she said, "It's about time! I can't believe you'd lose it in the first place!" I no longer felt good about finding it; I felt guilty for wanting to make a game out of something that was so serious.

   b. I was never told about the menstrual cycle at home, not even by my sisters; I learned everything from school. I was in the eighth grade when my first period started. I came home from school and got up the courage to tell Mom. I told her I had started my period at school and that I put my underwear in the bathroom. Her response was, "Did you wash them out with cold water?" I replied, "No, I used warm." "Well, you should have used cold." And that's all she said. She didn't even ask me how I was feeling, or if I needed anything. I felt really insignificant — less important than the underwear. As I looked at her face I realized that she was as scared as I, which made me feel like I had a rare disease or something. I felt very lonely with no one to talk to.

c. When I started college I was in the Nursing Program. I personally hated it, but I enrolled because my dad wanted me to. Well, that first semester I managed to fail every course I took. So I said, enough is enough and dropped out. I felt worthless, like I could not accomplish a thing. My father gave me no sympathy whatsoever. Finally I told him to back off and began seeking others' advice to figure out what I wanted from life.

Part IV., The Parent's Problem Area, page 143

1. Use the terms *discipline, correction* and *punishment* in sentences which clarify their meanings.
2. During your childhood and adolescence did your parents fit the description of powerful parents?
3. Think of persons who influenced your behavior. How did they do it?
4. What issues are involved in the following situation? Have you observed similar cases? What are your suggestions for dealing with such situations?

A congregation recently obtained a court order to bar a woman and her nine-year-old son from church services. According to news reports, the boy made loud noises, destroyed property, threw objects at members and set off a fire alarm. The mother "has been unwilling or unable to control the child despite many complaints and urgings" ("Church Cites," 1988).

When the mother and son arrived at the church the first Sunday after the court order was received, church officials barred her from entering. Before leaving the front of the church she prayed aloud, "Dear Lord, we know this is your house. We ask you to open your doors to let us in." Then she left and held a news conference before going to another church.

The pastor of the church from which she was barred also held a news conference. He said that the church worked with the mother for several months to try to restrain the son, but the efforts failed. "The level of disturbance moved from being merely annoying to being utterly intolerable," he said. Some church members had stopped attending because of the disruptions ("Woman, Child Barred," 1988).

5. Share examples of persons you have known whose Parent's Problem Area skills were out of balance (too strong or too weak relative to the other areas). What were their children like?
6. Assess your own Problem Area Skills.

Chapter 10, Providing Information: Facts and Feelings, page 147

1. Do you remember times when you unwittingly misbehaved because you didn't understand what was expected? What happened?
2. Share reactions to the following situation:
   My parents let me set my own curfew. I never really have had an exact time, but because I have been a good teenager, it hasn't been necessary. One time I still wasn't home by 1:00 on a school night. My father came looking for me. We met by a street near our house. He saw I was OK, and then told me I was grounded for two weeks. That would have been awful, because I'm a very social person. When we got home, he let me explain. I had gone out to Pizza Hut with a friend who was upset. It got late, and I didn't call because I didn't want to wake them up. After I explained, Dad took away the grounding and told me it was *never* too late to call.
3. Share memories about times when reasonableness worked for you (or your parents).
4. Describe parents you have known who exemplify the restricted and elaborated language codes reported by Bernstein. Have you observed the fight cycles reported by Patterson?
5. For practice, construct two responses for each of the following situations. First, respond with a You-message that parents likely would send, and then construct a less threatening and more honest I-message:
   • squabbling in the car
   • begging for candy at the grocery store

- bike left outside
- clothes on floor
- teenager coming in late
- dawdling in getting ready to leave

6. Do you agree that I-messages are hard to employ because they are confrontational and because they require vulnerability?
7. Have you known parents who relied too much on reasonableness? On feelings? What were their interactions with their children like?

Chapter 11, Taking Charge: Demands and Consequences, page 163

1. Role play the incident with the young child going down the steps and towards the street, using three different parenting styles. Role play it first with a parent who is meek (unassertive). Then, with a parent who is intimidating (aggressive). Finally, with a parent who is direct and firm (assertive) and who delivers the message with an assertive appearance.

2. Practice making statements which clarify the parent's position ("I want . . . ," "I would like . . . ," "I expect . . . ," "I will [not] . . . ," etc.) for the following situations. Make the nonverbal signals match the words.
   - young child gets out of bed repeatedly
   - siblings (elementary school age) pick on, fuss at and taunt each other at the table
   - early adolescent leaves without carrying out household chores
   - late adolescent uses family car without replacing gas or cleaning it

3. Choose one of the following situations, or a similar one, to role play. First, role play it in a manner in which the parent and child end up arguing. Then replay it so that the parent takes a position without arguing, by using the "fogging" and "broken record" techniques.
   - teenager talks for long time on phone
   - child doesn't want to go to family reunion
   - child wants to sleep over at friend's house and parent denies request
   - young child begs for junk food at grocery store

4. Have you known parents who were like the basketball official

who complains about infractions but does nothing to enforce the rules? What were the effects on the children? On the parents themselves?

5. Plan FFDC strategies for the following situations:
   - teenager ties up telephone
   - not doing dishes (or some other household chore)
   - fighting over which TV program to watch
   - poor table manners
   - teenager coming in late
   - quarrelsomeness in car

6. What successes or failures have you had with logical consequences?

7. How do you respond to this chapter, in general? How do you respond to the notion that firmness comes from within? That parents take charge by taking charge of themselves (moving their position on the seesaw)? That parents need to declare themselves, but don't need to persuade?

Chapter 12, Using Punishment, page 189

1. How do you personally respond to this chapter?
2. Were you punished as a child? How did your parents do it? Share specific memories—what happened, how your parents handled the situation and how you felt about it.
3. What do you think today about your parents' methods then?
4. Does punishment fit your parenting style? What are the conditions in which you do (or do not) punish?
5. For review purposes, illustrate each of the four uses of punishment with a personal observation or memory.
6. Does the use of logical consequences in the FFDC plan seem to you to be an alternative to retributive punishment?
7. Are you convinced by the argument that the proverbial rod does not need to be applied in a literal way by the modern reader?

Chapter 13, Applying Behavior Modification, page 209

1. For each of the following, fill in the blank with "positively reinforced," "negatively reinforced" or "punished."
   a. When Dwight reads a book from the library, he gets a gold star. His reading behavior is _____.
   b. Gregory ran to the house to get out of the cold rain. When

he got into the warm house, his running behavior was
_____.

c. Debbie's Uncle Bob sends her to the convenience store to get herself a treat whenever she gets so noisy he can't stand to have her around. Debbie's noisy behavior is _____.

d. When Susie refused to drink at the party she attended, the youth made fun of her. Her refusal to drink was _____.

e. Susie finally gave in to their invitations to drink, and they congratulated her for joining their fun. Her drinking behavior was _____.

f. The following morning, Susie did not feel well when she got up. Her drinking behavior was _____ the day after.

g. Susie's parents grounded her because she broke the family prohibition against drinking. Her drinking behavior was _____ by her parents.

h. Susie behaved so well during the time she was grounded, that her parents shortened the period by two days. Her good behavior was _____.

2. What behaviors are being learned in the following situations? Use the terminology of behavioral psychology in your analysis.

a. Marla gets sick and depressed and misses school quite often. On those days, her parents treat her especially nice; they buy her treats, help with her homework and require the other children to be quiet.

b. When Tonya's older brother does something she doesn't like, she cries and runs to her parents to tattle. When this happens, they usually reprimand or punish him and comfort her.

c. Sandy got in trouble with one of her high school teachers because she didn't hand her work in on time. The teacher refused to give her credit for the work because this was not the first time it had come in late. That night Sandy complained to her parents about how unreasonable her teacher was. The next day her parents called the principal to complain. The principal discussed the situation with the teacher involved, who decided to reinstate the grade.

3. Using the language of behavioral psychology, plan behavior modification programs for the following problems:
a. child is mean to little sister

   b. teenager ties up the phone
   c. child needs many reminders to do chores
   d. middle school child gets grades below potential
   e. child is slow to get dressed, stays in pajamas
   f. teenager uses family car inappropriately
   g. young child resists getting ready for bed
   h. child won't stay in bed
4. Did your parents intuitively understand and use the power of positive reinforcement? If so, how did they do it?
5. Do you have any experience in a classroom or institutional setting where behavior management techniques were used? Have you used them in a family setting? Share your observations.
6. What reinforcers have you found to be effective? Ineffective? Effective for a time, and then ineffective?
7. Would you use behavior modification? If so, in what situations? If not, why not?
8. Do you see value in studying behavior modification even if it is not used in a systematic way? What have you learned that is worth knowing?

plain to get what she wants.
then to solve her own problems. She also is learning to com-
parents. She is being trained to be dependent on them, rather
   c. Sandy's irresponsible behavior is being maintained by her
   b. Tonya is being trained to tattle.
2. a. Marla is learning to be sick and depressed to receive attention.
1. a. PR, b. NR, c. PR, d. P, e. PR, f. P, g. P, h. NR
Answers

Part V., The Mutual Problem Area, page 233

1. What did your parents teach you about conflict? How has this affected your relationships?
2. What would you like your children to learn in regard to conflict?
3. Do you recall instances in which your feelings about the parent-child relationship affected your reactions to specific situations? Describe what made the relationship strong or weak at that time, and how this affected the Mutual Problem Area.
4. Have you had experiences in which a relationship had grown

stale because of conflict and then, when the conflict was faced, was revitalized? Explain what happened.

5. What types of problems do you most frequently encounter as mutual problems?

Chapter 14, Managing Conflict, page 235

1. Do you agree that conflict in a relationship is inevitable? What difference does love make?

2. Assess your own strengths and weaknesses as manager of the conflict in your life.

3. Have you observed situations in which parents should have given up the problems they were concerned about? Describe the situations.

4. Family members often experience conflict with each other when they have other things on their minds. When are you and the other members of your family most likely to "pick a fight"? Does PMS (Premenstrual Syndrome) make a difference?

5. What is your opinion about how the Family Telephone Case was handled? The Homecoming Plans Case?

6. Role play the following examples of conflict. Play the parents' parts in different ways, and discuss the impact of each.

   a. Mom always talks about how she wishes her desk were not so messy, but she never gets around to tidying it up. I decided to help her out one day when I was cleaning. So I put everything on neat piles and put stuff away if I knew where it belonged. I thought I had it looking very nice and was proud of my work. However, when Mom got home she really flew off the handle. She sent me out of the room while she rearranged things again. When she was finished, it was just as untidy as before. I wish she would realize how much it matters to me that her desk is so cluttered. It's right in the kitchen where we see it all the time. I also wish she would understand that I was just trying to help.

   b. Six-year-old Lindsey has great difficulty swallowing pills. Her parents think it's important to take vitamin pills daily and expect her to do so. The moment for taking the pill is always filled with tension; Lindsey protests, chokes and cries. Her parents scold her, reason with her, wait her out and spank her, but the problem continues. Lindsey finally begins to lie about swallowing the pill. She hides the pill under her tongue and disposes of it later—down the toilet, behind some bushes, in a waste basket or in a drawer. One day her mother discovers a cache of pills in a drawer, and the problem comes to a head.

c. Marge, age 17, has become increasingly rebellious. Lately she has been coming in late and drunk on Saturday nights. On Sunday morning her mother yells at her to get up and get ready for church. Finally her mother says something like, "I don't know why you do this," and walks out. Marge rolls over and goes back to sleep.

d. Dan is the oldest of three children. During his high school junior year, his parents found out that he was drinking, which they opposed. They threatened to take away his car privileges if it continued, which seemed to keep him from additional drinking. Towards the end of his senior year, he began dating a girl from the neighboring town. Dan's parents were opposed to this and forbid him to see her. Dan continued to see her and began lying to them about his activities. Three days before he was to leave for college, they found out about this and expressed disappointment, hurt and anger. Dan's departure for college was a tension-filled moment.

Chapter 15, Changing the Family System, page 253

1. Explain how the following mutual problems possibly could be sustained by the families involved? Use the terminology of family systems in your explanations.

a. Charles and Jane have one child, a daughter Jamie. For the first five years of Jamie's life, they have followed the traditional pattern in which Charles worked full-time outside the home and Jane worked full-time in the home caring for Jamie. The three looked forward to Jamie's entry into kindergarten, taking pleasure in shopping for her school clothes and supplies. But when the school year began, Jamie became frightened. Her fear continued for several weeks. She would complain of a stomachache almost every morning. Jane guessed that Jamie's ailments probably were related to stress and was bothered that school should be so stressful for her daughter. Jane usually took Jamie to school in spite of the stomachaches, but sometimes she gave in to Jamie's protests and allowed her to stay home. Charles didn't know what to make of Jamie's fear of school. He left for work early in the morning and wasn't witness to Jamie's complaints or to Jane's struggles with Jamie's fear.

b. There are three children in the Wheeler family—Jim and Rob, biological children of the parents, and Trish, an adopted child. Trish seems to be the one who gets in trouble; whenever something gets broken or is missing, she is blamed for it. Her academic achievement gets worse during each year of elementary school, and her parents become increasingly frustrated and strict with her.

c. Four-year-old Heather behaves shyly around others, children and adults alike. When her family has guests, she observes the interaction from a distance, but if pressed to participate in conversation remains silent or disappears. Her mother worries that Heather might be so shy that kindergarten will be difficult for her. She begins inviting a couple of other preschool children to their home once a week so that Heather has some playmates. When they are there, Heather tends to play by herself.

2. Draw a diagram of your family which shows relative closeness and distance among family members. Draw lines between family members, using double lines to indicate over-closeness and wavy lines to indicate tension (as in Figure 15.7). Would you like to move your position relative to the others? How could you go about doing so?

3 Have you observed situations in which children exhibited problem behavior which probably was symptomatic of anxiety in the family?

4. To what extent are you able to be "nonanxiously present" with your children? Can you reduce the anxiety you feel in your relationships with family members? How do you do it?

5. Are you surprised to read that fusion is indicated by positive reactivity (for example, bragging about your child) as well as negative reactivity (for example, nagging your child)? Do you think positive reactivity poses a problem in your parent-child relationships?

6. If you tend to be over-involved with your children (or cut off), what do you think of moving towards the position of "mild interest" as a corrective technique?

7. What nicknames are used in your family? Were children named after other persons? How might these forms of labeling influence family interaction patterns?
8. Is it possible to think of each child as a separate, unique individual without labeling?
9. How do you make each child feel special without secrets and alliances?
10. Do you find yourself vying for position as favored parent? What are the usual circumstances in which this occurs?
11. What are the triangles which your family most easily falls into? Are they intense? Rigid?
12. What have you observed about being triangled into a problem? About getting out of a triangle?
13. Have you observed families in which children were confidantes of parents? Describe what you observed.
14. In general, how do you respond to the content of this chapter? To what extent do you find it to be helpful? Disturbing?

References

Abidin, R. R. 1982. *Parenting skills workbook* (2nd ed.). New York: Human Sciences Press.

Alberti, R. E. & Emmons, M. L. 1970. *Your perfect right: A guide to assertive behavior.* San Luis Obispo, CA.: IMPACT.

Augsburger, D. W. 1979. *Anger and assertiveness in pastoral care.* Philadelphia: Fortress Press.

Axline, V. M. 1964. *Dibs.* New York: Ballantine Books.

Bandura, A., & Walters, R. H. 1963. *Social learning and personality development.* New York: Holt, Rinehart & Winston.

Becker, W. C. 1971. *Parents are teachers: A child management program.* Champaign, IL.: Research Press.

Berkowitz, L., & Alioto, J. T. 1973. The meaning of an observed event as a determinant of its aggressive consequences. *Journal of Personality and Social Psychology* 28: 206–217.

Bernstein, B. 1971–75. *Class, codes, and control.* 3 vols. London: Routledge, Kegan, and Paul.

Bigner, J. J. 1979. *Parent-child relations.* New York: Macmillan.

Bryan, J. H. 1969, Dec. How adults teach hypocrisy. *Psychology Today* 3(7): 50–52, 65.

Bryan, J. H. 1971. Model affect and children's imitative altruism. *Child Development* 42: 2061–2065.

Bushnell, H. 1867/1973. What christian nurture is. In P. J. Greven, Jr. (Ed.), *Child-rearing Concepts, 1628–1861* (pp. 137–181). Itasca, IL: F. E. Peacock. (Original work published 1867.)

Christenson, L. 1974. *The Christian family.* Minneapolis: Bethany Fellowship.

Church cites disruption, bans mother, son from services. *The Wichita Eagle-Beacon,* 23 April, 1988, 11A.

Clifford, E. 1959. Discipline in the home: A controlled observational study of parental practices. *Journal of Genetic Psychology* 95: 45–82.

Cohen, S. 1980. Training to understand TV advertising: Effects and some policy implications. Paper presented at the American Psychological Association convention.

Corteen, R. S., & Williams, T. 1986. Television and reading skills. In T. Williams, (Ed.), *The impact of television: A natural experiment in three communities* (pp. 39–84). Orlando, FL: Academic Press.

Crary, E. 1979. *Without spanking or spoiling: A practical approach to toddler and preschool guidance.* Seattle: Parenting Press.

Curran, D. 1983. *Traits of a healthy family.* Minneapolis: Winston Press.

Dinkmeyer, D., & Dreikurs, R. 1963. *Encouraging children to learn: The encouragement process.* Englewood Cliffs, N.J.: Prentice-Hall.

Dinkmeyer, D., & McKay, G. 1976. *Systematic training for effective parenting: Parent's handbook.* Circle Pines, Minn.: American Guidance Service.

Dobson, J. 1970. *Dare to discipline.* Wheaton, IL: Tyndale House Pub.

Dobson, J. 1978. *The strong-willed child.* Wheaton, IL: Tyndale House Pub.

Dobson, J. 1982. *Dr. Dobson answers your questions.* Minneapolis, MN: Grason.

Dobson, J. 1987. *Parenting isn't for cowards.* Waco, TX: Word Pub.

Dodson, F. 1970. *How to parent.* Los Angeles: Nash Pub.

Drabman, R. S., & Thomas, M. H. 1976. Does watching violence on television cause apathy? *Pediatrics* 57: 329–331.

Dreikurs, R., with Soltz, V. 1964. *Children: The challenge.* New York: Hawthorn Books.

Drescher, J. 1979. *If I were starting my family again.* Nashville: Abingdon.

Erb, A. M. 1944. *The christian nurture of children.* Scottdale, Pennsylvania: Herald Press.

Eron, L. D., & Huesmann, L. R. 1984. The control of aggressive behavior by changes in attitudes, values, and the conditions of learning. In R. J. Blanchard & C. Blanchard (Eds.), *Advances in the study of aggression* (Vol. 1, pp. 139–171). Orlando, Fla.: Academic Press.

Faber, A., & Mazlish, E. 1980. *How to talk so kids will listen & listen so kids will talk.* New York: Avon Books.

Feiner, J., & Yost, G. 1988. *Taming monsters, slaying dragons: The revolutionary family approach to overcoming childhood fears and anxieties.* New York: Arbor House.

Fernandez-Collado, C., & Greenberg, B. S., with Korzenny, F., & Atkin, C. K. 1978. Sexual intimacy and drug use in TV series. *Journal of Communication* 28(3): 30–37.

Feshbach, N. D., & Feshbach, S. 1971. Children's aggression. *Young Children* 26(6): 364–377.

Feshbach, N. D. 1985, Spring. Learning to care: A positive approach to child training and discipline. *Society for Prevention of Violence Newsletter* 10(1): 1–2, 4–6.

Freedman, J. S. 1965. Long-term behavioral effects of cognitive dissonance. *Journal of Experimental Psychology* 1: 145–155.

Friedman, E. H. 1985. *Generation to generation: Family process in church and synagogue.* New York: The Guilford Press.

Gaulke, E. H. 1975. *You can have a family where everybody wins: Christian perspectives on parent effectiveness training.* St. Louis: Concordia Publishing House.

Gerbner, G., Gross, L., Morgan, M., & Signorielli, N. 1986. Living with television: The dynamics of the cultivation process. In J. Bryant & D. Zillman (Eds.), *Perspectives on media effects* (pp. 17–40). Hillsdale, N. J.: Erlbaum.

Gibran, K. 1923/1970. *The prophet.* New York: Alfred A. Knopf. (Original work published 1923.)

Ginott, H. G. 1965. *Between parent and child.* New York: Avon Books.

Gordon, T. 1970. *Parent effectiveness training.* New York: Peter H. Wyden.

Gordon, T. 1974. *Teacher effectiveness training.* New York: Peter H. Wyden.

Gordon, T. 1976. *P. E. T. in action.* New York: Peter H. Wyden.

Gordon, T. 1978. *Leader effectiveness training.* New York: Peter H. Wyden.

Gordon, T. 1980. Parent effectiveness training: A preventive program and its effects on families. In M. J. Fine (Ed.), *Handbook on parent education* (pp. 101–121). New York: Academic Press.

Harrison, L. F., & Williams, T. 1986. Television and cognitive development. In T. Williams (Ed.), *The impact of television: A natural experiment in three communities* (pp. 87–138). Orlando, FL: Academic Press.

Horton, R. W., & Santogrossi, D. A. 1978. The effect of adult commentary on reducing the influence of televised violence. *Personality and Social Psychology Bulletin* 4: 337–340.

Huesmann, L. R., Lagerspetz, K., & Eron, L. D. 1984. Intervening variables in the TV violence-aggression relation: Evidence from two countries. *Developmental Psychology* 20: 746–775.

Huizinga, J. 1949/1955. *Homo ludens: A study of the play element in culture.* (R. F. C. Hill, Trans.). Boston: Beacon Press. (Original work published 1949.)

Jennings (Walstedt), J., Geis, F. L., & Brown, V. 1980. Influence of television commercials on women's self-confidence and independent judgment. *Journal of Personality and Social Psychology* 38: 203–210.

Jeschke, M. 1983. *Believers baptism for children of the church.* Scottdale, PA: Herald Press.

Joy, L. A., Kimball, M. M., & Zabrack, M. L. 1986. Television and children's aggressive behavior. In T. M. Williams (Ed.), *The impact of television: A natural experiment in three communities* (pp. 265–301). Orlando, FL: Academic Press.

Kaye, K. 1984. *Family rules: Raising responsible children.* New York: Walker and Company.

Kerr, M. E., & Bowen, M. 1988. *Family evaluation.* New York: W. W. Norton.

Lepper, M. R., Greene, D., & Nisbett, R.E. 1973. Undermining children's intrinsic interest with extrinsic rewards: A test of the "overjustification" hypothesis. *Journal of Personality and Social Psychology* 28: 129–137.

Lerner, H. G. 1985. *The dance of anger: A woman's guide to changing the patterns of intimate relationships.* New York: Harper & Row.

Liebert, R. M., & Schwartzberg, N. S. 1977. Effects of mass media. In M. R. Rosenzweig & L. W. Porter (Eds.), *Annual review of psychology* (Vol. 28, pp. 141–173). Pal Alto, CA: Annual Reviews.

Locke, J. 1690/1973. Some thoughts concerning education. In P. J. Grever, Jr. (Ed.), *Child-rearing concepts, 1628–1861* (pp. 18–41). Itasca, IL: F. E. Peacock. (Originally written 1690.)

Lowry, D. T., Love, G., & Kirby, M. 1981. Sex on the soap operas: Patterns of intimacy. *Journal of Communication* 31(3): 90–96.

McIntire, R. W. 1970. *For love of children: Behavioral psychology for parents.* Del Mar, CA.: C. R. M. Books.

McIntire, R. W. 1985. *Losing control of your teenager.* Amherst, MA: Human Resource Development Press.

Meyerhoff, M. K., & White, B. 1986. Making the grade as parents. *Psychology Today* 20(9): 38–45.

Murray, J. P., & Kippax, S. 1979. From the early window to the late night show: International trends in the study of television's impact on children and adults. In L. Berkowitz (Ed.), *Advances in experimental social psychology* (Vol. 12, pp. 253–320). New York: Academic Press.

Myers, D. G. 1987. *Social psychology.* New York: McGraw-Hill.

Napier, A., & Whitaker, C. 1978. *The family crucible.* New York: Harper & Row.

Newswanger, D. E. 1977. Identifying rebellion in our children. *Eastern Mennonite Testimony* 9 (May): 54, 60.

Open road beckons to adventurer, age 5. *New York Times,* 5 December, 1987, 29.

Parke, R. D., Berkowitz, L., Leyens, J. P., West, S. G., & Sebastian, J. 1977. Some effects of violent and nonviolent movies on the behavior of juvenile delinquents. In L. Berkowitz (Ed.), *Advances in experimental social psychology* (Vol. 10, pp. 135–172). New York: Academic Press.

Parke, R. D., & Slaby, R. G. 1983. The development of aggression. In E. M. Hetherington (Ed.), P. H. Mussen (Series Ed.), *Handbook of child psychology: Vol. 4. Socialization, personality, and social development* (pp. 547–641). New York: Wiley.

Patterson, G. R. 1976. *Living with children* (rev. ed.). Champaign, IL: Research Press.

Patterson, G. R. 1984. Microscoial process: A view from the boundary. In J. C. Masters & K. Yarkin-Levin (Eds.), *Boundary areas in social and developmental psychology* (pp. 43–66). New York: Academic Press.

Peck, M. S. 1978. *The road less traveled.* New York: Simon and Schuster.

Phillips, D. P. 1983. The impact of mass media violence on U. S. homicides. *American Sociological Review* 48: 560–568.

Piaget, J. 1965. *The moral judgment of the child.* New York: The Free Press.

Robinson, J. P. 1972. Television's impact on everyday life: Some cross-national evidence. In E. A. Rubinstein, G. A. Comstock, & J. P. Murray (Eds.), *Television and social behavior* (Vol. 4): *Television in day-to-day life: Patterns of use* (pp. 410–431). Washington, D. C.: Government Printing Office.

Robinson, J. P. 1981. Television and leisure time: A new scenario. *Journal of Communication* 31(1): 120–130.

Rogers, C. 1980. My philosophy of interpersonal relationships and how it grew. In C. Rogers, *A way of being* (pp. 27–45). Boston: Houghton Mifflin.

Rosenthal, R., & Jacobson, L. 1968. *Pygmalian in the classroom.* New York: Holt, Rinehart and Winston.

Rousseau, J. 1762/1965. The child in nature (excerpts from *Emile*). In W. Kessen, (Ed.), *The child* (pp. 76–97). New York: John Wiley & Sons. (Original work published in French, 1762.) The saga continues: Children on airlines. *The Newton Kansan,* 16 April, 1988. 3.

Sanders, R. K., & Malony, H. N. 1985. *Speak up! Christian assertiveness.* Philadelphia: The Westminster Press.

Satir, V. 1972. *Peoplemaking.* Palo Alto, CA: Science and Behavior Books.

Scarf, M. 1987. *Intimate partners: Patterns in love and marriage.* New York: Random House.

Seligman, M. 1975. *Helplessness: On depression, development, and death.* San Francisco: W. H. Freeman and Co.

Shedd, C. 1970. *Promises to Peter.* Waco, Texas: Word Books.

Silberman, M. L., & Wheelan, S. A. 1980. *How to discipline without feeling guilty: Assertive relationships with children.* Champaign, IL.: Research Press.

Singer, D. G. 1983. A time to reexamine the role of television in our lives. *American Psychologist* 38: 815–816.

Skinner, B. F. 1938. *The behavior of organisms.* New York: Appleton-Century-Crofts.

Skinner, B. F. 1945/1972. Baby in a box. In B. F. Skinner, *Cumulative record: A selection of papers* (3rd ed., pp. 567–573). New York: Appleton-Century-Crofts. (Originally published in *Ladies Home Journal*, October, 1945.)

Skinner, B. F. 1953. *Science and human behavior.* New York: Macmillan.

Skinner, B. F. 1964/1972. Man. In B. F. Skinner, *Cumulative record: A selection of papers* (3rd ed., pp. 51–57). New York: Appleton-Century-Crofts. (Originally published in *Proceedings of the American Philosophical Society,* 1964, *108,* pp. 482–485.)

Sloane, H. N., Jr. 1976. *Dinner's ready.* Fountain Valley, CA: Telesis, Ltd.

Smith, M. J. 1975. *When I say no, I feel guilty.* New York: The Dial Press.

Sprafkin, J. N., & Silverman, L. T. 1981. Update: Physically intimate and sexual behavior on prime time television, 1978–79. *Journal of Communication* 3(1): 34–40.

Stark, E. 1985, April. Taking a beating. *Psychology Today* 19(4): p. 16.

Steinberg, C. 1985. *TV facts.* New York: Facts on File Publications.

Steinmetz, S. K., & Straus, M. A. 1973. The family as cradle of violence. *Society* 10(5): 50–56.

Steinmetz, S. K., & Straus, M. A. (Eds.). 1974. *Violence in the family.* New York: Dodd, Mead & Co.

Stinnett, N., & DeFrain, J. 1985. *Secrets of strong families.* Boston: Little, Brown and Company.

Tanner, B. 1988, February 16. Human TV guide on a 365-day fast. *The Wichita Eagle-Beacon,* pp. 1A, 12A.

Van Houten, R. 1980. *How to use reprimands.* Lawrence, KS.: H & H Enterprises.

Watson, J. B. 1914/1958. *Behavior: An introduction to comparative psychology.* New York: Henry Holt. (Original work published 1914.)

Wesley, J. 1783/1973. Sermon on the education of children. In P. J. Greven, Jr. (Ed.), *Child-rearing concepts, 1628–1861* (pp. 52–66). Itasca, Illinois: F. E. Peacock. (Original work published, 1783.)

heelis, A. 1973. *How people change.* New York: Harper & Row.

Villiams, T. H., & Handford, A. G. 1986. Television and other leisure activities. In T. H. Williams (Ed.), *The impact of television: A natural experiment in three communities* (pp. 143–213). Orlando, FL: Academic Press.

Winn, M. 1977. *The plug-in drug: Television, children, and the family.* New York: The Viking Press.

Woman, child barred from entering church in Topeka The Newton Kansan, 25 April, 1988, 2.

Wood, P., & Schwartz, B. 1977. *How to get your children to do what you want them to do.* Englewood Cliffs, NJ.: Prentice-Hall. You can bet your life, television. *Wichita Eagle-Beacon,* 12 August, 1986, 4C.

Zahn-Waxler, C., Radke-Yarrow, M., & King, R. A. 1979. Child-rearing and children's prosocial initiations toward victims of distress. *Child Development* 50: 319–330.

Index

Abidin, R., 58, 162
Active listening, 39, 110–119, 154, 236–237, 245
Adler, A., 177
Alberti, R., 166
Anger, 76, 103, 164, 239
Assertiveness, 42, 45, 145, 165–175, 234, 238, 241–242
Augsburger, D., 166
Autonomy, 125–142
Axline, V., 290
Bandura, A., 210
Barbeau, C., 75–76
Bateson, G., 253
Becker, W., 210
Becraft, S., 36
Behavior modification, 10, 40, 41–42, 44–45, 209–232
  baseline, 211–212, 222–223
  competing behavior, 216–217
  contingency contract, 222
  contributions of, 230–232
  criticisms of, 228–230
  extinction, 212–214
  Premack Principle, 219
  reprimands, 214
  self-modification, 231
  shaping, 41, 209, 217
  Time Out, 215–216
  token economy, 222
  types of reinforcement, 217–222
  types of reinforcement schedule, 223–224
Behaviorism, 40, 55, 210, 229
Berkowitz, L., 84, 85
Bernstein, B., 149
Bigner, J., 189
Birth order, 18, 204
Bowen, M., 253, 280
Broken record, 167–168, 172, 238, 245–246
Bryan, J., 52
Bushnell, H., 48, 53
Canter, L., 166
Catharsis, 102
Child abuse and neglect, 32, 44, 78, 127, 202
Child labor, 37
Child study movement, 37
Christenson, L., 290–291

Client-centered therapy, 37
Clifford, E., 151
Cohen, S., 91
Commands, 148–152
Competent children, 73
Compromise, 234, 241–242
Compulsory education, 37
Conflict, 235–252
Consequences
  logical, 145, 177–184, 238, 247
  natural, 145, 177
Corteen, R., 82
Crary, E., 215–216
Curran, D., 74–75
Delay of gratification, 130
Demands, 163–175
Dependence, 122, 140
Dinkmeyer, D., 141, 177
Discipline
  defined, 23–24, 49, 61, 145
Dobson, J., 10, 30–36, 42–44, 202
Dodson, F., 39, 202
Drabman, R., 83
Dreikurs, R., 132, 177
Drescher, J., 49, 51, 276
Durfee, M., 57
Elaborated language code, 150
Eliot, T., 208
Empathy, 153
Encouragement, 131–134
Erb, A., 151–152
Eron, L., 84
Expectations, 128–131, 145, 266
Faber, A., 111, 124, 132, 168
Family
  bedtime routine, 75–76
  celebrations, 67–68
  crises, 76–78
  leisure activity, 69–71
  mealtime, 74–75
  vacations, 65–67
Family Systems Theory, 10, 28, 244, 253–281
  anxiety, 10, 270–276, 306
  collusive bond, 267
  differentiation, 119, 138, 161, 238–239, 246, 264–267, 269, 279–280
  emotional cut-off, 262, 275
  fusion, 138, 260–265, 306
  generational boundaries, 276–279

invasive language, 267
over-responsible/under-responsible
    pattern, 126, 138–140, 297
personal boundaries, 262
problems in context, 254–260
reactivity, 161, 232, 244, 306
roles, 26–29, 267–270
togetherness and separateness forces,
    260–262
triangulation process, 270–276
Fathers
    traditional role, 11, 26–29, 125,
    267–270
Feiner, J., 279
Fernandez-Collado, C., 85
Feshbach, N., 154, 198
Fight cycles, 151
Fogging, 171–172, 238, 245–246
Freedman, J., 184
Freud, S., 102, 177
Friedman, E., 277
Friendly-Farmer-Drives-Combine
    (FFDC), 184–188
Gerbner, G., 83, 84
Gibran, K., 50
Ginott, H., 132, 290
Gordon, T., 30–32, 37–39, 44, 111,
    154–156, 161–162, 242
Haley, J., 253
Harrison, L., 82
Horton, R., 85, 91
Huesmann, L., 84
Huizinga, J., 94
Human nature, 33, 37, 40, 47, 46–48
Humanistic psychology, 37
I-message, 39, 154–162, 238, 245
Immanent justice, 191
Independence, 126, 134–136, 238
Jennings, J., 88
Jeschke, M., 49
y, L., 84
ye, K., 182–183
rr, M., 253
anders, A., 81
Lepper, M., 230
Lerner, H., 253, 275, 280
Liebert, R., 83
Listening skills, 101–124, 234, 236–237
Locke, J., 39, 41
Lowry, D., 85
Lucca, D., 39
McIntire, R., 108, 210, 239, 242, 244
McKay, G., 177
Meyerhoff, M., 74
Minuchin, S., 253
Modeling effect of parents, 24–25, 52,
    210
Moral development, 191–192
Mothers

traditional role, 11, 26–29, 125,
    267–270
Mullen, T., 242
Murray, J., 80
Mutual problem solving, 39, 242
Myers, D., 82, 88
Napier, A., 253
Newswanger, D., 290
No-Lose Method of problem solving,
    241–242
Nolte, D., 56
Nonverbal communication, 106–108,
    172–175
Parent Effectiveness Training (P.E.T.),
    10, 32, 39, 44, 111, 154, 156–157,
    161, 242
Parke, R., 80, 84
Patterson, G., 151, 210, 215, 290
Peck, S., 23, 62, 104
Peers, 70–71
Phillips, D., 84
Piaget, J., 191
Play, defined, 94
Problem ownership, 14–21, 39,
    288–289, 293–294
Procrastination, 182
Progressive Education movement, 37
Punishment, 23, 35, 38, 41, 45, 145, 148,
    189–208
    consistency, 197
    frequency, 197–198
    intensity, 196–197
    and parent-child relationship,
    199–200
    and reasoning, 198–199
    "rod" of punishment, 35, 53,
    206–208
    timing, 195–196
    to communicate displeasure, 201–204
    to inhibit undesirable behavior,
    195–201
    to make restitution, 193–195
    to render retribution, 190–193
Quality time, 61
Reasoning, 148–151, 198, 238
Reconciliation, 76, 203
Redmond, J., 175
Reflective listening, 111
Religion
    adult believers church tradition, 46–57
    age of accountability, 47
    baptism, 46–47
    beliefs, 46–57, 78–79, 288, 289–291
    child dedication, 49
    child evangelism, 47
    conservative Christian tradition,
    32–36, 42, 46
    doctrine of original sin, 33
    prayer, 75, 76, 203

and relationships, 24
  worship, 79
Restricted language code, 149
Rites of passage, 68
Robinson, J., 82
Rogers, C., 37–38
Rosenthal, R., 128
Rousseau, J., 36–38
Sanders, R., 166
Satir, V., 253, 256, 260
Scarf, M., 253, 265–266, 267
Seligman, M., 197
Shedd, C., 276
Silberman, M., 166, 167, 182, 230, 241,
  279
Singer, D., 80
Skinner, B. F., 31–32, 40–41, 195, 210
Sloane, H., 291
Smith, M., 166, 167, 171
Soltz, V., 177
Sports, 93–98
Sprafkin, J., 85
Stark, E., 189
Steinmetz, S., 204
Stinnett, N., 58, 59, 78
Strong family research, 59, 74–75, 78
Systematic Training for Effective
  Parenting (S.T.E.P.), 10, 132, 141,
  176–177

Tabula rasa, 39
Tanner, B., 82
Tattling, 127, 140
Teachable moment, 62
Television, 74, 80–92
  commercials, 87–88, 91
  and fear, 84–85
  and parenthood, 86
  preemptive effect, 82
  restrictions, 88–90
  and sex and marriage, 85–86
  and sex-role stereotypes, 86–88
  violence, 83–85
Twain, M., 201
Yost, G., 279
You-message, 156–157, 240
Van Houten, R., 214
Velde, L., 177
Watson, J., 40
Wesley, J., 33, 47
Wheelan, S., 279
Wheelis, A., 72
White, B., 73
Will of child, 33–35, 40, 42, 46–48, 51,
  152
Williams, T., 82
Winn, M., 81–82
Wood, P., 166
Zahn-Waxler, C., 159